Fine Print

FINE PRINT

Reflections on the Writing Art

James J. Kilpatrick

ANDREWS AND McMEEL

A Universal Press Syndicate Company

KANSAS CITY

James J. Kilpatrick's syndicated column "The Writer's Art" is distributed internationally by Universal Press Syndicate.

Fine Print: Reflections on the Writing Art copyright © 1993 by Op Ed, Inc. All rights reserved. Printed in the United States of America. No part of this book may be used or reproduced in any manner whatsoever without written permission except in the case of reprints in the context of reviews. For information write Andrews and McMeel, a Universal Press Syndicate Company, 4900 Main Street, Kansas City, Missouri 64112.

Library of Congress Cataloging-in-Publication Data

Kilpatrick, James Jackson, 1920-
    Fine print : reflections on the writing art / James J. Kilpatrick.
      p. cm.
    Includes index.
    ISBN 0-8362-8037-7 : $12.95
    1. English language—Usage.   2. English language—Style.
  I. Title.
  PE1460.K538   1993
  428—dc20   93–27736
                                           CIP

Book design by Cameron Poulter

Attention: Schools and Businesses

Andrews and McMeel books are available at quantity discounts with bulk purchase for educational, business, or sales promotional use. For information, please write to:
Special Sales Department, Andrews and McMeel,
4900 Main Street, Kansas City, Missouri 64112

For Aileen Lorberg of Cape Girardeau, Missouri,

who has loved our language all her life

and conveyed that love with authority and zest.

Contents

Preface

In the summer of 1981, for no particular reason, I began writing a weekly column on the use and abuse of English. The venture offered a pleasant respite from writing about the Supreme Court and the Reagan administration. My syndicate, which is surely the most amiable syndicate in the world, amiably agreed to offer "The Writer's Art" as a little lagniappe in a package deal. The column would go to subscribing newspapers along with my regular column, "A Conservative View." Editors could use it or spike it as they pleased. So we began.

I never had more fun. Not more than thirty-five or forty newspapers ever used the feature on a regular basis, but this limited exposure produced great bales of reader mail. In 1984, Andrews and McMeel, a subsidiary of Universal Press Syndicate, published a book based on my weekly columns. It too was titled *The Writer's Art.* I liked the book. A number of teachers wrote to say they were using it in their classrooms. Readers wrote to agree or to disagree with some of my magisterial pronouncements.

In the ensuing years since *The Writer's Art* came out, I have written another 450 columns based largely upon mail from readers. Every experience in one's life, I suppose, is a "learning experience," but the hackneyed phrase has had a special meaning for me. Readers of the column have sent me thousands of clippings. They have asked questions about a thousand points of usage. What is the difference between *healthy* and *healthful?* What is the rule on *take* and *bring?* I have learned from the Horrid Examples, and from the Good Stuff too, and I know that my own writing has perceptibly improved because of my readers' questions, comments, and occasional cries of, yanh, yanh, gotcha!

I began to write at the tender age of six. That was the spring of Lindbergh's solo flight to France. A precocious child, possessed even then of a writer's necessary ego, I took pen in hand and wrote a pome—not a poem, but a *pome*—about the heroic achievement. My sainted mother typed it up neatly and sent it to a children's magazine. I believe it was *Child's Life,* but maybe not. Anyhow, before long I received a congratulatory note from the poetry editor. My pome had been accepted! That was not all. Attached to the letter of acceptance was a shiny new 1926 dime.

Every professional writer knows the grand and glorious feeling. I was thunderstruck. It had not occurred to me that one could get *paid* for having such fun. I lost my amateur standing on the spot. I became a pro, and I have been a pro ever since.

After all these years, writing still strikes me as mostly joy, pure joy. God knows it can be a frustrating way to earn a living. Ten years ago I set as my goal to write one good sentence a month. I would strive to produce just one Rice Krispy line. It would go snap, crackle, and pop. It would raise the smoke from a catcher's glove. It would close with the thump of a Cadillac door. Ahhh, I would say, shamelessly admiring the beautiful thing, that is indeed a sentence for September.

Some months I met the goal. In most months I did not. In 1991 I hit a slump that lasted six months, and it was awful. But after a while the juice began to flow, and the weekly "Writer's Art" column kept reminding me that joy and frustration are inescapable parts of a writer's life. My hope in this second book is to pass along some of the pleasure and some of the pain, to hand down a few judgments on usage, and to trot out some ideas on what might be done to help good writers become better writers. These ideas are not much of a mystery after all.

Let me caveat you, as Alexander Haig used to say to Senate committees, by acknowledging that my judgments on usage are merely *my* judgments, and God knows they are not infallible judgments. They are no more than the distillation of experience—the kind of experience that comes from writing for publication every day for fifty years. Gentle reader, use what appeals to you, form your own stylistic judgments, and write as the spirit moves you. I wish you the inexpressible joy that comes to a writer when one good sentence turns out right.

—JAMES J. KILPATRICK

Charleston, S.C.
May 1993

1 How Must We Write? *Con Amore!*

The phrase carries a special meaning in Italian. A thing that is done *con amore* is not done merely "with love." It is done with a kind of rapturous enthusiasm that sweeps everything from its path. Good doctors go at the practice of medicine *con amore.* The best lawyers will talk incessantly, lovingly, of the law. Doubtless there are plumbers who look *con amore* upon gold-plated faucets. A cook of my close acquaintance makes poulet Marengo with a joy undimmed by half a century at the stove. Writers who write *con amore* are specially blessed. These are the fortunate ones.

Quite some time ago—this would have been in the autumn of 1939—Professor Roscoe Ellard welcomed incoming juniors to the School of Journalism at the University of Missouri. His required course was called "History and Principles of Journalism." Ellard was an interesting person. He had the generous build of a barrel of beer; he affected sports coats that might have been tailored by Jacob as a gift to Joseph; he stammered. He had little actual hands-on newspaper experience, but he was a great teacher. He was terrifying.

"Going into newspapering," he would begin, "is like g-g-getting married. Don't do it if you p-p-possibly can help it."

Year after year, that imperative line produced titters among the sorority girls down front. They weren't quite sure what Ellard was talking about. He was talking about love—about a man's loving a woman so much that he cannot imagine life without her. He was talking about the love of Iseult for Tristan, the love of Pyramus for Thisbe. He was talking about writers who write *con amore.*

Roscoe Ellard was under no illusions that such passion can be sustained, white hot, when a reporter is writing about a two-point drop in the day's Dow-Jones. A letter to one's beloved is one thing;

1

a letter to the school board is something else entirely. We use different vocabularies; we seek a different pitch; yet even in a letter to the school board, the principle applies. Good writers will fashion even the most pedestrian sentences with artful care. Love abides.

My thesis in this book lacks the virtue of novelty: Great writers may be born, I submit, but good writers can be made. To listen closely to Mozart, who wrote his First Symphony at seven years of age, is to marvel at the presence of genius. Shakespeare's plays endure because Shakespeare was born great. No teacher of the writing art can fiddle with a gene string. A hundred lectures on the uses of cadence will have small effect upon a writer who never marched on metric feet. But with practice, good writers can become better writers.

George Mason, one of the greatest of the Founding Fathers, said something in the Virginia Declaration of Rights that sticks in the mind. The blessings of liberty, he said, may best be preserved "by frequent recurrence to fundamental principles." It's a fine idea in any field.

What is a fundamental principle of writing? It is to convey a message. That is what counts first of all. Writing differs from speech only in the self-evident fact that the written word has some degree of permanence. It may not have much permanence. Most writers write on sand. Radio and television broadcasters, for their part, write mainly on the wind, but the identical considerations apply.

Broadcasting, indeed, provides a metaphor: Writer and reader must be tuned to the same frequency if the message, once transmitted, is to be understandably received. We must speak the same language.

In the International Morse Code the letter *S* is represented by three dots, the letter *O* by three dashes. The code long ago yielded to electronic wizardry, but there was a time when every mariner and Boy Scout well understood:

... ――― ...

Suppose the telegrapher, intending to send a distress signal, went through a moment of panic and sent instead:

-.. ――― ――.

Anyone in range would inquire in puzzlement, "What's this about a dog?"

Words are a form of code. It is astonishing how often writers, even good writers, fail to understand the absolute necessity of using a code that their readers can comprehend.

Communication fails for a host of reasons. A writer may employ familiar English words, but he may use them wrongly. In Oroville, Calif., in April of 1992, the Mercury Register interviewed an instructor in political science. The teacher was describing ways in which he lured his students into taking an interest in real-world politics. They could take surveys of public opinion; they could do research; they could work in a politician's campaign.

"If in that process they want to be a candidate for office," said the teacher, "that's their purgative."

Probably he didn't say that. Probably he said, "That's their prerogative," and the reporter got it wrong. Anyhow, the communication failed.

In January 1988, the office of the president of Linn-Benton Community College in Albany, Ore., sent a memorandum to staff. The subject was, "Semester Conversion Update." The memorandum read, in full:

> As you may know, due to information that became available to us prior to the first of this year, we delayed sending out the guidelines, procedures and timelines for the conversion process to a semester calendar. Based on what now appears to be the majority of community colleges in our region moving away from converting to semesters, internal college priorities relating to funding needed for college programs and facility maintenance, and discussion with instructional managers, staff and faculty, we have decided to postpone the conversion process indefinitely and determine what impact the State System conversion will actually have on our students when and if they convert.
>
> We would like to thank all of you who have been involved in the discussions about converting our calendar, and especially the Calendar Conversion Committee and John Carnegie's leadership. We would also like to see work continue

in reviewing courses and curriculum, especially in light of the articulation efforts that will have to occur between higher education and the community colleges when they convert their calendar.

A close look at that squirming swamp of words will tell us that all the words are English words, that they are spelled correctly, that the sentences have subjects and predicates, and that nothing is clear except that the president's office has decided "to postpone the conversion process indefinitely." The rest was gobbledygook. It was a sad articulation effort.

More often than not, communication fails solely for want of a common vocabulary. George Will, one of the most gifted essayists of our time, has a large talent for intellectual discourse, but he has small patience with intellectual inferiors. Writing in *Newsweek* in May 1992, he turned his icy fire on a newly published crime novel, *Rising Sun.* He didn't like it.

> *Rising Sun,* an intended thriller, is intensely boring because its RoboVillain—an entire race, caricatured—lacks humanity and hence lacks human interest. Today, as Japan's economy sags and its stock market crashes, the strongest American feeling about Japan is not fear but *Schadenfreude.*

Now, *Schadenfreude* was the key word in that second sentence. Those who couldn't comprehend the German noun couldn't comprehend the sentence. They could only guess at America's strongest feelings about Japan. For the record, *Schadenfreude* is "pleasure felt at someone else's misfortune" *(Random House)* or "enjoyment obtained from others' troubles" *(Webster's Ninth New Collegiate).*

Communication suffers from allusions that may be clear to the writer but are so much mud to the reader. Another gifted essayist of our time, Charles Krauthammer, wrote a column in the spring of 1992 scoffing at the prospective presidential candidacy of billionaire Ross Perot. What was Perot's solution to health care?

> Three novelties: Study foreign countries, bring experts together to work out the best plan, introduce pilot programs. Chauncey Gardiner lives . . .

Chauncey Gardiner? As *The New Yorker*'s Harold Ross was wont to say, Who he? The witty allusion to "Chauncey Gardiner"—I am surmising it was witty—must have been lost on a host of my brother's readers.

Communication often is not exactly lost; it is only mislaid. This can happen when a careless writer affronts his readers with misspellings, grammatical horrors, mangled syntax, bungled homophones and errors of fact. When we read of Queen Elizabeth's rein, or of an actor's remarkable flare for Shakespeare, or of a used boat wench for sale, we stumble but press on. We get the sense of the thing, but readers are entitled to something more.

Perfect comprehension, of course, isn't the only thing. Coleridge is authority for the proposition that poetry gives most pleasure "when only generally and not perfectly understood." A.E. Housman added his own shrewd comment that, indeed, "perfect understanding will sometimes almost extinguish pleasure." This may do very well for poetry, but the first rule of *prose* composition—the rule that must be mastered before it can effectively be broken—is, Be clear! Be clear! And yet again, be clear!

The good writers, the writers who write *con amore*, have a special obligation. As trustees of the English tongue, they have a duty to preserve the estate. (They also have a duty to enlarge the estate, by welcoming useful new words and accommodating new meanings of old words, but we will talk about neologisms later.) In these permissive times, the trustee's fiduciary duty is not easily discharged. Take-it-easy writers complain: If the first rule is to be clear, and if a given sentence clearly conveys its message, why must the sentence adhere to old rules? What's so hot about the old rule on nominative pronouns? Who cares if we spell it *potato* or *potatoe*?

Fair questions. Let me respond by example. In September 1989 a gentleman in Yakima, Wash., wrote to the Writers Guild of America. He wanted to know about similar organizations in England and Australia. His letter wound up in the West Hollywood office of Writers Guild of America, West, Inc. There an assistant administrator helpfully supplied the desired addresses. He added a paragraph:

The overseas counterparts has their rules and regulations. You would need to write to each of them individuals
for informations about their organization.

All right. The paragraph was clear. It was murkily clear, of
course, but the essential meaning was there. Isn't that enough?
The permissive teacher asks, Whassamatter? The guy in Yakima
found out what he wanted to know. Did'n he?

Everything was wrong with the response from West Hollywood.
The author displayed a carelessness that amounted, in Jacques
Barzun's phrase, to "a deliberate assault upon culture." Today's
writers have inherited only a few true *rules* of prose composition,
but one of those rules demands that subject and predicate must
agree in number. Why is it wrong to say that counterparts has
their rules and regulations? It is wrong for the same reason it is
wrong to wear a bikini to high mass. It is wrong to trample upon a
precious legacy. The careless error insults values that generations
of writers have held dear. To write in this slovenly fashion is to fall
into what we would call, in another context, bad manners. In a
civilized society, manners matter.

In their fiduciary capacity, good writers should labor to preserve good meanings. In an address on "The Press and the Prose,"
published in March 1992 by the Media Studies Center of Columbia University, Jacques Barzun cited a dozen words that once had
the durability of honest denim jeans: *preempt, ignite, mundane,
avid, arcane, meld, testament, fundament, cohort, controversial, volatile,
abrasive, strategy, scenario, legendary, conjuncture, sensitive, icon, argu-
able,* and *problematic.* Now the jeans have holes in the knees. They
are ragged around the cuffs. The adjective *fulsome* now is widely
understood to mean lavish, enthusiastic, extravagant. The descriptive lexicographers recognize this corruption of a word that
once meant—and still precisely means—*insincere.*

Barzun mentioned many other words that our trustees have
neglected. Even tolerably conscientious writers mistake *fortuitous*
for *fortunate* and *precipitous* for *precipitate.* The gassy tendency is to
pump helium into words, inflating their meanings. Thus *parameter,* which has a specific meaning, is pumped up to the point that

it now means boundary, or bracket, or limit, or topic, as in "the parameters of debate."

We must love words, collect words, arrange words, and re-arrange words. We must explore the penumbras of words—the shadowy groves of connotation and nuance. There is a great distinction between *immensity* and *enormity.* We ought to observe it. Clear lines define *assure, ensure,* and *insure.* We ought to obey them. A *list* is rarely a *litany.* Epidemiologists track *infectious* diseases and *contagious* diseases, but they are not necessarily the same diseases.

In our simple and direct way, which is so charming a part of the American character, we like to go at the English language in the innocent conviction that words—most words, anyhow—have but a single meaning. Asked for examples, we look about a room and say, "table." Everyone understands what is meant by *table.* It is a piece of furniture having a flat top. On examination we find a table of contents, a table of laws, a table of statistics, and a table of bricks. Underground is a water table. A table is a plateau; it is a facet of a gem. Idiomatically, and sometimes literally, we drink a man under the table. In parliamentary speech, we say that an amendment has been laid on the table, which is not what happens at all. On Capitol Hill, a measure that has been tabled is a measure that has been buried.

Play with the word *post.* It is part of a fence. It is where a horse race begins. It is a military station; it is the morning mail; it is a way of riding a horse. Or *book.* We all know what a book is. It is six tricks by declarer in a game of bridge. It is the libretto of a light opera. It is a pile of tobacco leaves. A pile? Why, a *pile* is a heap. It is an object of steel or wood that is hammered into the ground as a foundation. It is a brushy surface on carpeting or cloth. It is a hemorrhoid.

What meanings have we here! What is meant by *mean?* It can mean *to intend:* A procrastinator means to cut the grass on Tuesday. Perhaps, with emphasis, he really *means* it. The verb can mean *to signify:* A green light means "go." If my wife looks at an erring grandchild with a Look Full of Meaning, it means the little darling had better shape up.

It is no problem to understand what we mean by *mean*. The writer's pleasure lies in digging out subtle distinctions. Suppose our task is to describe something large. The indefatigable Laurence Urdang, in *The Synonym Finder*, suggests:

For starters: *big, great, huge, enormous, colossal, herculean, mighty, prodigious, gigantic, monstrous, monumental, stupendous, tremendous, towering, staggering, imposing, mountainous, tall, high, grandiose,* and *humongous.* Also, *sizable, considerable, goodly, substantial, excessive, titanic, cyclopean,* and *Brobdingnagian.* Not to mention *mammoth, jumbo, ponderous, massive, elephantine,* and *dinosaurian.*

Given such a menu, what does a writer choose? A large balloon cannot properly be described as *massive*, for *massive* bears a connotation of solidity. A wedding party ought not to be an *enormous* party, for *enormous* carries nuances all its own. A California redwood may be *tremendous*, but unless we are writing for comic effect it is not *humongous*.

Shall our word-loving writer write about love? Shall we describe something sexy? We have a choice: *suggestive, exciting, arousing, sensual, sensuous, erotic, risqué, ribald, bawdy, bedroom, off-color, indecent, lewd, lascivious, shameless, immodest, indecorous, obscene, pornographic, vulgar, foul, filthy, dirty, smutty,* and *raunchy.*

Is something that is "erotic" also "pornographic" or "dirty"? Maybe yes, maybe no. The Song of Songs which is Solomon's is certainly erotic. "My well beloved shall lie all night betwixt my breasts . . . Thy lips drop as the honeycomb; honey and milk are under thy tongue . . . Open to me, my love, my dove, my undefiled . . ." But it would be ludicrous to describe the Song of Songs as vulgar, foul, filthy, or risqué.

Words come in textures; words are hard or smooth or squishy soft. Words have colors; they are pastel, they are bold. They are neutral. They are colorless. Words have sounds derived from their meanings; *timid* is soft, *savage* is hard, *clamor* is loud. Words are sharp, words are blunt; words have edges that are keen. There are scalpel words and razor words and words that have a saber's slash. Words are dull, words are sparkling. Words are alive, they are languid. Words fly, sail, drive, race, creep, crawl. So many words! If we are patient—if we will work at the task—we will begin to find the right ones

The writer's art, of course, lies not in merely collecting words or in distinguishing among them. The art lies in stringing the right words together artfully. Newspaper reporters may begin by covering a luncheon speech at the Rotary Club, but if they are good reporters—reporters who write *con amore*—they will aspire to something higher.

Along the way they will discover that to embark upon a love affair with language is to take to heart a fascinating but difficult mistress. She can be frustrating, maddening, stubborn, filled with surly resistance. She can give great pleasure also, but she never can be wholly won. Language always holds something back from the eager writer.

Well, almost always. Now and then everything comes together. Sudden inspiration combines with observation; all the words fit nicely, and novelist John Logue, in such a moment, finds "a night as dark as the inside of a walnut." Robin Finn of The New York Times writes from Wimbledon that Michael Stich clung to Stefan Edberg "with the tenacity of a terrier to a pantleg." Ahhh, yes! Our seductive and elusive mistress seldom returns our love, but now and then, as I say, she turns and smiles.

2　How Fares the Craft of Carpentry?

It is an old metaphor, but it works: Writing is carpentry. At its poorest level we have Jack the local jackleg. At the highest level we have Tom Chippendale. Journalism may be a profession—in the newspaper business we like to think it's a profession—and the writing of poetry may be an art, but the fitting of words together is first of all a craft.

How fares our craft of carpentry? Not well. In the United States, it has not fared well at all. The second half of the twentieth century has produced a number of good writers and a few fine writers. Before long I will be quoting from some of them who dwell in my world, the world of the working journalist. The work of these journeymen craftsmen is every bit as good as the work of such long-ago English scribblers as Addison and Steele. I am thinking of Roger Rosenblatt, Lance Morrow, George Will, Charles Krauthammer, Meg Greenfield—the list could be much extended. As a superb reporter with a jeweler's eye, Shana Alexander stands with Rebecca West. In the writing of humor, science fiction and detective yarns, American authors head the parade. The American novel is off my beat, but I am agreeable to the assertion that a hundred years hence there will still be an audience for Hemingway and Faulkner. A substantial number of readers will dive into the deep waters of Thomas Pynchon.

The bad news lies mostly at the shallow end of the pool. The writing on smaller newspapers—those with a circulation under fifty thousand—may charitably be described as rotten. I venture this melancholy judgment on the basis of more than five thousand clippings that readers send to me every year. Overwhelmingly these clippings provide Horrid Examples of how not to write. They offer a depressing array of misspellings, grammatical howlers, and mangled syntax. Much contemporary journalism is patently the work of jacklegs who never have learned to saw a straight line.

How come? Heaven knows there is abundant blame to spread around. At bottom, perhaps, much of the blame may be laid broadly, intangibly, on the general decline of values that once America held dear. In a less permissive day, we valued discipline, we valued excellence, we had a high regard for the taking of pains. In life, as in the classroom, we tried not to blot our copybooks. Now in the arts, no less than in the manufactures, the standards decline.

In the newspaper world, my world, part of the blame for shoddy performance lies with newspaper owners who historically have paid shoddy salaries. The beginning schoolteacher, who once ranked at the bottom of the scale, now is paid more than the beginning reporter. Pay a second-rate salary, you get a second-rate writer. You get writers who write, in Mount Airy, N.C., "Much to the amazement of mother and I . . ." You get college graduates who never met a gerund, a nondefining clause, or a dangling participle. Some of their publishers never have met these strangers either.

The schools cannot escape responsibility for the sad state of our carpentry. Some schools, to be sure, are doing outstanding jobs. For the most part the record is poor. One study after another has reached this same conclusion. Levels of achievement in reading and writing should make us weep.

Periodically the National Assessment of Educational Progress (NAEP) reports on how our students are doing in the public schools. In 1988 NAEP looked at levels of writing in the fourth, eighth, and twelfth grades. The survey covered twenty thousand young people who were asked to try their hand at writing informative, persuasive, and narrative pieces. The survey also inquired into the teaching of writing.

It transpired that instruction in the writing art is not exactly intensive. At the eighth-grade level, students typically spend no more than one hour a week on written assignments. Half the twelfth-graders had written no more than two papers for school during the previous six weeks.

Given this limited instruction, it is not surprising that the NAEP study found that writing skills also were limited. Pupils improved their writing as they grew older, "but even at grade twelve, on almost all of the writing tasks, most students were unable to give adequate responses—that is, responses judged likely to accomplish the purpose of the writing task."

Asked to write an informative composition, more than half of the students at every grade level failed abysmally. Only 36 percent of the students could write a persuasive paragraph. Narrative writing proved somewhat better, but even here, "no more than 56 percent of the students at any grade level wrote adequate or better responses."

The survey graded papers as unsatisfactory, minimal, adequate, and "elaborated." A fourth-grader submitted this informative paper. It was judged unsatisfactory.

> We went to the zoo and seen a tiger. It was orange with black dots. We also seen a loine. It was ugly. We seen a ap. We also seen a zebra. It was brack wite. It weat 2,00000 ponds.

This was a fourth-grader's minimal response:

> Bear's can Be mein But They won't bother you if you Don't Bother Them. Bear's are Derent in many ways for instens Bear's sleep ontol spring and many other ways.

This was judged adequate:

> The Beta is a fish. The Beta comes in different colors. The Beta gets jelouse whenever he sees another fish like it. The Beta fans out and starts to fight. When the Beta lays its egg its nest is bubbles. When the eggs hatch you can save all of them so the mother won't eat them but you can only save a few. But keep them in separate jars.

Only 1.5 percent of the fourth graders' papers were given the highest rating of "elaborated." One such paper began:

> The Arctic Fox is a very tough animal. It thrives through long and cold winters. It reproduces more when there is more food. For instance, the average number of kits in one family is 10. Last year scientists studies came out 14 kits a

family! The arctic fox ranges from Northern America Eurasia and the northern islands.

At the eighth- and twelfth-grade levels, samples of "informative" student writing followed the same general pattern.

In a second part of the test, students at every grade level were asked to submit an example of their "persuasive" writing. The idea was to express an opinion and then to support it with reasoned argument. Note the results among high school seniors: unsatisfactory, 24.1 percent; minimal, 37.6 percent; adequate, 24.6 percent; elaborated, 2.7 percent. Put another way, barely one student in four could produce a "persuasive" paragraph that was even "adequate." This was an adequate paper, cast in the form of a letter to a senator:

> I strongly urge you to make the proposed cuts in spending for the space program. There are so many other problems wich desperately need to be solved before we start worrying about something as frivalous as colonies in space. The drug problem in our country is overwhelming. A lot of progress has been made but its been just a drop in the ocean. So much more is needed in helping these people. Our children are being effected by this at younger ages than ever before. We must have funding to educate the children on the dangers of drugs before its too late.

A few more dispiriting findings from the NAEP survey will suffice for the point at hand. In the final part of the test, students were given ten to fifteen minutes to write an imaginative narrative about a ghost. In the fourth grade, only 9.1 percent of the pupils turned in papers that were adequate or better. Eighth-graders did better: 32.5 percent scored adequate or better. Slightly more than 40 percent of the twelfth-grade ghost stories made the grade.

All this strikes me as a sad commentary on the state of the writing art in our public schools. A different report by the Educational Testing Service concludes that "students are poor writers, they do not like to write, and they like it less as they go through school."

It would be grossly unfair to put all of the blame, or even most of the blame, upon the classroom teachers. I hear from teachers all the time. Typically they work sixty hours a week, earn less than a trashman in Manhattan, and often toil in fear of their lives. They are overwhelmed by the demands of an educational establishment that piles upon the teacher more than a teacher should be asked to carry—drug education, driver education, sensitivity education, education for the handicapped. They are charged with sex education ("This is how he should put on the condom, darling"). In New York a manual for fifth-graders had a section on anal intercourse. After some parents objected, the material was removed from the fifth-grade manual. It was put in the sixth-grade manual instead. A teacher's life is one damned form, test, or questionnaire after another, and these time-consuming demands come on top of education in English, mathematics, history, and the sciences. It is small wonder that teachers are too weary to give a critical reading to themes and stories.

To a considerable extent, teachers are victims of the teachers' colleges. They learn to swim in polluted waters. From their professors, they learn how to teach the writing art. An NAEP report explains: "Process approaches to writing instruction emphasize the active, meaning-creating aspects of writing." Yes. Here they are taught that the teaching of grammar is old hat. Black English is not *inferior* to standard English; it is only *different,* and diversity must be encouraged. Except in a few schools, spelling bees have gone out of style. Teachers of reading use phonics as a tool, but the tool stays mainly in the toolbox. The whole word method, also known as "look and guess," remains the predominant vogue. When I once grumbled that diagraming sentences has become a lost art, a Midwestern teacher—a teacher of the old school—put her pupils to work on a special task just for me. They bought a fifty-foot roll of butcher paper and diagramed the whole of the United States Constitution and the first ten amendments, beginning with "We, the People" and ending with "to the people." Their work arrived in a mailing tube that had once contained a flag. I could have wept.

Having thus spoken in defense of teachers, I have to add that many teachers are incapable of teaching students how to write well for a self-evident reason: They write poorly themselves. Writing in The New York Times (June 12, 1991), Rachel Erlanger cited a paper on "Rhetoric and Ideology" prepared by a professor of English at Purdue University. The paper was published by *College English*, the magazine of the National Association of Teachers of English:

> It is true that some rhetorics have denied their imbrication in ideology, doing so in the name of a disinterested scientism . . . More recently the discussion of the relation between ideology and rhetoric has taken a new turn. Ideology is here foregrounded and problematized in a way that situates rhetoric within ideology, rather than ideology within rhetoric.

At the 1988 meeting of the Modern Language Association, a professor of English at Berkeley delivered a paper on American literature. She discussed a theory involving the organization of "discursive space around a circulatory system of power relations that can be tracked across the boundaries dividing the literary from the extraliterary." The model is not without difficulty.

> If power is absolutized as a transhistorical force which always produces and recontains subversion, then any resistance to such power presents itself as already neutralized. By focusing too exclusively on domination, we risk reinscribing marginalized groups as a reified "other," a category in which their voices can be treated as always appropriated by a dominant discourse.

How is anyone to learn writing from a teacher of writing who writes such bilge?

Academics are like lawyers. As a breed they are terrible writers. In North Carolina a professor in 1985 undertook to teach a "workshop." Someone sent me a copy of the professor's brochure. His students could expect:

> A brief definition will be given of the concept of human service "models," and the (commonly unconscious) assumptions that underlie and control such models . . . Examples of model-coherent and model-incoherent services will be given, and it will be brought out how important it is that human service models be congruent with social role valorization (formerly called the principle of normalization), and

that as much as possible, they emulate culturally valued analogues within the larger society.

The workshop was titled, "The Concept of Model Coherency as a Key to the Construction of High Quality and Maximally 'Social Role-Valorizing' Human Services." Until the moment that the brochure arrived I had never met *to valorize,* but *Webster's Ninth New Collegiate Dictionary* says that since 1906 it has meant "to enhance or try to enhance the price, value, or status of by organized and usually governmental action." All clear?

In Colorado, the school superintendent in Poudre District R-1 sent a questionnaire to members of his community asking for their "input." The respondents were to rate different "behaviors" from 1 to 5 in their importance. How important was it, for example,

to develop exit outcomes for graduates including periodic benchmark indicators supporting assessment and reporting systems?

to explore differentiated diplomas, weighted grades, for exit accountability?

to implement a plan for participatory management at each site that improves school climate, educational delivery, and student achievement and operates from a central direction with a shared district focus and set of educational beliefs?

Gene Amole, columnist for the Rocky Mountain News, remarked that this was the kind of input that made him want to upthrow.

In 1985 Jonathan Nicholas, a columnist for the Portland Oregonian, served as a judge for an essay contest among 170 Oregon teachers. He was appalled. He and his fellow judges stumbled over such misspellings as *villans, delt, liazon,* and *posible.* One teacher regarded herself as a "strong roll model." Another spoke of an "espectatious" classroom environment. Yet another remarked sagely about the feelings "that all humans are err to."

These 170 Oregon teachers, it should be noted, were applying to be chosen for a trip into space. Nicholas voiced his "terrible fear that what we had graded was the work of the best and the brightest." His experience was not at all unusual. Whenever teachers sit for a written examination, the same phenomenon appears. A significant number of teachers cannot write even five hundred words without an embarrassing error. So Little Patsy can't write? Big Patsy can't write either.

Perhaps these Horrid Examples are atypical. Surely there are many teachers in the elementary and secondary schools who love the writing art and teach it effectively. God bless them one and all.

If we are attempting to apportion blame for the lamentable writing skills of our schoolchildren, a substantial part of it, of course, should be assigned to the children themselves. They could learn to fashion a coherent idea into a coherent sentence if they applied themselves. In 1992 a couple of genetic biologists announced a startling discovery: The mastery of grammar, they concluded, is controlled by a single gene. Without the gene, a child is likely to go through life inviting his friends to a party for my sister and I. Really? The genetic theory has the feel of a flimsy excuse.

Poverty of course is a contributing factor. In most inner cities and in much of rural America, families have few books beyond the Bible and few publications beyond an occasional magazine. With little to read in their homes, and not much motivation for a child to find the local library, perhaps we should be gratified that the NAEP findings are not more melancholy still.

Taking all these considerations into account, we ought to be amazed that America produces any good writing at all—yet our country produces great quantities of good writing. It turns up in such national media as The New York Times, The Washington Post, and The Wall Street Journal. It also turns up in such fine regional papers as the Portland Oregonian, Seattle Times, and Miami Herald. Jerome Lamb, a gifted master of the mignonne essay, writes from Fargo, N.D., of all places. No American need apologize for the quality of writing in *The New Yorker, New Republic,* and *National Review.* The *Atlantic* magazine continues to publish some top-notch writing. Small journals of poetry survive, though only Calliope, Erato, and Clio could tell us how they make it.

It is the quality of everyday writing that worries me. If it is to improve, it will be up to parents, teachers, students, editors, publishers, private foundations, and—yes—lexicographers to help the cause along. Writers need all the help we can get.

3 Notes on How Not to Do It

Imagine, for a moment, that you are visiting Manhattan, and your immediate purpose is to jaywalk across Seventh Avenue at rush hour. Taxis stream past in yellow-jacket swarms. Drivers yell imprecations. Lights flash, sirens scream. It seems a long way to Penn Station, and the path is filled with hazards. So it is with the writing art. Just getting across a tough paragraph can become an act of survival.

As writers, we survive the scramble in two ways. The first is to avoid error. That is the theme of this chapter. The second is to get beyond the mere avoidance of error and to strive for something more. I will get to that in the next chapter.

First there are things we ought *not* to do, and the first of these is—

Don't mess up on grammar.

For those who think seriously about their writing, this must seem the most elementary advice that could be given. Perhaps so, but a great many professional writers appear to have forgotten their elementary lessons. They may never have learned them in the first place, for grammar, as such, seldom is taught in our public schools. Teachers and pupils alike tend to regard the subject as a colossal bore.

In some ways, grammar is a bore. I open Professor Curme's masterwork on syntax, and my eye falls upon a section dealing with "sentence dative of reference and interest." Here is an extensive analysis of "functions of the genitive." Here is a discussion of the objective predicate. The eye glazes over.

My own heretical thought is that the teaching of grammar

should be pretty well confined to the simplest rules: Subjects and predicates should agree in number. A singular antecedent cannot take a plural referent. Get straight on nominative and objective pronouns. That is about the size of it. It is not necessary to get into arcane maxims of Latin construction. Many distinctions between *who* and *whom* are fading so rapidly that by early in the twenty-first century they will have vanished altogether. Let 'em go.

But hold on. There are indeed levels of "good grammar" that ought to be diligently guarded. I am reminded of a true story involving a rough-cut gentleman who made a fortune—a very large fortune—in roofing materials. He said "it don't" and "between you and I," and he tramped roughshod through fields of double negatives. One day his daughter, a schoolteacher, reproached him.

"Daddy," she said lovingly, "you really must try to use good grammar."

"Honey," said he, "good grammar never made me no dollars."

Perhaps so, but "bad grammar" cost the fellow in all kinds of ways, in the amusement of his better-educated associates and in the impression he made upon others. What we provisionally call "good grammar" is among the hallmarks that identify a civilized society. Sterling silver is better than tinware. To write at the level of a plastic fork amounts to communication of a sort, but it is not the kind of writing that appeals to cultivated readers.

Ponder, if you will, a few Horrid Examples.

"As far as Terry and I's situation, it's behind us," said Clemens, who is now 5–0 after leading Boston to a 7–2 triumph against the Chicago White Sox.
—South Bend Tribune

Spanish is the tongue of her native Argentina and Scotland the ancestral home of both she and her husband.
—Bloomington (Ind.) Herald-Times

During a window of detente in 1980, she received the necessary permission for she and her children and their families to leave.
—San Antonio Express-News

Such blunders can be avoided by mentally leaping over words
that get in the way. The writer in Bloomington would not have
spoken of "the ancestral home of she." The writer in Texas would
not have written, "permission for she to leave."

Old rules of grammar may be bending and yielding, but the
rule on number endures. Let us flinch together:

> The scenes of mayhem from Los Angeles and other cities
> has led to a lot of talk . . .
> —The Wall Street Journal

> The rioting and arson in Los Angeles has left many Amer-
> icans shocked and outraged.
> —Rocky Mountain News (Denver)

> It are the statewide ballot propositions that are generat-
> ing the lion's share of interest.
> —The Olympian (Washington)

Some writers have trouble remembering that *neither/nor* and
each almost always demand singular verbs.

> Each of these thick, juicy filets are hand-selected for their
> blue ribbon quality.
> —ad for Blue Ribbon Beef

> Neither Congress nor the White House are likely to push
> for a permanent replacement for Mr. Garrett before the No-
> vember elections.
> —The Wall Street Journal

Antecedents and their referents must agree in number. Violation of this cardinal rule leads a writer into saying that when fire
broke out, everyone kept their head. In Cumberland, Md., a
Methodist church advertised its day care program: "Do you want
your child to develop their potential? To increase their speaking
skills? To enrich their vocabulary?" At the University of Notre
Dame, an academic librarian discussed ways to promote "his or
her role in the educational process by demonstrating a command
of the literature in their area of specialization." Clumsy, clumsy!

Don't fall into misspellings.

The owner of a dress shop received a flier from one of her wholesale suppliers. She was offered a "rabbet hair sweater," a "strait skirt" from Ellen Tracy, and a "fushia top" and "cummerbun" from Anne Klein II. The supplier also could ship a "high wasted" skirt and some "cruse wear" from Calvin Klein. If the supplier keeps books as carelessly as he spells, he will be broke before long.

A gentleman in Nebraska, eager to become a syndicated columnist, sent me three samples of his work. In the first he confused *capital* with *capitol*. In the second he spoke of a base drum. In the third he asserted that a low interest rate is the lynch pin of our economy. Back went his samples. The fellow won't make it. He won't even get past the front door.

Spelling matters. At the professional level, a misspelled word is the outward and visible sign of a careless writer. Why should an editor or publisher look at a manuscript that has been carelessly written? First impressions count.

Misspellings cannot be excused. They cannot convincingly be explained. Most word processing software includes a program for identifying misspelled words. The programs will not catch such homophones as *bazaar* for *bizarre,* or *feat* for *feet,* and they will be of no help on most foreign words and phrases, but within their limitations they are a poor speller's best friend.

Under the thundering pressure of a newspaper's deadline, a reporter may not have time to run her copy through a check on spelling. Those who prepare their material well in advance of publication lack even that excuse. In an article about figurines, *House & Garden* three times admired "dalmation" bookends. That firehouse dog is a dalmatian. Comic strip artists work weeks in advance. It is pure carelessness, nothing more, when a wildlife artist gives us *wild beast* for *wildebeest,* and *main* for *mane.* Advertising agencies have abundant time to check their copy for blatant errors, but misspellings constantly turn up in magazine displays.

Some misspellings are wildly original. The Young Americans for Freedom once wrote of the "hare's breath defeat" of Nelson Rockefeller. Classified advertising is a rich source of Horrid Examples. Here one finds Chip 'N Dale furniture, Floor Shine shoes, 14–carrot gold chains, coo-coo clocks, a krenlin bridal skirt, and a rod iron étagère. It's jus' hard to fine good rod iron anymore.

The best advice for writers is to cultivate a strong sense that a given word may . . . be . . . spelled . . . wrong. Be wary, be suspicious, be leery! Learn to be doubtful! It helps.

Don't use foreign phrases foolishly.

One of the great comic scenes in Shakespeare comes in the last act of *Love's Labour Lost*. The schoolmaster Holofernes takes on the curate Nathaniel in a battle of big words. They rattle along in dog Latin; they speak learnedly of a thrasonical nobleman whose behavior is peregrinate.

The two are having a balmy time when Moth, a page, breaks in with an aside: "They have been at a great feast of languages," he says, "and stolen the scraps."

The scene came back to mind some years ago, when Newsday carried a long piece on Arizona's controversial governor, Evan Mechem. The writer came to this conclusion: "A direct result of Mechem's fifteen months of tsuris is that Arizona is now a far better place to live."

Tsuris? What in the devil, I wondered, is *tsuris?* It was the key word in the sentence. The noun does not appear in *Webster's Ninth Collegiate* or in the massive *Webster's III*. It does appear in the *American Heritage* Second College Edition and in the *Random House Unabridged*. It may be spelled *tsouris* or *tzuris*. Spelled *tsores*, it appears in the 1986 supplement to the *Oxford English Dictionary*, where a first printed usage is dated from 1901. Not to keep you in suspense, *tsuris* is Yiddish for "trouble, woe, aggravation."

This leads me, as faithful readers will have guessed, to one more eruption on the use of foreign words and phrases.

There was a time, a century or so ago, when all educated Englishmen (and many educated Americans) were fluent in Latin, Greek, and French. They could adorn their manuscripts with quotations from Seneca and Thucydides and get away with it. We had scholars then in public life. Thomas Jefferson had strong feelings about the use of an ablative case in Greek. Daniel Webster decorated his oratory with filigrees of Latin maxims. In recent times, Ezra Pound larded his cantos with Chinese ideograms, but only God and Ezra Pound knew what they meant.

I pray you, beg you, beseech you, and implore you: Stick with English! Stick with English! Stick with English!

This is the rule: Unless you are absolutely certain about the aptness and the spelling of a foreign phrase, *forget it!* Suppress the impulse! Of course, if you have command of the phrase, if you believe its use would add a nice touch of elegance, and if you believe that 90 percent of your intended readers will understand the phrase and applaud your wit and erudition—all right, go ahead, you reckless fool. Be forewarned: The accurate use of such a phrase may add to your reputation as a writer. The bungled use surely will add to your reputation as a phony.

William F. Buckley, Jr., during the years he served as editor in chief of *National Review,* used foreign phrases with a sure and certain hand. He speaks fluent French and Spanish, and he can find his way across the perilous minefields of the dative case in Latin. Yet even my beloved brother had a way of falling into excess. In 1988 a reader complained mildly that in a single issue of the magazine, he had to grapple with—*perestroika, ad nauseam, vere dignum et justum est, ad infinitum, cogito ergo sum, märchen, sum ergo cognito, credo quia absurdum est, anima, nomenklatura, glasnost, magnum opus, soi-disant, de haut en bas, a fortiori, Kraft durch Freude, Ordnung, Achtung, jeu d'esprit, tour de force,* and *billets-doux.*

Buckley responded to the complaint by saying that foreign words and phrases, delicately used, "bring little piquancies and *aperçus* with them." True enough, but before we serve our readers *aperçus* like *aperitifs,* we ought soberly to consider whether we are achieving net gain or net loss in understanding.

Something in the American character pathetically envies the French. In the back of our minds there crouches a humbling notion that the French are literate and sophisticated fellows, and we Americans are rubes. From this foolishness there emerges an insane desire to garnish our writing with sprigs of Française.

This is almost always a mistake. God did not make the American tongue to curl into the French "u," and God did not make our noses to produce the subtle nasalities, somewhere between a honk and a whinny, that distinguish the French *en* from *on* and *an* from *en*. When we stab at French phrases we are likely to produce the "chase lounge" and the "horse de combat." What we do with *lingerie* brings tears to Gallic eyes.

To judge from the clippings that are sent me, not one writer in a thousand knows the meaning of *coup de grâce*. It is a stroke of mercy; it is the finishing stroke, the death blow. In the days of chivalry it was the final sword's thrust that instantly dispatched a mortally wounded foe.

But in Trenton, N.J., a retiring superintendent of schools said he was most proud of his students' gains in math and English. Their achievement, he said, is his *coup de grâce*. In Savannah, Georgia's chief medical examiner testified in a murder trial. He got it right: He said the deceased had been shot once in the chest and then shot twice more as he lay on the floor. The final two shots, he said, "appear to be *coup de grâce* wounds." Alas, it came out in the Evening Press, *coup de grâs* wounds. A *coup de grâs*, if it means anything, might mean that a fat person had managed to lose thirty pounds.

Half a dozen other *coups* may lure the writer. There is the stroke of good fortune called a *coup de bonheur,* the brilliant exploit called the *coup d'éclat,* and the surprise attack known as a *coup de main*. When conspirators attempted to overthrow Mikhail Gorbachev in August 1991, they were attempting a *coup d'état*. They failed. It was rather a *coup manqué*. Do 90 percent of our readers comprehend *coup d'état*? Maybe yes, maybe no.

In December 1983, a sportswriter for Newsday turned out a story about a three-way trade involving twelve players. After describing the deal, the writer continued:

> The *menage a trois* trade appeared to set the stage for another three-club deal involving the Cubs, Padres and Royals.

Where did he get this stuff? A *ménage à trois* is usually a living arrangement involving a husband, his wife, and his mistress—or less often, we may suppose, a wife, her husband, and her lover. And to show you how things can get bolixed, the Portland Oregonian once described a cassata cake. It is "an amazing *ménage* of amaretto, sweet marscapone cheese and dark chocolate icing." Melange, maybe?

Cooking seems to bring out the worst of our fractured French. The Miami News, in a moment of inattention, identified TV's Chef Tell as "a four-time Cordon Blew winner." A restaurant in Culpeper, Va., now fortunately defunct, listed beef "with a cup of au jus on the side." *Better Homes & Gardens,* which is old enough to know better, presented a recipe for roasted veal: "While the au jus simmers . . ."

In Birmingham, Ala., a country club promoted its gourmet candlelight dinner. This was to begin with consumme Rothchild, followed by Northern pike cressonier, accompanied by a bouquetierre of vegetables, lettuce with radoichio, Lindenburg cheese, demi-tas and petit-fores. This was at $30 per person.

Someone should have told the menu chairman that the soup is consommé, the gentleman's name was Rothschild, "cressonier" must mean with watercress, radoichio presumably is radicchio (an Italian red chicory), the cheese may have been Limburger, though it seems a smelly choice, the little cup of coffee is a demitasse, and those tiny cakes are petit fours (or petits fours, take your choice).

A restaurant in Harrisburg, Pa., advertised its menu in the Sunday Patriot News: "Hord'derves of selected seafood items included with all dinners." Halfway across the continent, in Topeka, the Greenery Lounge offered music by Jeannie Dieball: "Come and listen and enjoy our free hor'devours." In Washington State, a writer on the Olympian promoted a party to welcome the season's beaujolais. The piece de resistance was "coca vin."

Well, those tasty tidbits are *hors d'oeuvres.* The Olympian chicken purportedly, but doubtfully, was *coq au vin.*

For the record, the late Agatha Christie was not a "grand dame." She was a *grande dame.* An epileptic spasm is not a "grandma seizure," but an attack of *grand mal.* The Dallas Cowboys and the Washington Redskins were not engaged one December in a "malay," but in a *melee.* The soup is the *soup du jour,* not the *soup de jour.* A sauce is made from Grand Marnier, not Grand Manier. A boxing writer for Sports Form reported that Julio Cesar Chavez

won a bout in Las Vegas because he has "a chin that is non-peril
for any weight division." It doubtless would be a great asset for
any pugilist to have a chin immune from peril, but the chin of
Señor Chavez was probably *nonpareil,* a chin without compare.
The ladies at a Portland (Ore.) bridge club do not pass "bons
mot" over their cucumber sandwiches; they pass *bons mots.* The
birds in an AP photo do not fly off in mass, but *en masse.*

The Gannett News Service quoted a sociologist on contemporary marriage: "It's become almost a social moray to marry someone close to your own age." I never met a moray, except in the eel
clues of a crossword puzzle. Neither have I met a singular form of
mores. I don't believe there is one.

Yogi Berra once said, or so it is said he said, that something was
"déjà vu all over again." A lovely line. In 1990 Lee Trevino and
Jack Nicklaus were fighting it out for prize money in the U.S.
Open. They had known such battles before. Said a writer in the
Bridgeport (Conn.) Post: "It was like deja vous." Not such a
lovely line.

Matters of gender give unceasing trouble. A columnist for the
Los Angeles Times Syndicate wrote of her friend "Crocodile (nee
Lenny) Schwartz." Women are *née,* men are *né,* though I can't
recall a citation of any such usage. Would we speak of Muham-
mad Ali, *né* Cassius Clay? Probably not. When the Mets' Doc
Gooden resurfaced, having had his tsuris with drugs, The New
York Times welcomed him back in a headline as "Nouvelle Doc
on Opening Day." The doc is *nouveau;* tennis star Gabriela Saba-
tini would be *nouvelle.* The Boston Globe's man in Ankara offered
an interesting description of a Turkish masseuse—a "burly man
with close-cropped hair and a walrus mustache." This was a *mas-
seur,* monsieur. In the Indiana Daily Student in March 1989, a
freshman undertook to defend horse racing and dog racing:

> And to say that people who enjoy the sport have no concern
> for animals? Oh, contraire!

Even hello and good-bye give trouble. In a northern Virginia
county, when two members of the board of supervisors resigned,
the local headline read: "Ms. Maddox, Owings, Say Their Ados."
In 1990 the AP in Paris provided a story on the startling defeats

suffered by tennis stars Stefan Edberg and Boris Becker in the French Open. They were eliminated by relatively unknown players in the very first round. Headline in the Denver Post: "Edberg, Becker Bid Bonjour in Paris." *Bonjour? Sacre bleu!* (That is French for *aaargh!*) What the copy editor wanted was *adieu*, or *au revoir*, or *à bientôt*. Or just "farewell."

In Wooster, Ohio, a feature writer for the Daily Record went to a hair stylist who works with computer images. It was quite an experience. She felt like a new woman. "Viola!" the writer cried.

Viola? Who she? How did Viola get into the parlor? The word she wanted was *voilà!* A writer for the Seguin, Texas, Gazette Enterprise once had the same problem. When her brother solved a problem for her, she cried *wallah!*, which may be how you spell it in Seguin, Texas.

French is not the only language, of course, that gives us trouble when we try to show off. A long time ago—this would have been about 1939—the playwright William Inge was teaching English at Stephens College in Columbia, Mo. I was then a staff photographer at Stephens, earning my way through the University of Missouri. Inge was living with another member of the English faculty, Austin Faricy, in some very Bohemian digs just off the campus.

One evening Inge invited me and my current young lady, a fetching and intellectual Chi Omega, to come for an evening of listening to opera. Other students also arrived. It was an evening of dim lights, jug wine, and candles in wickered chianti bottles. I was an 18–year-old from Oklahoma City.

The conversation turned to opera, and Inge said something about a basso buffo. Eager to appear sophisticated, I puffed desperately on a pipe and volunteered that I had heard some of Buffo's recordings. "Magnificent artist," I said. Inge and Faricy exchanged a Meaningful Glance. There followed a Pregnant Pause.

As I was walking my date back to her sorority house, she gave me a look that combined pity, scorn, and affection in equal parts. She was a music major. A basso buffo, she gently informed me, is a bass singer who specializes in comic parts. I said, "Oh."

These things happen, but they ought not to happen. Some dictionaries run foreign phrases right along in the principal alphabetical text. Others list them separately. The *Random House*

Unabridged provides a concise dictionary in French, German, Spanish, and Italian. I rely constantly on the Berlitz-Mawson *Dictionary of Foreign Terms,* published by Crowell in 1975. Writers who find themselves in doubt can always find somebody—a local teacher, a Catholic priest, a rabbi, an immigrant—to help with spelling and usage. Mistakes are not unavoidable.

But mistakes abound. A Houston bank runs an advertisement "in memorium." It's *in memoriam.* A weekly in Buena Vista, Va., speaks of an ad hock committee to study local fire service. That's an *ad hoc* committee. A Maryland manufacturer offers its digitizer for sale at $1,000: "Limit one per bonified dealer." *Southern Living* interviews a "bonafied World War II ace." I offer these Horrid Examples with my *bona fides.* I did not make them up.

Horrid Examples could continue ad nauseum, but the spelling is *ad nauseam.* The phrase is not per say. It's *per se.* The Port St. Lucie (Fla.) Tribune fielded a question from a curious reader: "Did pumpkins come from Europe?" The Tribune had a snappy answer: "No, sir, vice versa," i.e., Europe comes from pumpkins.

The *i.e.* you just skipped over is an abbreviation for *id est,* that is. I am thus reminded to express a word of caution on the language of footnotes. The rules defining endnotes and footnotes are meticulous and demanding. Don't do as I say. Do as your professor says. To introduce a series of examples, horrid or otherwise, the word is *videlicet,* abbreviated for some reason to *viz.* The four-dollar word for "see" is *vide.* The scholarly phrase for "for example" is *exempli gratia,* abbreviated to *e.g.* An italic *supra* means "above." Manifestly, *infra* is "below."

There is a difference between *opere citato* (op. cit.) and *ibidem* (ibid.). An *opera citato* is an Italian opera with an urban setting, such as Mozart's *Le nozze di Figaro.* An *ibidem* is a shore bird common to the Florida Gulf Coast. I wanted to see if you were paying attention. In scholarly papers, *op. cit.* identifies a second reference to a particular source; *ibid.* identifies further references to the same source, provided there have been no intervening notes on some other work. The hell with it.

Latin plurals are booby traps. The plural of *et al.* is not *et als* but rather *et alia* or *et alii.* Data *are,* and media *are,* and honoraria *are.* These are plural forms. One bacterium, two bacteria. The male graduate is an alumnus; two male graduates are alumni. A woman is an alumna; she and her sister are alumnae. It's curriculum, curricula.

In March of 1989 the Coffeyville (Kans.) Journal carried a page-one photo of Mrs. Ollie Brocaw engaged in spring trimming. "She got outside last week and did some pruning on her exterior flora and fauna." Fine for the flora, hell on the fauna.

Greek plurals also cause problems. Even so gifted a writer as columnist Ellen Goodman remarked in a piece about Richard Nixon that "there is a criteria for rehabilitation." One criterion, two criteria. One rookie infielder may be a phenomenon; two would be phenomena. One encephalon; two encephala. You can take your choice of automatons or automata, but *automatons* looks better and will not suggest a dish cooked with tomatoes. The plural of helicon is *helicons*. A *gonfalon* comes from Italian, not from Greek, and more than one gonfalon is quite a vexillogical show. You could look it up.

I mentioned earlier that some writers have tsuris with Yiddish. Indeed they do. In Oregon the Willamette Writers Conference announced an unusual program: "We will be offering panels, short and long workshops, and time for kibbutz with other writers." A kibbutz is an Israeli community farm. These writers wanted to kibitz, i.e., to give unsolicited advice to one another.

German presents a problem in trying to spell *Gemütlichkeit* without an umlaut, but *Gemuetlichkeit* will do. The Seattle Times once identified Marianna Sagebrecht as "a middle-aged Pollyanna in liederhosen." These would be singing jeans. The lady was wearing *Lederhosen*.

To sum up: The use of foreign words and phrases has much in common with cooking. Used sparingly, deftly, accurately, and with consideration for the sophisticated or unsophisticated tastes of our guests—yes, herbs and spices can greatly improve a sauce or a marinade. No doubt about it.

But the foreign phrase that is used inaptly or ignorantly is the banana peel that brings on a pratfall. A few years ago a writer for a West Coast weekly set out to do a serious piece on local music groups. The Portland Camerata, he said confidently, is "a 16–voice acapulco choir." A writer for the Cleveland Plain Dealer once described the ball gown of a local matron. It was "a black, strapless silk organza over cafe ole silk." On that note I will subside. As we Italians say, *chow!*

Don't fool around with dialect.

In his hilarious essay on the literary offenses of James Fenimore Cooper—an essay that every novelist should take to heart—Mark Twain laid down eighteen rules that govern the writing of romantic fiction. This was Rule Seven:

"It requires that when a personage talks like an illustrated, gilt-edged, tree-calf, hand-tooled, seven-dollar Friendship's Offering in the beginning of a paragraph, he shall not talk like a Negro minstrel in the end of it."

Twain was a master of dialectal writing. He worked at it. He began *Huckleberry Finn* with an explanatory note:

> In this book a number of dialects are used, to wit: the Missouri negro dialect; the extremist form of the backwoods Southwestern dialect; the ordinary "Pike County" dialect; and four modified varieties of this last. The shadings have not been done in a haphazard fashion, or by guesswork; but painstakingly, and with the trustworthy guidance and support of personal familiarity with these several forms of speech.
>
> I make this explanation for the reason that without it many readers would suppose that all these characters were trying to talk alike and not succeeding.

Twain's example is a hard example to follow. Even the most skilled writers have trouble with dialect. My beloved brother pundit, William F. Buckley, Jr., ran headlong into Rule Seven in one of his delightful Blackford Oakes novels. Lyndon Johnson was a major character. Buckley undertook to capture the president's Texas speech. He might with equal success have attempted to capture a bubble in a butterfly net.

Thus the reader observes that sometimes Lyndon says "I," and sometimes Lyndon says "Ah." At one point in the novel Johnson is thinking of sending a note to Hanoi: "Ah know we never done it before." At another point he is thinking of getting in touch with Brezhnev: "Who knows how to work the hot line? I don't; never used it." Over the course of two pages, Lyndon says "Ah" six times and "I" nine times.

In one of his Sackett novels, *Lonely on the Mountain,* the late Louis L'Amour toppled into the same pitfall. The narrator, William Tell Sackett, sometimes is *thinkin'* and sometimes is *thinking.* He is alternately *ridin'* and *riding.* We find Tell Sackett *scrapin',* *diggin',* *drinkin',* *talkin',* *shootin',* *settin',* *lookin',* *studyin',* and *gold minin'.* At the same time, Tell is *remembering, wondering, glancing, squatting, telling, trading,* and *learning.*

Owen Wister had his problems. Off and on throughout *The Virginian,* Wister spelled "you" as "yu." It is not clear why he used this peculiar orthography, for 99.99 percent of English speaking people pronounce "you" as "yu." On one page Wister spells the familiar conjunction *an'.* On the same page the hero spells it *and.* Like Lyndon Johnson, the Virginian talks cowhand part of the time, saying "it don't" and "he don't," and then he forgets and for no apparent reason, with the same companions and in the same rough surroundings, the Virginian says "it doesn't" and "he doesn't."

Robert Louis Stevenson couldn't stay consistent. In *Kidnapped,* David Balfour befriends Alan Breck. Stevenson could not decide whether Alan says *you* or *ye.* Sometimes Alan speaks hoot mon Scottish, and sometimes not. D.H. Lawrence's amorous gamekeeper shifted in and out of dialect. Stephen Crane could not keep one of his soldiers consistently saying *th'* or *the.*

Writing good dialect demands an ear as sensitive as the most delicate microphone. It demands surpassing skills of orthography. It is fearfully difficult to transcribe speech. A long time ago I sought advice on how to spell the exchange of greetings between two young ladies of Richmond who meet on Grace Street. This is as close as native Richmonders could come:

"Hah, hower you?"

"Ah'm fahn, har're you?"

And that is not close at all.

Some writers, notably William Faulkner and Margaret Mitchell, handled the speech of Southerners, white and black, with a sure hand. I have lived all my life in the South, and I believe I know something of the cadences of Southern speech, but I wouldn't tackle the assignment without compelling reason.

It is not enough to listen intently and to spell phonetically. Far more is required in the writing of dialect. If we are to get it right, we must know what kind of razor our fictional hero uses in the morning, what kind of underwear he wears, what he likes for breakfast. I remember reading in some forgotten novel about a woman's bathroom. In a mirror-fronted cabinet over the sink was a bottle of Listerine and a brush choked with hair. The bathroom, and the woman, came alive. Her accent became believable.

We must recognize that speech patterns change according to circumstance. Essayist David Cohn once laid down Cohn's Law on the Thickness of a Southern Girl's Southern Accent. The law postulates that the thickness increases by the square of the distance she travels north of the Mason-Dixon Line. By th' tahm she gaits to Bosson you can ba'ly unnerstan' a wuhd she says.

This was certainly true of Lyndon Johnson. When he was in his molasses mode, seeking to pour syrup on a waffling senator, Lyndon spoke as if he had a ripe plum in his mouth. On state occasions his grammar was impeccable. On other occasions, when the cactus juice was flowing, he spoke barroom Texan. I doubt if even the most meticulous writer could spell out Johnson's nasalities. The president had a large nose, filled with resonant cavities, and the sound chambers of his sinuses did odd things to his speech.

Experts in the branch of linguistics that is known as dialectology pursue the role of Henry Higgins in Shaw's *Pygmalion*. Their art is to identify regional speech by variations in nomenclature. In some areas the container we use for bringing home the groceries is a bag; elsewhere it is a sack; elsewhere a tote.

Some years ago Professor Marvin Carmony of Indiana State University in Terre Haute studied variations in the speech of Indiana. He found that some Hoosiers speak of a quarter *till* eight, and some of a quarter *of* eight. Well-educated men tended to speak of a quarter *to* eight. In some parts of the country people speak of roller *shades*. In Indiana they are *window blinds*. One woman, reflecting the influence of her Tennessee-born mother, spoke of a *parlor.* In Indiana the room is a *living room.* Older people use a *skillet;* younger people use a *frying pan.* Indianans who emigrated from Pennsylvania put potatoes in a *gunny sack.* Others put taters in a *burlap bag.*

In writing dialect, as in so many other areas, the trick is to listen *intently.* If your purpose is to write in Swedish dialect, or Mexican or French-Canadian or Cajun dialect, you must listen with total concentration to people who speak the Swedish or Spanish or French of a given region. You must listen with total concentration to the rhythms of speech and to the regional choice of words. You must take into account the circumstances in which the speech is to be reproduced. A farmhand is likely to speak in one voice when he is courting his girl, and in quite another voice when he is coaxing a mule.

Within these guidelines of time, place, and circumstance, a writer of dialect must stay in his lane. As I have remarked elsewhere, if his stage Irishman says *fwhat* the first time, he must say *fwhat* till kingdom come, though it may drive his editors to *dhrink.*

Don't get careless with trademarks.

For more than twenty years I lived up in the Blue Ridge Mountains of Virginia, about eighty miles west of Washington, D.C. Our post office was at Woodville, but when I began writing an occasional country column I latched on to the dateline of Scrabble, Va. Before long, a stuffy letter arrived from lawyers representing Selchow & Richter, manufacturers of the word game of the same name. They demanded that I abandon the dateline instanter, or face horrible consequences in the courts of law.

Aha! I responded happily by suggesting what the lawyers could do with their injunction. Scrabble was, and is, a very real community in Rappahannock County. The name appears on Civil War maps of the area in which Ranger Mosby made his raids. It appears on maps of the Coast and Geodetic Survey. It appears on the county's official map. The community had its own post office until Jim Farley economized it out of existence about 1937. The name of "Scrabble" appears on a highway directional sign. (I know, because I put it there.) In sum, Scrabble, Va., existed long before anyone put *xiphoid* on a triple word score, and if the lawyers wanted to make something out of my cherished dateline, just let 'em try. I never heard another word.

I probably should not have replied in such a bellicose fashion, for the lawyers were only doing their job. Trademarks are precious possessions. The lawyers' responsibility is to prevent the unauthorized use of trade names lest the names become common property. The writer's obligation is to respect trademarks and to see that the trade names are capitalized on publication.

At one time such familiar words as *thermos, cellophane,* and *deep freeze* were the trademarks of their manufacturers. They long since passed into generic use and now may be lower-cased. A thousand familiar trade names are still under trademark protection, and we ought to be careful with them. A current list may be obtained from the U.S. Trademark Association, which in 1992 could be addressed at 6 East 45th St., New York, NY 10017. The association then maintained an afternoon hotline (212) 986-5880, for the convenience of writers and editors.

These are only a few of the trademarked names that must be capitalized on publication:

Adidas footwear	*Day-Glo* paint	*Muzak* music
Advil analgesic	*Dixie* paper cups	*Naugahyde* fabric
Alcoa aluminum	*Dumpster* containers	*Palm Beach* suits
Alka-Seltzer antacid	*Erector* sets	*Popsicle* ices
AstroTurf turf	*Grape-Nuts* cereal	*Princess* phones
Band-Aid bandages	*Jacuzzi* baths	*Realtor* broker
Brillo scouring pads	*Jeep* vehicles	*Spam* meat
Bromo-Seltzer antacid	*Jiffy* mail bags	*Stetson* hats
B.V.D. underwear	*Kotex* napkins	*Teflon* coatings
Chap Stick lip balm	*Levi's* jeans	*Tinkertoy* blocks
Cool Whip topping	*Loafer* shoes	*Twinkies* snacks
Crayola crayons	*Mace* tear gas	*Xerox* copiers

It isn't likely that a minister, drafting a Sunday sermon for publication, will get in trouble for writing band-aid instead of Band-Aid, but you never know. Reporters, ad writers, novelists, and editors should mind their manners.

Don't coin words wantonly.

The key word here is *wantonly*. There is nothing wrong, and a great deal that is right, about coining new words. One of the lovely things about our lovely language is that it grows. The metaphor of spring is irresistible. Everywhere we look, new shoots are coming forth; hybrid formations appear; exotic creations suddenly flower. Many of them may be dandelions, but at least for a while they add a touch of color.

Autumn follows spring and summer. Our language accumulates deadwood. Some words disappear altogether. Some barely survive with notations of *arc.* and *obs.* During long lexicographical winters—seasons that may last a few centuries—primary meanings change. *Gay* becomes a noun. Spellings change, so that *publick* sloughs the *k* and *towne* loses its *e.* Alternate spellings gain recognition; we may spell it *sluff* if we please. Verb forms go through metamorphosis; in such reputable publications as The New York Times, the past tense of *sneak* becomes acceptably *snuck*.

All this is wonderful. Writers ought to revel in neologisms. Shakespeare coined hundreds of new words. Lewis Carroll's jabberwock came whiffling through the tulgey wood and burbled as it came. The late Wallace Stevens (1955), a poet with a kaleidoscopic eye, contrived his own words when he couldn't find one to suit him. Thus he wrote of nincompated pedagogues, clickering syllables, and pennicles of frost. His pittering images dulcied and pampaluned in bazzling floraisons and halidoms. H.L. Mencken, who died in 1956, left amid his legacy the classic formulation of *ecdysiast,* i.e., a dancer who does the striptease.

But Shakespeare was a genius, Carroll was a genius, and Stevens and Mencken were men of remarkable talents. Gentle reader, if I may fall into apostrophe, you are probably not a genius. Therefore, do not *wantonly* coin words! You will find 460,000 words in *Webster's III,* and surely that compendium should suffice for every day.

Happily, I may add, coinages continue, wantonly or not. Most of the neologisms that come my way are verbs. Some of them are great, some are not so great, and some of them I hope never to see again. A movie critic in the Terre Haute Tribune-Star summarized the plot of a movie: "Lorie is attracted to Dan, but she is, naturally enough, obnoxed by his ego." In Omaha, an angry woman wrote the editor: "When will the news media be revulsed enough to tell the story of rescue workers at abortion clinics who get brutally manhandled by police?" One of Dear Abby's readers complained of conduct "that really nauses me out." Columnist Judy Markey watched the Persian Gulf War on TV: "You are very weirded out by this," she said. Gracious! There are four verbs that strike me as right for interment. And to borrow a verb from the San Antonio News-Express, they ought not to be unburied any time soon.

On the other hand, *to dainty* seems to me a thing of beauty. It turned up in 1989 when the Omaha World-Herald carried a feature on wall coverings. Wallpaper designers "now acknowledge that wallpaper shouldn't be daintied to death." Accord it a permanent place in the language!

I like *to bleaken,* as in "Czechoslovakia Bleakens U.S. Hockey Hopes." The AP revived *to coronate* when Queen Juliana ascended to the throne of the Netherlands. It's a useful verb, and it's not for monarchs only: The Rock Island (Ill.) Argus has reported the coronation of a Grand Champion Angus steer. The Charlotte Observer revived another useful verb: "Broyhill Richens Campaign Fund." Miss Manners has breathed new life in *to neaten.* A garden magazine advertised a product that will "lushen up your foliage." These are splendid verbs.

I like *to biograph.* It popped up in the Fort Worth Star-Telegram, where a book reviewer commented that Ring Lardner had survived "to biograph his remarkable family." I would admit it to *Webster's* gates.

The next dictionaries that come from the press surely will recognize *to hub,* which is what USAir does in Charlotte and United does in Chicago. If we may forward something, may we also backward something? NBC weatherman Willard Scott said he "just backwarded" into wishing a happy birthday to centenarians. A doubtful nomination came from a weatherman in New York. He told Newsday that Hurricane Gloria "just kind of mediocred out."

An ad in appeared in Miami in 1984: "Term papers accurated." In Oregon, a physician assessed the damage to the Achilles tendon of a basketball player: "It's all a matter of quantitating the amount." An automobile manufacturer sent a memorandum to regional dealers: A decision had been made "to deproliferate the following low volume, slow-moving models." Maybe *accurate, quantitate,* and *deproliferate* will make it. I can think of a lot of things that ought to be deproliferated.

Not much can be said in favor of *to subterfuge,* as in the special diet that will "subterfuge your weight loss efforts." Other noun transformations seem as feeble. In Mount Airy, N.C., the News reported that Commissioner Frank Lowey *chagrined* at the deposit of state funds in distant banks. In Vero Beach, Fla., "Microwaved chili provides kids first *chefing* experience." From a book critic at the Chicago Tribune came a note on Dostoyevski's *The Brothers Karamazov.* The novel recently had benefited "from a badly needed new *Englishing.*" In Oregon the Portland State University offered prospective teachers a course in *"Sciencing* for Kids."

Readers have cited quite a few *uns* and *ups.* A developer in South Carolina offered to *upfit* a building to suit a buyer's needs. In Florida, police *uprighted* tombstones after vandals toppled them. In Greer, S.C., neighbors were urged to *upkeep* their property. In Tacoma, a reader of the News Tribune wondered why a crime bill "is still *unenacted.*" In Las Vegas, a prosecutor assumed that a hospital was seeking to *unpublic* certain documents. I can think of ten thousand bills that ought to be unenacted, and I have concluded that many aspects of the private life of a public person ought to be kept unpublic.

The acceptability of a neologism is a matter of editorial judgment. I like an item from Potter County, Tenn., where the local prosecutor urged a judge to send a burglar to prison. He said it would send a message to every other person who takes it upon himself "to break into someone's business and *ramshackle* it." Right on! But I can't say much for an item from Campbell County. A local historian acknowledged his debt to manuscripts that never had been available except to random members of the public who *plummage* through the archives.

One verb strikes me as perfect for the occasion. It cannot be improved upon. Stand back for a moment and marvel at a writer for the Columbia (S.C.) State who summarized the plot of the

1963 movie *Cleopatra*. In all of English literature a more compact sentence has never been composed: "Queen of Egypt seduces Caesar, sees Mark Antony, asps herself."

Newly coined verbs that end in *-ize* are in a class by themselves; most of them ought to stay there. There is something frantic in a lawyer's announcement that he will *statementize* his witnesses on a given day. The poor fellow is so desperately rushed that he cannot take a fraction of a second to write that he will take statements instead. An executive who wants to *concretize* a proposal is headed for mush. Nothing is gained by *perennializing* a garden. Let us say simply that perennials should be planted there.

This is not to condemn all *-ize* verbs out of hand. The process of thus converting virgin nouns into bastard verbs has been going on for at least five hundred years. *Harmonize* dates from 1483 and *memorize* from 1591. Our language would be poorer without *sermonize* (1635), *criticize* (1649), *signalize* (1654), and *anthologize* (1892). In a tolerant humor, I would concede that a useful purpose is served by *privatize* and even by *finalize*, which carries a meaning not served by *to complete*.

As for the rest, let it be left to one's editorial judgment. A Baptist paper in Louisiana announced in 1984 that "the evidence of the blessed is always *tangibilized*." The Indianapolis Star editorialized that "many of us automatically *catastrophize* when a crisis approaches." We learned from some source—I have mislaid the clipping—that the first presidential debate in 1984 *respectabilized* the candidacy of Walter Mondale.

A reader of the Omaha World-Herald wrote the editor about the role of NASA (the National Aeronautics and Space Administration). "NASA tries to answer the question of how we can live and work together without the *sardineization* of Earth's most populated cities." The commander of Fort Bliss, Texas, wrote to the family of a recruit: "I am pleased to inform you that Michael has arrived safely and has begun the *soldierization* process."

Professional football, it appears from the Los Angeles Times, has been *corporatized*. A California minister offers drive-in services on Sunday mornings to *positivize* attitudes about going to church. In Las Vegas, a reader of the Sun reacted to news that the Pentagon was experimenting with "psychic force." This was a lot of baloney, he said, intended for those "who are easily *suggestionized.*" In Tempe, Ariz., a professor of math told a reporter that "the world is becoming more and more *mathematized.*" The normally sane *New Yorker* magazine has given us *to Broadwayize.* From *The New Republic* comes *Manhattanize.* A letter writer in San Diego feared all of California would soon be *Los Angelized.* In 1991 a magazine called *Association Publishing* let us know that in the multifaceted world of marketing planning "tactics will need to be *calendarized* to be truly useful." Absolutely.

Early in 1991 the Palm Beach Post reported on a new movement in biblical scholarship. Led by black professors, the effort is to explore evidence that Noah's son Ham and others, including Egyptians and Canaanites, were black. A divinity professor at Howard University asked us not to worry. This is not an attempt, he said, "to *blackenize* the whole Bible."

Aileen Lorberg of Cape Girardeau, Mo., a top-ranking word maven, has recorded a citation of *awfulize,* an awful verb indeed. Columnist Mary McGrory of The Washington Post also collects these things. She told the heart-warming story of a family that adopted a Down's syndrome baby, even though friends warned the parents that they would *disasterize* their life. In Alaska, a contributor to the Anchorage Times said unkind things about environmental lobbyists: "Nattily attired in green sweat shirts, freshly talcumed sneakers and backpacks in position, their week's agenda will *strategize* on how to coerce or convince Congress." There was an agenda for you—an agenda in backpack and freshly talcumed sneakers.

Enough already. These are other *-ize* verbs of fairly recent vintage. Vote up or down as you will: *agendize, civilianize, condominiumize, chronicalize, credentialize, directionalize, restaurantize, reprioritize, amenitize, accessorize, dignitize, peripheralize, securitize,* and *funeralize.*

My own favorite comes from columnist Jeffrey Hart, who reminisced about the long-ago sex and espionage scandal in England that involved defense minister John Profumo and call girl Christine Keeler. It is not clear, said Hart, whether Keeler *horizontalized* her way to the information she sought.

The last word on this subject profitably may be left to the editors of *American Heritage Dictionary.* The *-ize* suffix is well established, but it can be ambiguous. They note, for example, that to *computerize* may mean "to furnish with computers," as in "computerizing an office." It may also mean "to enter data into a computer." Many recently coined *-ize* verbs are acceptable, but be wary: "Coinages of this sort should be used with caution until they have passed the tests of manifest utility and acceptance by reputable writers."

That sound advice applies not only to *-ize* verbs but to newly minted nouns, adjectives and adverbs as well. In 1984, TV's friendly Hugh Downs tried to launch *vidience* (people who watch TV) as something more than an *audience,* but the coinage never caught on. The Seattle Post-Intelligencer came up with "the *fabulosity* of Broadway." Out of the space program, sadly, came *teachernaut.* In Indian River County, Fla., an ordinance fixed a level of *opaquity* for fences. An automobile dealer advertised cars for *matures* who want more interior room. We matures also want seats with greater *recline.* We may not be so interested in "*galores* of hardwood furniture," but who knows? A member of the Southern Baptist Alliance rued the growth of a new *creedalism.* In Nebraska, a headline reported that "sisterly *loathe* keeps warring siblings apart." A monthly newsletter called *Who's Mailing What!* reported a loophole in laws governing federal campaign contributions. As a result, abuses could create "a rampaging monster of such *terribility* as to rival Dr. Frankenstein's." We matures are not going to buy *terribility.*

Not all our newly coined nouns are clunkers. Some strike a crystal chime. *Time* magazine invented *trendlet,* an excellent word for the little movement that is not big enough to wear knickers and become a trend. I like *mushification,* a word used by P.R. man Jody Powell to describe much revisionist history. There is something to be said for *mediability,* coined by Richard Roeper of the Chicago Sun-Times in a piece about globe-trotting Governor Jim Thompson. Some politicians have it, and some don't, and the ones with enduring mediability get in the papers all the time.

Two truly delightful nouns came along early in the 1990s. I love both of them. In Seattle, a real estate agent commented upon life in a run-down section of the city. "There's a lot of nervousness and upsetedness," he said. It occurs to me that I have spent my life in newspapering covering upsetedness. It abounds.

My other favorite came from Allen Nixon, a state highway trooper in Oklahoma. He covered a tornado that injured a woman in a mobile home near Laverne. The AP asked for details. "I don't have the exacts," he said, "but I understand she had a broken leg." Trouble is that most of us, most of the time, "don't have the exacts."

Three adjectives merit nomination. Professor Robert Schmuhl of Notre Dame wrote that some people are handy, "but I am *thumby*." His name should be Legion, for he is many. I also like a line from an old salt who recalled for the Portland Oregonian a voyage around Cape Horn in World War II. He went through seas that were *sharky* with German submarines. My favorite comes from a free safety for Clemson University in South Carolina. He was talking to a reporter for the Greenville News about defensive tactics in a coming game: "It will be a very *thinkative* thing," he said.

The new adverbs that have come my way are a mixed lot. There's not much to be said for *secludedly*, which is how Alexander Solzhenitsyn has lived in Vermont since 1976. Someone else lives *remotely* in Wyoming. The Vatican has criticized theologians who *novelly* apply their teaching authority. The Daily News of Northwest Florida reported that "Eastern is *fastly* becoming a shrinking airline," suggesting correctly that soonly it would be in real trouble.

I like *blanketly*. It has turned up in two citations. One involved former Attorney General Ed Meese who wanted to reverse a policy that *blanketly* favored refugees. The other concerned Nevada State Senator Ray Shaffer, who got in trouble when he was running for treasurer in 1990. He was quoted as saying that some handicapped people might be unable to handle duties in his office. Thunder rolled about his head. Belatedly, he told the Las Vegas Review defensively, "No way would I blanketly include all the disabled."

Two citations also have come along for *majorly*. In 1989 the Kraft cheese people conducted a contest. Something went badly awry, with the result that every entrant inadvertently became a Big Winner. Evidently the company handled the matter poorly, for an expert in public relations had Monday morning advice:

"Kraft should have gone majorly public." During the Christmas season in Bloomington, Ind., when students at Indiana University head for their homes, business at Bloomington's beaneries falls off. The manager of Garcia's Pizza-in-a-Pan complained sadly. Business, he said, "has slacked off majorly."

The adverb *painterly* dates from around 1580. Its cousin *lawyerly* also has respectable age, but new cousins keep coming along. A columnist in the Seattle Times reported in 1991 that a Polish fashion designer had taken on her greatest challenge. She hoped to make Lech Walesa look "more presidential and less workerly." The thought inspires imitation. A good public relations adviser, seeking to create an outdoorly image, might make a politician look more fisherly. Given the right duds, one could look golferly, hunterly, riderly, or sailorly. Such an image surely would be *studly,* an adverb admiringly extended to a placekicker at Southern Methodist University. He was "one studly kicker," said a sportswriter. Fine with me.

Don't be redundant!

In *The Elements of Style,* which is the second book a writer should buy (a good dictionary is the first book), E.B. White recalled one of the rules laid down by his old teacher at Cornell, William Strunk, Jr. This was Professor Strunk's Rule 13:

> Omit needless words. A sentence should contain no unnecessary words, a paragraph no unnecessary sentences, for the same reason that a drawing should have no unnecessary lines and a machine no unnecessary parts. This requires not that the writer make all his sentences short, or that he avoid all detail and treat his subjects only in outline, but that every word tell.

Rule 13 is a great rule, provided one gives a broad interpretation to *needless.* Not all cholesterol, the doctors tell us, is bad cholesterol. There is good cholesterol also. So it is with redundant words. Most redundancies are on the bad side. They leave fatty deposits in the arteries of prose. *Drop that metaphor!* The editors of *Webster's Dictionary of English Usage* make the point in distinguishing between the Redundancy Useful and the Redundancy Wordy.

The editors offer thirteen examples of the Redundancy Useful. As it happens, I disagree with them on six of the thirteen, but so it goes. By way of example, the editors find nothing amiss in a sentence noting that ownership of the Panama Canal will *revert back* to Panama. Let us wince together.

Why the *back*? The Buffalo News in 1991 headlined a piece of nostalgia, "Columnist Reflects Back on 12-year Partnership." What is gained by *back*? Nothing is gained by *back*. In an editorial early in 1992, the Seattle Post-Intelligencer commended the Washington State Supreme Court. It had *remanded back* the case of a man convicted of burglary. The P-I is wedded to *back*. In another instance, the U.S. Court of Appeals for the Ninth Circuit had *remanded back* a case involving Indian fishing rights. Unnecessary word! An appellate court doesn't *remand back*. It plainly and simply remands. The *back* is a Rule 13 incrustacean.

Such barnacles grow. The AP reported from Tampa that an 11-year-old boy had written General Norman Schwarzkopf in Saudi Arabia; the lad received a *reply back*. The Mexican American Legal Defense Fund appealed in 1990 for funds to buy a computer: "We cannot *revert back* to using pencils, calculators and road maps." A correspondent for the Portland Oregonian filed a feature on Rock Creek, where a movie was being made: "The tavern will *revert back* to its original state immediately after filming ends."

O my aching back! Let us not remand back, revert back, reply back, or reflect back. Let us strike the little adverbs that ride like pilot fish on the back of verbs: *cancel out, saddle up, close up, type up*. In Biloxi, the Sun Herald noted that Orange Grove has become a heavily churched area: "Churches of all different denominations have sprouted up." In what other direction may a denomination sprout? It's not going to sprout down.

The editors at Merriam-Webster approve a line from Norman Mailer: ". . . one's past history was going to be removed." Is there any kind of history, unknown to me, that is other than *past* history? The editors extend their benediction to William Thackeray: ". . . let us begin with a true and authentic story." With deference to old Bill, I submit that *true* adds nothing useful to *authentic,* and *authentic* adds nothing useful to *true.*

These are not Redundancies Useful. They are Redundancies Wordy, and the world is full of them. Masters of ceremonies thank *each and every one.* Politicians oppose higher taxes *in any way, shape, or form.* Lawyers love conduct that *in and of itself* may not be unlawful. They ask: "What is the defendant's reputation for truth and veracity?" When I was covering trial courts I hungered for the moment when a witness would reply, "He's okay on truth, but he ain't much on veracity."

Redundancies Wordy run on and on: *basic fundamentals, hot water heater, invited guests, cooperate together, long chronic illness, new recruit, early pioneer, little hamlet, pastoral country place,* and *prerecorded.* In Redmond, Wash., a restaurant advertises a *free complimentary* dinner. The Corning cookware people advertise a saucepan with two sets of *perforated holes,* which presumably are better than unperforated holes. An attorney for the Sierra Club says that certain new regulations will not be *sufficient enough* to abate a lawsuit. Let us denounce one more time, all together, *at this point in time.*

The Hutchinson (Kans.) News covered a track meet at which team scores belatedly were tallied. The meet director said the scores would stand as announced "unless we find an erroneous error we didn't realize." Erroneous errors are the very worst kind.

In August 1991 the AP filed a report from Gulfport, Miss., about a rogue who had fourteen *phony aliases.* In Las Vegas, the Review-Journal noted an employment policy of a telemarketing company: The company fires any employee who makes *false misrepresentations.* A reader of the Greenville (S.C.) News wrote the editor to complain that the *true facts* about abortion are being suppressed.

Headline in Olathe, Kans.: "Murder Charge Filed in Man's Fatal Death." The headline echoed the boast of a bug bomb that "kills bugs dead." The AP has reported the testimony of *live witnesses,* who certainly are preferable to dead witnesses. In Florida a lawyer prepared a divorce agreement: "Wife is to execute an affidavit that she is not now married to any living person."

The old Washington Star, God rest it, once carried an obituary in which we learned that the deceased "left no living survivors." And no dead ones, either.

Thinking of affidavits, let me holler once more against *sworn affidavits*. At the time of the William Kennedy Smith rape trial in Florida, The Washington Post reported from West Palm Beach that the prosecutor had released "87 pages of sworn affidavits." The Post knows better. If an affidavit isn't sworn, it isn't an affidavit. Let us forthwith abandon such Redundancies Wordy as *old adage, old saw, old proverb,* and *old cliché.* And let us swear never to write of some event at 8 p.m. tonight or 11 a.m. in the morning. We can do better than to ask invitees, "Please RSVP by the enclosed card."

In 1991 the Terre Haute Tribune-Star, reporting on an historic property, noted that the property had been deeded in 1937 to 74-year-old John Bradford, "the only remaining male son of the family." In Mount Airy, N.C., the News reported that in coach Mike Royster's office is a photograph of his two twin sons. The Palm Beach Post informed us a few years ago that "Jack Nicklaus set the nine-hole record in 1978 when he birdied the last five holes consecutively." Golf is not my game, but perhaps some golfer could explain how Nicklaus could birdie the last five holes in any other fashion but consecutively.

Writers and editors will disagree on whether particular couplings are useful or wordy. I have disagreed with myself. In 1985 I set out to check the spelling of *hors d'oeuvre.* You know how it is. No writer who browses in a dictionary ever stops at one word; it would be like stopping at one pretzel. The wandering eye touched briefly on *horrent,* an adjective I had not seen before and have not seen since, and then settled lovingly on *horripilation.* It means goose bumps. At the first opportunity I wrote that when a kiss on the nape of the neck makes the short hairs rise and everything go tingle-tangle, that's horripilation.

"You disappoint me," wrote Dorothy Robinson of Portland, Ore. "'Nape of the neck' is redundant."

Sure enough, it is redundant. To write of the nape of the neck is to write of the back of the neck of the neck. I was about to confess error and promise to sin no more. Then I got to thinking.

The first purpose of prose is to convey thought from the writer to
the reader. Does the redundant *of the neck* help to convey thought?
I believe that it does. Not everyone may be wholly familiar with
the nape. Suppose:

> He pulled her close to him and then, gently, but with in-
> creasing pressure, he began to caress her nape. His eager
> fingers pushed aside the fine hair. She moaned with plea-
> sure as his lips touched her. "Don't stop," she gasped, "don't
> stop."

I submit that many a reader, plowing through that passage,
might surmise that the nape is located further south. My doubts
were later confirmed when a professor of English at Miami-Dade
Community College ran a test. He asked 111 of his freshman
students to identify the nape in the sentence, "He kissed her on
the nape." Fifty-four students got it right, thirty made guesses
ranging from the forehead to the lower back; twenty-seven confessed total ignorance.

On another occasion, in the summer of 1991, I set out to
instruct a reporter who had written about "psorosis" of the liver.
I gently suggested that he spell it *cirrhosis* of the liver, whereupon
I was jumped by a gentleman in Connecticut. He admonished me
stiffly that the fellow who suffers from cirrhosis is bound to be
suffering from cirrhosis *of the liver,* for cirrhosis is found nowhere
else. Sure enough, that's what *Random House* says; it's a chronic
disease "of the liver." *Webster's* equivocates; it is a disease "esp. of
the liver." *American Heritage* says cirrhosis is "chronic interstitial
inflammation of *any* tissue or organ." If there's a redundancy in
cirrhosis of the liver, so what? Let us give the reader a break.

Other redundant combinations are so firmly planted in English usage that a battalion of perfectionists could not root them
out. It is time to surrender on *rice paddy* and *conniption fit,* though
paddies are inherently *rice* paddies and conniptions are certainly
fits. Nothing is gained by writing of *component parts* that couldn't
be achieved by *components* alone, but *component* and *parts* now go
together like horse and carriage. The acronymic *WASP* is here to
stay, though it is difficult to imagine an Anglo-Saxon Protestant
who is not white. It still seems absurd to speak of *shrimp scampi* or

tuna *fish* salad, but only the most captious critics will continue to banish *grand total, sum total,* or *final stop.* There may be several subtotals before one gets to a grand or a sum total, and an arriving plane may stop several times before it comes to a final stop at the gate.

Two more blatant redundancies, *close proximity* and *convicted felon,* also qualify for parole. By definition, *proximity* is "the state, quality, sense, or fact of being near or next; closeness." One cannot be a *felon* until one has been convicted of a felony. Both terms grate upon the sensitive ear, but perhaps they don't grate badly. Let the grumbling subside.

It is not necessary to write of a *bowl of hot soup* if a *hot bowl of soup* comes more easily to mind. It is likely that not only the soup but also the bowl is hot. In an uncharacteristic mood of tolerance, I yield on *self-confessed* spy, even though I do not understand how anyone else could confess for the spy. The AP permits *HIV virus,* though HIV stands for the Human Immunodeficiency Virus. Not all chitchat is necessarily *idle* chitchat. Some chitchat may have an ulterior purpose. Wanna come upstairs and see my campaign buttons?

The point of all this is that conciseness is a virtue, but conciseness is not the only virtue. Sentences have weight. Sentences have cadence. If the structure of a sentence is weak, a couple of redundant two-by-fours may shore it up. If a sentence is clumsy, the addition of an extra word may add a touch of grace. Professor Strunk was right. *Omit unnecessary words!* But beware of a rigid rule against redundancy. We would not write that Willard Scott became bald-headed as he grew older; we would write that he became bald. But I would see nothing wrong in referring to a bald-headed bowler if the redundant *headed* added a grace note to the cadence of the passage. We have to think upon these things, for indeed they are thinkative.

One more Horrid Example, and then we move on. In 1987 the Hebrew Orphan Asylum Association asked permission to dedicate a plaque in the gymnasium of P.S. 192 in New York City. The principal of the school was agreeable. He could not have been more agreeable. "We are pleased," he responded, "to answer with an affirmative yes!" Surely that is the nicest kind.

Don't fall into clichés.

Thetis, the silver-footed sea nymph, was a good mother. She sought to make her newborn son invulnerable, so she dipped the infant Achilles in the River Styx. Alas, she held him by one heel. None of the magical water touched the spot. Years passed, the Trojan wars wore on, and one day Paris shot an arrow toward Achilles. Apollo guided the arrow surely to the warrior's heel, and that was the end of Achilles.

Not really the end. The heel of Achilles lives on and on. In The Wall Street Journal, Amtrak's continuing need for a federal subsidy is the rail line's Achilles' heel. Brokers convicted of insider trading exposed an Achilles' heel. In 1992 a modest gun control provision proved to be the Achilles' heel of a crime bill. During the presidential campaign of that year, the slumping economy was George Bush's Achilles' heel. Democrat Bill Clinton had his Achilles' heel in his draft record.

Isn't it time to let Achilles go? And may he take the vaunted Hercules along? The clichés drawn from mythology are stale herbs; they have lost their savor. Not one reader in ten thousand is likely to grasp an allusion to the labors of Sisyphus or the frustration of Tantalus. John F. Kennedy once described the atomic bomb as a nuclear sword of Damocles hanging over the world. The controversial tax bill of 1990 presented a Gordian knot that could not be quickly severed. Were the images clear to an untutored generation of readers?

Most clichés have less Olympian origins. In the presidential campaign of 1992, vice president Dan Quayle became "an albatross around the neck of President Bush." Mr. Quayle had not passed muster. He had a hard row to hoe. Pundits speculated that Bush might take his colleague to the woodshed or make him walk the plank. In 20–20 hindsight Bush never should have chosen Quayle at all. If he hadn't been blind as a bat, Bush wouldn't have touched Quayle with a ten-foot pole, but it was now too late to cry over spilt milk. He was being hoist on his own petar. Maybe Bush himself would throw in the towel.

For quite some time in that election, the Bush campaign moved at a snail's pace. Its chickens had come home to roost. The president was over a barrel. He was skating on thin ice and had to get into high gear. Bill Clinton had two strikes on him and was throwing nothing but hardballs. Well, nobody ever said that campaigning is a bed of roses.

A thousand phrases from Shakespeare were fresh when the bard of Avon coined them. Three centuries of hard usage have made most of them weary, stale, flat and unprofitable. The world of sports creates lively images and then ruins them by repetition. Surely imaginative writers could draw more from the world of business than a sea of red ink and the bottom line.

The Bible is a rich font of beauty—and a great source of the banal phrase. Correspondents who cover Washington, D.C., have a way of dressing their articles in threadbare allusions. Housing Secretary Jack Kemp once was a thorn in Bush's side. On Capitol Hill, that tower of Babel, legislators who sowed the winds of arrogance reaped whirlwinds of defeat. Their house was built upon sand. Even by the skin of their teeth they could not escape the voters' wrath. If they had possessed the wisdom of Solomon, things might have been different, but they sold their reputation for a mess of pottage. Now their constituents would hang them higher than Haman. Lo, how hath the mighty fallen!

Some writers cherish the illusion that by tinkering with a stale phrase, they may come up with freshness born again. In the Los Angeles Times, we learn something about people on low-cholesterol diets: "Experts say they might want to jump on the fish oil capsule bandwagon." The AP finds that "too many entrepreneurs are ignoring significant untapped markets woven throughout the state's economic fabric." Miss Manners remarks that "restrained booing" at a sports event is "the other side of the applause coin."

In Utah a few years ago, a politician "dangled a severance pay carrot before low-seniority members." This was not the same politician who was "sticking his political neck out," though perhaps he was relighting a flickering torch of reform. Other legislators turned off the state's money faucet. They wielded a budgetary axe, and they gave a fiscal cold shoulder to some low-priority projects. The financial outlook was as bare as Mother Hubbard's cupboard, but an influential senator said, "There may be a silver lining in the state's no-money predicament."

The compounding of clichés in this fashion amounts to putting a fedora on a mule. Underneath the hat is the same old mule. Not all clichés, of course, are tedious and tiresome, and some clichés are irreplaceable. No combination of words beats the early bird, the turning worm, and the white elephant for the succinct conveyance of an idea. But when the political writer succumbs to the wearies, and tells us that a dark horse is expected to throw his hat in the ring, let him be properly ashamed. When a drama critic recalls some old thespian trodding the boards, let her be hustled off stage. The verdant fields of English have grown up with weedy masses of maxims, adages, proverbs, and saws. By definition they are already old. Use them if you must, but don't use them if straightforward prose will do the job.

Don't scramble your syntax.

A reader sent me an article from the Pittston (Pa.) Gazette of July 2, 1868. The article was captioned "Newspaper Errors." It began:

> Grammatical errors in punctuation and composition, and typographical absurdities, are of such common occurrence in the everyday literature of the age as to excite no feeling in the reader's mind, except it be one of wonder at the carelessness of the printer, stupidity of the proofreader, or ignorance of the writer . . .
>
> We copy the following from the Advertiser's Gazette, a collection it has for several months been gathering from various exchanges. Erroneous in construction, and of such a nature as at best to defy the printer's art, we may unquestionably set down such as these:
>
> "The classic London Spectator makes a curious slip when it speaks of Matilda Griggs who 'was stabbed by a lover to whom she had borne a child in thirteen places.'
>
> "A Wisconsin paper says: 'During a fierce thunderstorm near Mount Desert, the lightning came down through the

roof of a house and a bed, upon which lay a husband and
wife, throwing the man out of bed, thence into the cellar
and out through the drain, and then plowed up the ground
to the barn yard, where it killed a cow.'"

Mind you, these were Horrid Examples from 1868. Poor Matilda
Griggs, who bore a child in thirteen places, exemplifies what I
call the Hedgehog Phrase. The appellation comes from Alice's
famous game of croquet, in which flamingos served as mallets
and hedgehogs served as balls. The hedgehogs were forever un-
rolling themselves and wandering away.

This is what happened to Dave McTeague, a candidate for
reelection to the Oregon legislature. The author of a campaign
flier lost sight of the ball:

> When the Oak Grove community was facing a nude danc-
> ing saloon in a residential neighborhood, Dave helped pass
> a constitutional amendment to regulate nude dancing through
> the House.

As The Washington Post used to be inordinately fond of saying,
the picture boggles the mind. Could members of the House dance
in the nude during roll calls? Probably not. During quorum calls?
Perhaps so. During morning hour? Only by unanimous consent.
The prospect is enchanting.

Here the troublemaker was the errant prepositional phrase,
"through the House." The hedgehog phrase unrolled itself. Then
it wandered off to the end of the sentence where it had no
business being. The only escape from such a maze lies in recasting the sentence and separating its elements, e.g., "When an
unwanted go-go saloon opened in the Oak Grove neighborhood,
Dave went to work in the House. He pushed through a constitutional amendment to regulate nude dancing," and so on.

Let us learn from Horrid Examples. These are ripe for
recasting:

> (Quoting a Red Cross official): "We do use sterilized nee-
> dles and a new needle for every blood donor that is dis-
> posed of after use."
> —Akron Beacon Journal

The prostitution problem came to light in June, when health officials reported a high rise in gonorrhea cases due to prostitution at the regional health clinic here.
—Salem (Ore.) Statesman-Journal

A Boulder judge yesterday refused to disqualify himself from hearing the case of a woman who sued the city over the death of her son because he dates a city official.
—Rocky Mountain News (Denver)

The new bridge replaces one heavily traveled by tourists to the shore that was declared structurally unsound.
—Birmingham (Ala.) News

Deputies roped off the scene where Rivers may have been stabbed with yellow tape yesterday.
—Miami Herald

Several readers have pointed out an explanation of how soda neutralizes odors that appeared in an apparently syndicated column in their local newspaper.
—Chemical & Engineering News

There are apocryphal stories, going all the way back to John McGraw when the home team supplied the balls to the umpire one-by-one, of home team managers storing the balls to be given the umpires when the visiting team was at bat on ice.
—*The Physics of Baseball,* by Robert Kemp Adair

President Reagan watched with amusement as Baryshnikov danced with Mrs. Reagan, wearing a polka-dot and salmon dress with ruffles.
—Associated Press

Reported homosexual activity in past months in a city park has triggered a heated campaign against all forms of adult entertainment led by Arlington Councilman Jim Norwood.
—Associated Press

The House of Representatives voted overwhelmingly yesterday to adopt a ban on Dial-a-Porn services proposed by Sen. Jesse Helms, R.-N.C.
—Winston-Salem (N.C.) Journal

Tower admitted to breaking his wedding vows during his confirmation hearings.
—Associated Press

"I got influenced by Dinesen when I discovered some great photographs of her riding in duster coats and britches and standing around with two dogs wearing riding boots and safari jackets."
—United Press International

Victoria Parker has the title role in "Medea," a 1948 adaptation of Euripides' play about betrayal and revenge at Portland State University.
—Portland Oregonian

Notice again, if you will, how such wounded sentences may be healed by judicious trimming and stitching. In Akron, "For every blood donor we use a new sterilized needle that is disposed of after use." Such a recasting recovers the poor blood donor who otherwise might have been summarily disposed of.

The item about prostitution in Salem might similarly be recast so as to salvage the reputation of the clinic: "The problem came to light in June, when officials of the regional health clinic reported a high rise in gonorrhea cases owing to prostitution."

We might untangle the Boulder judge by taking hedge shears to the sentence: "A Boulder judge, acknowledging that he dates a city official, yesterday refused to disqualify himself from hearing a suit against the city. The case was brought by a woman who sued the city over the death of her son."

A couple of commas might have improved the photo caption in Birmingham: "The new bridge replaces a bridge, heavily traveled by tourists, that was declared structurally unsound."

Rough sentences may be smoothed by breaking them in two: "There are apocryphal stories, going all the way back to John McGraw, of home team managers storing balls on ice. These balls would be supplied one-by-one to the umpire when the visiting team was at bat."

Often the trouble may be repaired simply by recasting an offending sentence to move a modifying phrase to a sensible place:

"President Reagan watched with amusement as Mrs. Reagan, wearing a polka-dot and salmon dress with ruffles, danced with Baryshnikov." The recast sentence needs a little balancing weight after "ruffles," but I put off a discussion of balance to another chapter. A better approach would lie along these lines: "Mrs. Reagan took to the floor wearing a polka-dot and salmon dress with ruffles. The president watched with amusement as she danced with Baryshnikov."

Let me leave the remaining Horrid Examples to your remedial hands, with a prayer that your editing will rescue Jim Norwood, Jesse Helms, and John Tower from the critical avalanche that otherwise would fall upon them. The rule for Hedgehog Phrases is to roll them back where they belong.

Beware the dingle-dangle.

From time to time, every writer wearies of the same old orderly sentences, in which predicates trail subjects like pachyderms on parade. We want to break the monotony by beginning a sentence with an introductory phrase or a participial clause. The idea is sound. Of course we should try for variety in our construction of sentences. But if the thought is attractive, the results sometimes are startling. An ad for Hardee's Food Systems began, "Hot and juicy, we start with real American beef . . ." Some hanging phrases get downright ugly:

> Smeared with oil and infested with fleas, the detectives bundled up Benji and Bandit and carted them off to the Broward County Animal Control Shelter.
> —Miami Herald

Remarkably, the same curious image appeared in the Canton (Ohio) Repository in a story about an aged man who horribly neglected his forty dogs. Social workers took the old fellow to a hospital for treatment of gangrene.

> The dogs weren't as fortunate. Diseased, flea infested and weakened from years of in-breeding, a court ordered them destroyed.

Now there was a court that had seen better days. Such hanging phrases have to be carefully watched.

Last seen heading to Bloomington to visit Meisberger July 31, Sawyer's decomposed body was discovered August 6.
   —Bloomington (Ind.) Herald-Times

Dilapidated and time-worn in 1982, Brenda Greene and Scott Mitchell set about buying the old cafe from Willie.
   —*Texas Weekly Magazine*

Clothed in raincoats and holding umbrellas, the chicken crisped to its usual golden goodness.
   —Fulton (Ill.) Journal

After 136 years of remaining relatively the same size, Chester Mayor William Cranford thinks it's time for Chester to grow.
   —Chester (S.C.) News & Reporter

"As a Christian minister, the Lord has been dealing with me in many areas of my life."
   —Fredericksburg (Va.) Free Lance-Star

Perched on a white divan in her airy, sunny Benedict Canyon home, Jacqueline's smoky eyes were thoughtful as she contemplated the role of Anna.
   —United Press International

After burning over 89,000 acres of forest and range land in Wallowa County the past two weeks, the Forest Service Monday was demobilizing thousands of firefighters.
   —Wallowa County (Ore.) Chieftain

Weighing nearly four pounds, with almost three times the content of his earlier work, the author enables you to manage your money . . .
   —Ad in *New York Times Book Review*

Long thought to be relatively flat and shaped like huge frisbees, the scientists have found that some galaxies are actually oblong in shape.
   —*Science Newsletter*

> While walking between the Hyatt Hotel and the Visitor In-
> formation Center, my wallet fell out of my purse.
> —Letter to the San Antonio Express-News

> Cleaning out the garage over the weekend, a headline in
> an old newspaper caught my attention.
> —Columnist, The Washington Post

In each instance, an orphaned phrase was crying for a friendly
subject to hang onto. Revisions may take several forms.

In the first Horrid Example, a recasting might go this way:
"The detectives bundled up Benji and Bandit, smeared with oil
and infested with fleas, and carted them off . . ." In the second,
we would make it clear that the old café, and not the new owners,
was dilapidated and time-worn. In the third, having to do with a
picnic of the Lions Club, we must take the raincoats and umbrellas away from the chicken.

And so on. We must let the town of Chester, and not Mayor
Cranford, do the growing. We should assign the Lord a ministry a
bit upscale from Fredericksburg, Va. We should leave Jacqueline,
and not her smoky eyes, perched on that white divan. In the final
example, the sentence easily could be tidied: "As I was cleaning
out the garage over the weekend," etc., or, "Cleaning out the garage
over the weekend, I came across a headline in an old newspaper."

Don't let me discourage you from trying different constructions. No rule of composition decrees that all sentences must
leap from their starting blocks with a proper subject out in front.
Do as the Germans sometimes do, and put the subject down a
kilometer or two. One word of caution: I would avoid the introductory *that* clause, as in, "That George Washington had false
teeth is a well-known story." The reader wonders if there is another
George Washington besides *that* George Washington. I never
have seen a *that* clause I really liked. Otherwise, move elements
around until a sentence delights your eye and ear.

Don't misplace the time angle.

As any city editor will tell you, the time angle of a story is important. Readers want to know the who, what, where, why, and how

of a given event, but they rightfully ask: *When* did it happen? The time element gives writers a great deal of trouble.

Thus the AP reported that "a convicted sex abuser was sentenced to life in prison with the possibility of parole on Monday." The Monterey (Va.) Recorder similarly reported that "a Highland County man was sentenced to twelve months in the county jail for the sale and distribution of marijuana in Highland County Circuit Court last Thursday."

The Bradford (Pa.) Era advised readers that "the public hearing for a Johnsonburg high school teacher allegedly involved in a barroom brawl that was scheduled for Thursday was canceled."

The Canton (Ohio) Free Press announced that "the Grief Support and Education Center is sponsoring a series of meetings for persons who have experienced the death of a loved one on Wednesdays from 5:30 to 7 p.m."

In Birmingham, the Post-Herald provided a feature on teenage cruising: "It's a popular pastime among those old enough to drive on Friday and Saturday night."

Themes of death and resurrection recur: Headline in the Buffalo News: "For second time in 12 days, priest slain in Buffalo." From the Chicago Sun-Times: "A recipient of a living-donor liver transplant has died for the first time in the pioneering program at the University of Chicago Hospitals." From a photo caption in the Greenville (S.C.) Piedmont: "Sister Wylie, left, and Sister Jacynta walk near the cemetery on the ten-acre grounds at the monastery, where sisters serving in the monastery are often buried."

Clearly, when you come to think about it, the sex abuser, sentenced to life, will not be eligible for parole on Tuesday. The fellow in Highland County was not selling cocaine in court on Thursday. In Pennsylvania, the hearing was scheduled, not the brawl. Presumably the North Canton Center counsels those whose loved ones die at any time. Teenagers who are old enough to drive in Birmingham on Friday and Saturday night doubtless are old enough to drive in Birmingham on Monday and Tuesday night as well. Let us bury one priest at a time! If we would not repeatedly inter organ donors and nuns, we must *Pay Attention!*

The time element gives surprises in other ways. The Motion Picture Association of America once reported the conviction of a video pirate. In addition to serving two years in prison and five years on probation, the felon was required "to perform one thousand hours of community service within the first forty-eight hours of his probation." It was the trick of the week.

Headline in the Indianapolis Star: "Ex-female ump files discrimination suit." Item from Mississippi in the Eugene (Ore.) Register-Guard: "A U.S. district judge has ordered the state to pay $4.7 million to about 760 former black and female clients of the employment service's Cleveland office." Dispatch from the AP, about settlement of a class action in Chicago: "The suit was filed on behalf of case aides and case aide trainees, more than 80 percent of whom were black when the suit was filed."

It is a fair guess that the female umpire is still female, and those black and female clients in Cleveland are still black and female. The aides in Chicago, who were black when the suit was filed, remain as black as ever.

Also keep in mind, if you will, the clear distinction between *ancestors* and *descendants*. We ought not to read that certain ancestors of Martha Custis Washington are now living in Mobile where they are members of the D.A.R.

Avoid the ambiguous adjective.

Innocent adjectives have a way of leaving our readers startled. In Minnesota, the New Ulm Journal carried a classified ad offering a "huge selection of good boys' clothes." Perhaps good boys' clothes are better than bad boys' clothes. Columnist Andy Rooney had the same thought. For years, he said, "Brooks Brothers has set the standard for good men's clothes."

In Amarillo, Texas, a classified ad sought "an experienced two-year-old teacher." Elsewhere the classified ads have offered for sale such remarkable furniture as "an adjustable kid's drafting table." It would be nice to have adjustable kids. An Atlanta store offered shoes "for children made in Italy." A store specializing in sporting goods assured prospects that a particular rifle "has a large following among dangerous game hunters." These would be hunters to follow at one's peril.

In the same vein, *Modern Maturity* carried an advertisement: "Your unwanted man's wristwatch could be worth hundreds of dollars!" In Omaha, a reader of the World-Herald commented that some collectors are interested in "old men's watches." Young men's watches will have to age. Headline in Salem, Ore.: "Archbishop Favors Larger Women's Role," a sentiment that said little about smaller women's roles.

From the Indianapolis Star: "Fourteen years of flat beer sales turned around last year in Germany." The Associated Press observed the same trend in North Carolina: "After several years of flat beer sales, a growing number of people with discretionary money to spend and the migration of people from states where people drank more beer led to increased sales." It seems a remarkable demand for an undrinkable product, but in 1988 perhaps the beer wholesalers were doing better than the dress shops of Miami. In Miami, the Herald reported, "Researchers predict flat women's apparel sales throughout the '90s."

Another ambiguous adjective turned up in the Las Vegas Review-Journal in an item about actress Bridget Fonda: "Her roles so far have included a mistress to a British politician in *Scandal* and a racy preacher's daughter in *Shag*."

The moral of all this is to read one's copy as if it never had been read before. Such a second reading (or third, or fourth reading) may prevent our describing an ebony lady's writing table. Some ladies are ebony, and some tables are ebony, but we ought not to leave readers in doubt.

Shun the evasive amphibology!

Writers must remain constantly on guard against sentences that have more than one meaning. Some of these are known as amphibologies, or in a simpler spelling, as amphibolies. My own favorite came from a popular country Western song: "If I told you you had a beautiful body, would you hold it against me?"

What is one to make of this recipe for oatmeal bread? "Knead the dough for about ten minutes, but you cannot knead too much."

The Associated Press put together a feature story in 1991 marking the fiftieth anniversary of certain events in World War II: "In London, the government announces that men too old for military duty and women will be drafted for factory work." The gentlemen deserved it.

A spinster advertised in the *Senior Spectrum* of Nevada: "Christian lady will pet and house sit. Excellent credentials."

In Las Vegas, a fast-food beanery used its cheeseburger as a fund-raising attraction: "Help a Las Vegas child! Eat one today!"

Such misadventures occur everywhere. In Washington State, a slogan of dubious merit promoted the campaign of Sen. Brock Adams: "He'll win the tough fights with integrity." An enthusiastic reader wrote in praise of a columnist: "I wouldn't miss Ellen Goodman's column." In El Paso visitors are either welcomed or warned: "Nothing is better than Mexican food." In the same vein, a soap manufacturer proclaimed, "No soap is better for your skin than Zest!" In Mobile, a eulogist sadly reported that "the death Wednesday of Max Rogers leaves a void in this community which will be difficult to replace."

At one uneasy point in the Reagan administration, a headline writer impaled the president on an amphibolous verb: "Reagan Determined to Have Cancer." In Florida, artists staged a fund-raising exhibition. The headline in Naples read, "Artists rush in to help abuse shelter." The AP reported in 1986 that former Attorney General Griffin Bell had been rebuffed in an attempt to meet with a client in Nicaragua. The Washington Times seemed a bit confused: "Bell denied meeting with Hasenfus."

Some writers have a fondness for non sequiturs. Readers of a suburban paper in Seattle must have been puzzled, but well informed, by an item about teachers Ellen and Bill Hofman. "While on their honeymoon they climbed the pyramids of Egypt and now have two children." The same cryptic nexus has appeared elsewhere:

> Sheik Dahlawi has a 1962 degree in economics and political science from the American University in Cairo. He was an avid squash player until he had a heart operation, and he and his wife Diana, who is English, have five children.
> —Miami Herald

Like Mr. Tauke, who gave up the seat for an unsuccessful
Senate bid, Mr. Nussle is married and the father of one
child, a moderate Republican who is antiabortion.
   —The Wall Street Journal

For the fortieth time—I may get to the four-hundredth time—
let me commend to you the beautiful act of carving by which an
experienced writer slices one sentence into two sentences, or
even into three sentences. In the process we may lose ambiguity
while we gain comprehension. These are purposes not to be
spurned.

Be not backward.

To the embarrassment of their authors, some sentences wind up
with dismaying reversals of meaning. A helpful item on airline
safety appeared in the Seattle Post-Intelligencer: "Here are several ways travelers can reduce their chances of staying alive." This
is the kind of advice we all can use.

   In 1988 Newsday carried an obituary on a beloved teacher of
English at Bayport–Blue Point High School:

   Her colleagues described her as a special, inspired teacher
   who never tired of her subject or gave up on convincing
   students that developing skills in writing or an appreciation
   of literature was a waste of time.

An automobile dealer in Wilmette, Ill., sought to attract customers with an offer they couldn't refuse:

   Last shipment of 1987 Camry. Least trouble free car sold
   in America.

It was quite a party in Summerville, S.C., in October 1990 at
the local Holiday Inn.

   The occasion was the third annual Celebrity Waiters Luncheon sponsored by the Leukemia Society to raise funds to
   combat research.

The Myrtle Beach (S.C.) Sun-News carried a classified ad of remarkable political candor in 1990. The Georgetown County Water and Sewer District wanted to buy some new cars, but only with this understanding:

> We reserve the right to reject any and all bids deemed to be in the best interests of the District.

How's that again?

Some delightful mangles and dangles have an element of what might be called sober surprise. The attentive reader doesn't know quite what to say. So it was when a correspondent for the Birmingham Post-Herald in 1991 interviewed Major Rhonda L. Cornum on her release from Iraqi captivity: "Today is the first day in twenty-two days I've brushed my own teeth," the major said. It was something to think about.

We also may meditate over the sound advice from a leading herpetologist: "People should watch out where they step in the woods, so they won't step on a snake, which will cause them to bite someone."

The AP's man in Chittagong provided a vivid statistic at the time of the 1991 cyclone: "The pressure on land is enormous in Bangladesh, a nation of 110 million people the size of Wisconsin."

In Newsday, readers learned of a suit "brought against the estate of Rock Hudson, who died of AIDS, two advisors and three doctors."

Writing in the Las Vegas Sun, Hank Greenspan warned of the hazards that lie concealed in the apparently harmless oleander. The poisonous plant is not indigenous to Nevada. It ought to be uprooted wherever it has been planted. Exposure to oleander, Greenspan made clear, is a serious matter:

> If you sometimes experience irregular heartbeats, high blood pressure, dryness of the throat, convulsions, heart failure or even death, blame it on public officials who have done nothing to ban or eradicate oleanders from our midst.

It was also difficult to know quite what to make of a report in the News-Star of Monroe, La., about fatalities on the highways in 1987:

Only three fatal accidents involved a victim who was wearing a seatbelt and two of those were pedestrian fatalities.

The Wheeling (Ill.) Daily Herald gave its readers a moment's pause in 1991 with a close-up of Frank Allgauer:

The secret to staying in the hotel business is liking people, says Frank Allgauer, who happens to own two.

Another nonplusser appeared at about the same time in *This Week* magazine, courtesy of the Frugal Gourmet. Critic Jeff Smith was describing *Focaccia Romana:*

Craig, my cooking assistant, and I tasted this at the Forno Campo de'Fiori, the bakery in the great market center in Rome. People line up to buy this fabulous bread and they are baked throughout the day.

Late in January 1990 the UPI provided a story from Guam about the death of the island's former governor, Ricardo J. Bordallo. It was not altogether clear what happened.

Bordallo, 62, apparently committed suicide about 3 p.m. and died 90 minutes later at a U.S. Navy hospital, police said.

At the University of Colorado in Boulder, students confronted a peremptory notice on the doors to the campus cafeteria: "Shoes are required to eat in the cafeteria." To which a literalist appended a clarifying note: "Socks may eat wherever they want."

Every part of speech and every syntactical arrangement carries Seventh Avenue perils for the unwary writer. Reflexives give trouble. In Rapid City, a classified ad made an offer that many readers might well refuse: "Two-year-old buffaloes for sale in Badlands. Can shoot yourself." Another classified ad, this one in Milwaukee, promoted a catering service that "cooks meals for those who don't want to cook themselves."

To return to the point of departure: The reporter who compiled that list of blunders in 1868 attributed such errors to "the carelessness of the printer, stupidity of the proofreader, or ignorance of the writer." In our current era of cold type and computers, it is futile to blame blunders upon printers and proofreaders. They have gone the way of rumble seats and running boards.

Don't let your mind wander.

This is the hardest of all my *don'ts* to obey. Most of the goofs, boo-boos and Horrid Examples result not from abysmal ignorance but from sheer inattention. Writing is like any other occupation that demands intense concentration. The shortstop takes his eye off the ball, and the balls scoots between his legs. The carpenter hits his thumb. The pianist plays B-natural when the score requires B-flat. A lawyer misses a filing deadline, and there goes his case. So it is in our craft. The author of a medical newsletter meant to advise doctors not to be patronizing. What he said was that doctors should not treat their patients "with condensation."

Don't keep on writing when you're too tired to pay attention.

4 Getting Beyond the Rough Edges

The first thing to be said about "style," which is the general subject of this chapter, is to say what style is not: Style is not ketchup. It is not a sauce that can be sloshed on to a composition after the first draft is done.

A writer's distinctive style results from a dozen characteristics all put together, but these are the writer's own characteristics. Style is the outward and visible manifestation of whatever a writer has within. Elizabeth Drew, for many years Washington correspondent for *The New Yorker,* writes about politics. So does Mike Royko of the Chicago Tribune. The one writes designer prose, neatly stitching every sentence. The other writes as if he were talking to the boys at a lakefront bar. Both are stylists, but if they tried all night, neither one could write in the style of the other.

Henry Mencken, newspaperman, had an unmistakable style. It was a product of his personality, his diverse interests, and his lifelong love of the American language. Mencken influenced a whole generation of newspaper writers who vainly sought to be as brash, as audacious, as colorful as the Sage of Baltimore. I myself went through a Mencken period. I used Mencken's favorite words—such words as *booboisie* and *brummagem*—and I spoke mockingly of *the Hon.* Sam Rayburn. I sought to imitate the hammock swing of a Mencken sentence, rolling lustily from one grand impudence to another.

It is hard to remember the sequence of these things, but after Mencken came my Gibbon period, and after Gibbon, Macaulay. Any schoolboy should have known better. The effort was bound to fail. Writers who ape the style of their idols will always look like monkeys. We may parody the style of Faulkner, hanging subordinate clauses like Spanish moss from the limbs of a sentence, but

65

the result is just that: parody, and generally not very good parody. Writers must be themselves.

Very well. We must not imitate the stylists we admire, but we still can learn from them. The carpentry of words is not an especially arcane undertaking. The writer with a simile is cousin to the carver with a chisel. If we are writing a sermon or making a chest of drawers, we begin in the same way, with a plan, and toward the end of a task we employ the same techniques. We sand with the grain of the wood, or with the grain of a sentence, and after a time of sanding and rubbing and polishing, the job is done.

I will tell you a secret. This is all there is to the writing art: having something to say, and saying it well.

When a passage of writing fails, it fails for one reason or the other. We truly had nothing to say that was worth saying, or we said it poorly. Or both. All of us have read editorials in which the editorial writer could think of nothing useful to say beyond the powerful pronouncement that, egad, sir, *Something Must Be Done!* All of us have read Horrid Examples of mangled syntax, poor grammar, misspelled words, murky allusions, and clumsy phrasing. To write well, one must work at writing well.

I cannot help you with the initial task of having something to say that is worth saying. That is your job. Think about it.

The second part of the formula is to say what we have to say "well." For a writer, the process begins in the cradle and goes on to the grave. All along the way we must read voraciously. We must write incessantly. We must use every sense intently. This is at the core of the writing art: We must look intently, and listen intently, and we must taste and smell and touch with all the concentration we can bring to the task. If we do this consciously, deliberately, and with an abiding curiosity about the world around us, in time we will build a kind of pantry. We will fill it with images, similes, metaphors, characters, scraps of revealing conversation. When we need a jar of chutney, the chutney will be there.

Something more. Thomas Wentworth Higginson, who served as critic and friend to Emily Dickinson, wrote a "Letter to a Young Contributor" in the *Atlantic* in 1862. He offered some sound advice: "Charge your style with life." It is a great exhortation. I once had a journalism teacher who said the same thing: "People who lead dull lives will write dull copy." We ought to think about that, too. I'm not encouraging anyone to try a love affair, buy a boat, or take a bungee jump, but the writer who stays in a rut will never see a far horizon.

These are a few imperatives:

Know your audience.

I have touched on this before, in commenting upon the use of foreign words and phrases, but the importance of establishing a bond between writer and reader cannot be emphasized too often. Forging a bond isn't easy; it's only essential. A writer should strike for the goal of Goldilocks. She tried one bowl of porridge; it was too hot. She tried the second bowl; it was too cold. The third bowl was just right, so she ate it every bit. If we write over the heads of our prospective readers, they will find us pretentious. If we write down to a supposed level of ignorance, they will find us condescending.

For whom are we writing? For twenty-eight years I wrote a nationally syndicated column on politics and public affairs. At its peak the column appeared in 538 newspapers from Florida to Hawaii, from Texas to Alaska, with a combined circulation of more than twenty million readers. Thinking of that potential audience, I set as my target a hypothetical reader. I would write to be understood by the high school graduate in his most intelligent moments.

Most of the time I must have found the third bowl of porridge, for the complaints I received were evenly balanced. Some readers protested that in covering the Supreme Court I used too many hard words; others grumbled that my comments on the federal budget were too elementary to be interesting. Now and then I let a *damn* or a *hell* creep into my copy. Nice old ladies would urge me to refrain from such profanity. We can't win 'em all.

Who's out there? In the summer of 1992 *The New Republic* carried a review of a volume of poems by C.K. Williams. Because

I am fond of poets and poetry, and because I had barely heard of the gentleman, I turned to the review with interest. There I learned that Williams broods upon the fluctuating data of consciousness, quarreling with itself.

> No other contemporary poet, except perhaps John Ashbery, has given us a more textured or pressurized rendering of what it feels like to think—to try to think—through a situational or mental problem moment by moment: to bring the unconscious into the available light of language, to anatomize the psyche with a continual tally of internal and external evidence.

Wrong bowl of porridge.

Apply your editorial judgment to a few examples. William Safire, writing in The New York Times, criticized the weltanschauung of Republican Pat Buchanan for his position against foreign involvements. In Cheyenne, Wyo., directors of the Civic Center sent out a flier: "Kudos is an idoneous name for the 1991–92 season." In North Carolina the pastor of a Baptist church reminded his flock that, "At best, the finite can only adumbrate the parameters of the infinite." All clear?

Bret Harte, in *The Outcasts of Poker Flat*, used such words as *vituperative, prescience, bellicose, celestial, anathema, malevolent,* and *querulous.* Too tough? Pat Conroy, in *The Prince of Tides*, challenged his readers with *minatory, circumvallated, magus, frissons, flense, chasubles, numinous, anapests,* and *pastille chinoserie.*

One of my readers got into a suspense novel, *Death Sweet*, by T.J. MacGregor. On one page she found the maniacal murderer holding up a knife like a corban. On another, she learned of the fulgent tunnelings of Quin's thoughts. Ruth was a perdurable fixture. "The brief mention of food triggered a splanchnic reaction." The cool night air alleviated the crescive pressure in a character's head. The novel spoke of ignescent heat, eidolous joggers, an esurient beast, a caliginous light, and a stench of death that inspissated the air. At about this point, Gentle Reader stumbled over a laciniated sky and a calcareous glow and gave up.

In the Chicago Tribune, a writer spoke of anthropomorphizing New York City. The brokerage house of Merrill Lynch cautioned its customers about utility earnings: "Don't extrapolate when you see some of the earnings that will be reported for the summer." An AP reporter at the U.S. Supreme Court said that Justice O'Connor had recused herself; a reader said the reporter must have meant "excused herself." The manufacturer of a silk dress attached a tag to the garment: "The occasional slubs and shadings in the fabric should not be regarded as defects." Did buyers understand *slubs?*

U.S. News describes James Reston of The New York Times as "the doyen of capital journalism" who has rarely committed "acts of lese majesty." Was this the right level for readers of *U.S. News?* The Scripps Howard News Service commented upon the "expressive physiognomy" of actress Lesley Ann Warren. *Time* magazine spoke of Wilson Phillips' eponymous debut album of 1990. The Wall Street Journal commented that a building on Wall Street was "chockablock with white-shoe investment and law firms." Do most of the Journal's readers understand what is meant by a *white-shoe* law firm? I don't.

Newsweek magazine speaks of *dystopia. Time* speaks of *macaronic* ideas and a *steatopygous bauble.* The Miami Herald speaks of the city's *indigenous* park. In my own column I have spoken of word *mavens* and of headlines in *72-point* type. Did most of my readers know that a maven is an expert and that 72 points make an inch?

These questions of editorial judgment cannot be resolved by some rule that is tacked to a bulletin board. I might have written of *inch-high* type instead of *72-point* type, but type is measured not in inches but in points. Should we use the exact word, which may not be clear, or a precise word that may be murky? Do we need to consider our readers at all? James Joyce never considered his readers. He wrote to please himself. Should we let our own rich vocabularies flow like wine, while the reader stays sober and we get drunk?

Every writer knows the temptation to use an exotic word. The best advice I can offer, knowing full well that it will rarely be taken, is to resist the impulse—except, of course, when the temptation is irresistible.

Err on the side of modesty.

Several years ago (1986) I heard from a maiden in distress in South Carolina. Fresh out of journalism school, she had just been fired from her first newspaper job. How come? She had been assigned to review the movie *Cocoon*, which had to do with a couple of elderly gentlemen who swim in a miraculous pool and find their virility restored.

In her review my young friend identified the old fellows as "a couple of old—" and here she used a word that has been part of the English language (a vulgar part, to be sure) at least since Chaucer wrote *The Miller's Tale*. The word denotes flatulence. In college, she wrote me, her sorority sisters used the word all the time. In her innocence she supposed that *everyone* uses the word all the time.

Alas, she was unaware that one does not use *fart* in a family paper in Greenville, S.C. Chaucer knew his audience. She did not know hers. Farewell, my lovely.

When I went to work as a cub reporter in 1941, we could not write of syphilis or gonorrhea; we could not even write of a *venereal* disease. When a reference clearly could not be avoided, we called it a *social* disease. It would have been incredible to speak in the columns of the Richmond News Leader of a woman's breasts, even in the context of breast cancer. There was, in print, no such thing as a penis, an erection, or a condom. If women were possessed of a vagina, clitoris or uterus, the fact was unknown to newspaper readers. No one, male or female, even had a buttocks. The whole human body was airbrushed out of the paper. Call it modesty, delicacy, prudery, or diffidence—those were the rules.

As recently as 1976, a crisis arose. President Jimmy Carter promised publicly to "whup Senator Kennedy's ass." Every reporter in the traveling press corps heard him. This was undeniably news. Most of the reporters bucked a policy decision to the home office, whereupon editors and publishers met in solemn conclave. Some looked to the navel for inspiration. Some looked to the ceiling for direction. They all bit their knuckles. Especially in the Bible Belt, the general feeling was that readers would tolerate *ass* only in the sense of Numbers 22:21–23. But this was *the president!* In the end, most editors sighed, took a chance, and quoted Jimmy Carter verbatim.

A similar crisis arose in 1984. After a debate with Geraldine Ferraro, Democratic candidate for vice president, George Bush remarked to some dockworkers, "We tried to kick a little ass last night." He was unaware that a nearby microphone had picked up his words. An AP reporter gave him a chance to regret the statement, but Bush refused to retreat. "I stand behind it. I use it all the time. My kids use it. Everybody who competes in sports uses it."

Six more years passed. In 1990, few editors hesitated when President George Bush said of Iraq's Saddam Hussein, "If we get into an armed situation he's going to get his ass kicked." I am advised that most television news editors decided against using the quote, and doubtless some small newspapers found *ass* still too offensive for their readers, but the noun seems to have been admitted to newspaper columns where once it would have been forbidden.

As I write in 1993, it is not at all unusual to see references in daily newspapers to oral and anal intercourse. Diseases of the prostate, cervix, and rectum are routinely reported. We have restored all the body parts, but the old rules against vulgarity remain generally in effect.

Editors worry about giving offense. At The Wall Street Journal, the rule is to avoid vulgarities and profanities "except in direct quotes and for compelling reasons." When such circumstances arise, the Journal uses a first letter followed by a dash. In 1992 the Journal quoted the director of a child care center in Lynchburg, Va. A two-year-old child, said the director, "had called a teacher a 'g-d—m m——f——.'"

The San Francisco Chronicle has no formal policy, but in practice it draws the line at vulgarities "having to do with defecation and fornication." Matthew Wilson, managing editor of the Chronicle, puts it this way: "Our general rule is to respect standards of civilized behavior. Our readers have invited us into their homes for breakfast, and we don't aim to be discourteous by serving profanity along with their toast."

This is also the rule at the Rocky Mountain News in Denver. Managing Editor Chris Cubbison comments:

"We're very careful about using vulgarity. As a metro daily, we have a mass audience. We're trying to appeal to literally every reader in Denver and Colorado. You don't win many readers over by printing obscene language. The fact is that vulgarity offends a large number of readers. We think there ought to be a hugely compelling reason to print it in our paper."

The Miami Herald directs reporters and editors not to use obscenities, profanities and vulgarities "unless they are part of direct quotations and there is a *compelling* reason for them." The Herald's policy is to use hyphens, as in *bulls- - -*, but if reporters are doubtful about proprieties, "*He muttered a profanity* is a convenient substitute."

In the Charleston (S.C.) Post and Courier, not even a first letter is used. A young man, waiting his turn for a bungee jump, saw one customer get tangled in the cord. "That scared the - - - - out of me," he told a reporter.

That is about as far as most daily newspapers will go with blatant vulgarities. One or two large papers will spell out *son of a bitch*. The Washington Post softens the epithet: Congressman Bob Dornan referred to Bill Clinton as a "draft-dodging, womanizing sonuvabitch." (Dornan denied ever having said it.) A few papers go further. In Shreveport, La., the Times shocked some readers in its coverage of a canceled rock concert. A few disgruntled fans protested. "Some motorists passing by City Hall honked in support. Others rubber-necked at protestors' 'Butthole Surfers' T-shirts, combat boots and spiked helmets."

Magazines generally are more worldly. *Newsweek* in 1992 was still using mostly first letters and hyphens, e.g., "Chao called Diller a 'f- - -ing liar.'" In the same issue that carried the Chao story, *Newsweek* reported that Secretary of State Jim Baker was angered over premature reports of his departure to lead the Bush campaign. The magazine said Baker's top aide, Margaret Tutwiler, had conferred with White House press secretary Marlin Fitzwater. "Baker is livid," she told him. "He is pissed off . . ."

That same phrase appeared in midsummer 1992 in *Men's Health* magazine. "Spikes [a short-term jump in blood pressure] can be caused by a multitude of things, including being pissed off." The *World Press Review* goes further. It carried an article in

August 1992 about Quebec film director Jean-Claude Lauzon. A Hollywood producer had asked him to do a movie with a big-name star as a small start toward bigger achievements. Lauzon said, "I don't want to make a little pile of shit to be able to make a big pile of shit."

The New Republic goes further still. The editors have no aversion to *asshole,* and in its coverage of the 1992 presidential campaign the magazine sanctioned a gratuitous parenthetical phrase.

> Even some Democrats who attended NP [New Paradigm] dinners now emphasize that they did it mainly to make contacts. ("It was a clusterfuck," one puts it.)

If I had been editing that article, I would have argued that the parenthetical sentence added nothing of value and would need-lessly offend some readers. I would have killed it. *The New Republic's* editors manifestly thought otherwise; they felt the sentence added a touch of vivid color, so they left it in. You pays your money and you takes your choice.

The writing of books presents an entirely different matter. It would be fatuous to limit one of Elmore Leonard's seedy charac-ters to saying "aw, shucks," and "dear me." The screenwriter engaged in turning out a script for an R-rated movie is virtually required to put foul language into the mouths of his people. A person who buys *Penthouse* or *Playboy* expects to see the Seven Dirty Words on every page. This is part of a free society.

My admonitions are addressed to those who write for everyday publication in newspapers and magazines of general circulation. Have care! It is far better to err on the side of modesty than to offend on the side of frankness. It is stupid to risk driving away readers by the pointless use of vulgar language. Those of us who write for money need all the readers we can get.

If you reasonably can, avoid sexist phrases.

There was a time, and the time lasted for several centuries, in which a neutral antecedent required a male referent: "Does *everyone* have *his* book?" This is still the rule. Even so, it is evident that the rule offends some readers, both male and female, who view the custom as a sexist practice. My subversive thought is that even more readers are offended by the stylistic bilge that results from unctuous efforts to avoid offense, but I put the thought aside.

Some writers try pathetically, absurdly, not ever to be accused of sexist writing. Given a singular antecedent, they lunge for a plural referent. "To me," says Dr. Christian Barnard, "more important than how long a person lives is how well *they* live." The *Christian Advocate* observes that, "If someone stole the $4.9 million Gutenberg Bible, *they* couldn't sell it without revealing *themselves* as a thief." Kodak advertises a new product with an illustration, "This picture was taken by *someone* who didn't bring *their* camera." In a house ad, the Canton Repository asks a question: "What kind of parent lets *their* child work for nickels & dimes?"

Other writers, clumsily striving for public virtue, take recourse in *him or her. Historic Newspaper Archives* advertises in this fashion: "Just think how he or she will thrill when reading of the other events that occurred on the day they were born." In desperation, some take to the virgule: "Tell the reader what you want him/her to do." An inventive fellow suggests tennis lessons for h/her or h/him.

Some revolutionaries have proposed radical steps. At the Mayo Foundation, a gentleman in the section of publications suggested *thon* and *thon's* as substitutes for *he, she, her, him,* and *his, hers.* "Thon picks up thon's pencil and writes 'thon.'" In the Roanoke Times & World News some years ago, a columnist earnestly promoted *hier,* as in, "Everyone has a right to represent hierself in court." In Oregon, the editor of the state's official manual on real estate hit upon a Solomonic solution. "Our decision was to balance gender—every other chapter the singular pronoun feminine, and every other chapter masculine. It was randomly decided that odd-numbered chapters would be feminine, even-numbered masculine."

Jody Powell served as press secretary to President Carter. He was the best of all the press secretaries I have known. We remember him not only for his stellar performance but also for his wit.

"My duty," he once told us, "is never unintentionally to deceive you." In the same way, a writer has a duty never unintentionally to offend readers who are sensitive to what they perceive as sexist language. (I can't imagine why we would want intentionally to offend them, either, but doubtless it happens.)

Commentators have written whole volumes on ways to avoid offense. Some of the ways involve such an affected torturing of the language that we should reject them out of hand. Let me nominate as abominations:

chairperson	flagperson
waitperson	freshperson
bellperson	weatherperson
alderperson	barserver
elder statesperson	access hole
midshipperson	utility hole
snowperson	

I am not making these up. Readers have sent me other examples of balminess. A *yes man*, it appears, should be a *yes person*. The Jack of all trades is the *person of all trades*. A wholesaler should not be identified as a middleman, but as a *middleperson*. In North Carolina, a jury's verdict is brought in by the *foreperson*. On a shabby street in Portland, Ore., one may meet a *bag person*. Dear Abby advised Dear Heartbroken to consult a *clergyperson*. Marshall, Tex., has a facility for teenage *pregnant persons*. Purdue's Parent Advisory Council was headed by a *chaircouple*. This is madness.

Public speakers are admonished not to begin, "Ladies and gentlemen," but to begin, "Good evening, gentlepersons," or just plain, "Good evening." The words *widow* and *widower* should be abandoned in favor of *surviving spouse*. No more husbands and wives, only *spouses*. Instead of *showmanship, showship*. Farewell the Po'Boy sandwich; hail the Poor Person sandwich. The words *boy* and *girl* (and *lad* and *lass*) should be driven into exile, to be replaced by *baby, child, youth,* and *youngster.* The same eradication is recommended for *sister, brother, aunt, uncle*—gone, all gone— along with *fathering, mothering,* and *siring*. In many Protestant denominations, God the Parent is replacing God the Father.

Well, God the Parent knows this is linguistic rubbish. The very word *man* has two senses. It defines the male of the species, of course, but more to the point, it generically encompasses all humankind. There is something eerie in demands that *chairman, manslaughter,* and *masterpiece* be sterilized. These terms are as sexless as concrete blocks.

Moreover, some of the synthetic rubber substitutes are not usable substitutes at all. In 1986 an academic study group put forth a four-page list of approved terms. A *businessman,* said the Guide to Nonsexist Language, should be identified as an *executive,* a *cameraman* as a *photographer,* and *statesmanship* as *diplomacy.* These won't do. A *manmade* pond is not a *manufactured* or a *handmade* pond. A television *weatherman* cannot be promoted to *meteorologist* without credentials. Ridding English of a thousand inherited masculine constructions is no easy task.

Yet there is no sense in offending any substantial body of readers if reasonable ways can be found to avoid "sexism" without appearing ridiculous. This is how it can be done:

• Use plurals. Five times out of seven, in my own experience, I can hook slide around the annoyance of *everyone/their* by recasting a sentence to read, "All the pupils had their books." "Writers should read their copy." "Artists should learn their anatomy lessons."

• Accept reasonable substitutions of neuter nouns for nouns of gender. Without yielding on principle, writers and editors can go along with *firefighter, mail carrier, cave dweller, night guard,* and the like. With a little forethought we can write around *man-hours, common man,* and *man-sized job.* Not all the proposals advanced by the reformers are loony. As society changes, and women move into new areas of the work force, such deadwood as *mailman* properly can be pruned.

• Abandon sexist suffixes. Copy editors would howl if ever they were deprived of *heiress, actress, priestess,* and one or two others, but surely the time has come to get rid of *sculptress, poetess, executrix,* and the like. These have become excess baggage.

• Kill the offending pronoun. "The student who is troubled about his grades" can give way comfortably to, "The student who is troubled about grades." This is not the same thing, of course, but in context it is seldom likely to cause confusion.

• Change the pronoun to a neuter adjective. "Every graduate

should have a picture taken" is about the same thing as, "Every graduate should have his picture taken." ("All graduates should have their pictures taken" works better.)

• Try *its.* "An infant who sucks its thumb . . ."

• Repeat an antecedal noun. "First the city editor looks at the copy. After the copy has been read for style by the copy desk, the city editor marks it for publication . . ."

Other devices may occur to the writer who is sensitive about these things. The general rule is to assuage tender feelings, but not to make a fool of yourself.

Every conjurer, every lawyer, every statesman and poker player has a bag of little dog tricks. Writers have their little dog tricks also. These are artifices, or devices, or rhetorical gimmicks. None of them is especially difficult to master. Let me offer a few suggestions.

Change the pace of your prose.

A succession of simple, indicative sentences soon gets to be monotonous. There's no rule against long sentences, but the writer who wants to keep his readers awake will intersperse long sentences with short ones. In the same fashion, a string of sentences in the passive voice will be more easily digested if the string is salted with sentences in the active voice. Learn to write *fast.* The trick is to use short sentences and vivid verbs. This is how one of Louis L'Amour's Western heroes fought an Indian:

> He threw himself to one side and felt the cold steel of the blade as it grazed him. His rifle in his left hand, he hit low and hard and up with the blade. It struck, something ripped and then he was hit hard on the shoulder. He rolled back, throwing up his feet to catch the Huron as he dove at him. His feet churned, smashing hard into his attacker's face, and then he was up, swinging his rifle with both hands.

Note the verbs: *threw, grazed, hit, struck, ripped, rolled, dove, churned, smashing, swinging.* The paragraph races along.

We may want to write *slow.* One of England's most gifted masters of the detective story, a proper successor to Agatha Christie,
is P.D. James. She has a way of putting on the brakes now and
then, or in a better image, downshifting her gears. In *Devices and
Desires,* she slows the action to describe an interdepartmental
meeting at a plant directed by Dr. Mair.

> The weekly meeting was held in his office at the confer-
> ence table set in front of the south window. Darkness was
> falling and the huge pane of glass was a black rectangle, in
> which he could see their faces reflected, like the gaunt,
> disembodied heads of night travelers in a lighted railway
> carriage. He suspected that some of his departmental heads
> would have preferred a more relaxed setting, in his private
> sitting room next door, the low, comfortable chairs, a few
> hours of chat with no set agenda, perhaps a drink together
> afterwards in a local pub. Well, that was one management
> style, but it wasn't his.

Note her verbs. There isn't a strong one in the lot.

Use the active voice.

Every manual on the writing art will give you this advice. All these
patented programs of computer hardware, purporting to teach a
person how to write, will sneer a computerized sneer when you
employ a passive verb. In general, the advice is quite sound. In
general, you should take it. If an editorial writer in Charleston,
S.C., had followed this advice, we would not have read:

> When asked about the reports of an anti-Castro coup in
> Cuba by a reporter, the diplomat said: "I've been talking to
> Elvis and he hasn't heard anything about it."

The editorial writer might have recast the sentence to read, "When
a reporter asked about reports of an anti-Castro coup in Cuba,
the diplomat said . . ."
    Active verbs, by their very nature, are livelier than passive verbs;
they have better muscles. "He broke his arm playing polo" is

surely a better sentence than, "While playing polo his arm was broken." Not many arms play polo anyhow.

To be sure, you can overdo the bit about active verbs. Sometimes it is better to be passive than to be hyper. Your ear should tell you when enough is too much.

Work hard on your lead.

Every professor who teaches the writing art should devote a couple of weeks each semester to a single topic: the lead sentence. In the writing of prose, a conclusive ending is desirable and a well-developed middle is essential, but it is the lead that can make or break a composition.

Memorable leads have one thing in common: They are generally short. Not many people have read *Moby Dick* all the way through, though millions of liars have said they have, but almost every student of American literature can quote the first line: "Call me Ishmael."

James M. Cain began *The Postman Always Rings Twice* with nine words: "They threw me off the hay truck about noon."

Billie Holiday began her autobiography with a perfect one-two punch: "Mom and Pop were just a couple of kids when they got married. He was 18, she was 16, and I was 3."

"Brevity," said Polonius, "is the soul of wit," and so it is. Dickens began *Bleak House* with sentence fragments:

> London. Michelmas Term lately over, and the Lord Chancellor sitting in Lincoln's Inn Hall. Implacable November weather.

Aldous Huxley used the same device in opening his *Brave New World:* "A squat grey building of only thirty-four stories."

Emerson was fond of putting short leads on long essays. From his essay on love: "Every soul is a celestial Venus to every other soul." From his essay on friendship: "We have a great deal more kindness than is ever spoken." From his essay on manners: "Half the world, it is said, knows not how the other half lives."

Essayist Lance Morrow has a way with leads. He began an essay on the work ethic with a captivating come-on:

When God foreclosed on Eden, he condemned Adam and Eve to go to work. Work has never recovered from that humiliation.

Many writers use the lead to set the scene. In *Another Country*, novelist James Baldwin began: "He was facing Seventh Avenue, at Times Square." George Orwell launched into *1984* with a memorable sentence: "It was a bright cold day in April, and the clocks were striking thirteen." Garry Wills began *Nixon Agonistes* with a dateline: "February 1968. It is early morning in Wisconsin, in Appleton, air heavy with the rot of wood pulp."

Some good leads have a beguiling quality. In *Citizens*, Simon Schama lured his readers into the French revolution: "Between 1814 and 1846 a plaster elephant stood on the site of the Bastille." John Dos Passos, in *The Shackles of Power*, grabbed us with a come-on opening line: "Thomas Jefferson was an early riser."

Now pay attention to this one:

The annual labour of every nation is the fund which originally supplies it with all the necessaries and convenience of life which it annually consumes, and which consist always either in the immediate produce of their labour, or in what is purchased with that produce from other nations.

That was Adam Smith's lead to *The Wealth of Nations*, which explains why everyone lies about having read the whole of that one, too.

The lead is vital to any writing, whether one is writing a novel, a short story, a book review, a term paper, a newspaper editorial, or a homily to be read in church on Sunday morning. The lead sentence is the writer's baited hook. If it is skillfully cast, the fish will bite.

I don't mean to suggest that every good lead should be short, but as a working rule, short is better than long. For this reason: Many readers have a natural resistance to reading. Other diversions and occupations press upon them. They may be reading out of a compulsion that is real or implied. Certain things are known as "must reading."

To overcome this resistance, the concise lead performs a useful function. In one tug, it pulls the reader across a threshold. The most difficult step has been taken. It remains for the writer to develop that lead, and sometimes this proves a real obstacle. The story is told of a wannabe novelist who ran a clean sheet of paper into his typewriter and boldly began: "Naked, Elaine stood at the window watching John come up the walk." It was one helluva lead, but alas, it was the end of the novel.

Work just as hard on your cracker.

The last sentence of a piece of writing, known in the trade as a cracker, is almost as important as the first. It is the snap of the ringmaster's whip, the slam of a young lady's door. In the writing of essays and editorials the crafting of a final sentence is an art in itself. "No self-respecting bee," said a venerable editor in North Carolina, "ever sat down without leaving a sting."

Sometimes a single word will suffice. Lord Macaulay knew how to do this. In his essay on Warren Hastings, Macaulay recalls (probably unfairly) how Hastings dealt with a difficult judge in India: He bribed him. "The bargain was struck; Bengal was saved; an appeal to force was averted; and the chief justice was rich, quiet, and infamous." So much for Hastings.

Macaulay speaks of William Pitt, an incorruptible statesman who silently tolerated corruption around him. At one point a coalition of good men and evil men rallied to his side: "The coalition gathered to itself support from all the high and low parts of human nature, and was strong with the whole united strength of virtue and of mammon."

Notice, if you will, the trochaic cadence of the final two prepositional phrases. Take away the "of" before "Mammon," and the cadence collapses like a struck tent. Little words count.

One of the tricks of the trade is to end a piece of writing on an accented syllable. Sen. Pat Moynihan of New York wrote a light-hearted piece for The New York Times. He was talking about the correlation of public funds and academic achievement. He said:

> The president was right enough in stating that "the major cause of problems of the cities is the dissolution of the

family." But it is not just the slum families: affluent families, too—the self-destructive poor and the self-indulgent affluent.

The senator had a lovely, lilting sentence going—and then he muffed it. How much better it would have been if only he had written of "the self-destructive poor and the self-indulgent rich."

If your concluding sentence ends on an accented syllable that provides a long vowel or a diphthong, it sometimes lends a desirable note of finality. The two best editorial pages in the country, 180 degrees apart on most issues, are the editorial pages of The Washington Post and The Wall Street Journal. On a given day in August 1992 the Post had an editorial on the declining value of the dollar. It ended:

> To put it in political terms, you could say that the current decline of the dollar is Adam Smith's comment on the way the campaign is going.

The Post had another editorial on worldwide indifference to events in Lebanon. It ended:

> This is Lebanon's fate. Its best way to avoid it is to take every chance—even a half-chance—to go down the democratic road.

The Wall Street Journal editorialized on the scandal involving movie director Woody Allen, who was accused of having an incestuous affair with his adopted daughter. Quoting the Democratic platform, the Journal concluded that even liberal Democrats found the story revolting.

> Democrats get it. Republicans get it. Woody Allen, in our judgment, never will. Even the media elite, in reaction to Mr. Allen's troubles, displays some capacity for shock, or at least sensation. We guess there's hope.

The Journal's other editorial that day commended President Bush's decision to bottle up Iraq's air force in an effort to protect the Shiite Muslims.

> It represents movement away from the old-fashioned *Realpolitik* of deals among strongmen, and toward an information-

world-order in which ideals such as legitimacy and ultimately democracy play a central role.

It was not by accident, but by design, that all four editorials ended with the bell-ringing sound of a good strong vowel—*going, road, hope, role.*

Develop a strong sense of cadence.

In *My Life as Author and Editor,* H.L. Mencken praised Lilith Benda, who contributed fiction to the *Smart Set* in 1916. He especially praised a novelette: "There was little overt movement in it, but it was packed with sharp observation and searching understanding, and there was a fine surface to the writing and a keen sense of the music of words."

The music of words! We must listen for it, for we read not only with our eyes, but also with our ears. It is therefore desirable that our sentences both read well and sound right. A writer—a serious writer—must cultivate an awareness of life's rhythms. They are all around us, in the sound of waves, in the changing of a traffic light, in the phases of the moon. Often we can achieve a sense of cadence by the shifting of a mere word or two. At a given point two syllables may be better than one. We must listen—*listen!*—to what we write. If a sentence can be made to read rhythmically, without altering its meaning, it is likely to be a better sentence.

A few years ago a political writer had occasion to mention the senior senators from Massachusetts, Georgia, and New Jersey. After a moment's thought he wrote of Kennedy, Bradley, and Nunn. How come? In that order he got a little lilt in his sentence. He had bagged a wily dactyl.

Notice what happens if the order of senators is changed to: Kennedy, Nunn, and Bradley. Or Bradley, Nunn, and Kennedy. The references are equally clear, but listen again to the reporter's first choice. He wrote of KEN-ned-y, BRAD-ley, and NUNN, and his sentence rippled along. You can slip a dactylic beat into almost anything. We may write about CARD-in-als, THRESH-ers, and JAYS. Or HICK-o-ry, POP-lar, and PINE. Or OR-i-oles, YANKees, and BRAVES. In each instance we wind up with an accented word at the end of the phrase.

You can go iambic. In the first casting of an editorial, the writer says, "The damning facts require a Senate investigation." Nothing wrong with that. Now let us change one word: "The damning facts require a Senate probe." Or perhaps: "The SENate MUST pur-SUE the DAMN-ing FACTS." The sentence no longer dribbles off. It closes like a rat trap.

If the mood is upon you, take an anapest to lunch: "With the VOTE in Ver-MONT, Mis-ter LEA-hy was JUB-i-lant." Surely that beats, "Mr. Leahy was jubilant at the outcome in Vermont."

Like anything else, this sort of thing can be overdone. If a rhythmic effect is to be achieved, it is best achieved without calling attention to it. Anyhow, the matter affords an opportunity for me to say that writers should write verse for the same reason that boxers jump rope. It keeps the mind nimble.

Avoid using nouns as adjectives.

In football they call it "piling on," and the violation carries a penalty. In prose composition, the piling on of modifying nouns amounts to the same thing. A few examples will make the point.

> Four justices said the ruling may undermine some prison reform efforts.

Try recasting the sentence to read, "Four justices said the ruling may undermine some efforts at prison reform." For the price of a single added word, the preposition *at,* we get a better, smoother sentence.

> So what if *The Sum of All Fears* lacks credibility? This is, after all, a suspense novel, not a political science text.

Try that sentence again, but make the same kind of change: "This is, after all, a suspense novel, not a text in political science."

> The Trump Shuttle could not turn a profit because of ferocious competition from rival Pan American and an overwhelming debt load.

Same thing: ". . . an overwhelming load of debt."

Let me ask you to sandpaper these jagged edges:

No note was made that the prospects for congressional passage are about equal to the New England Patriots' Super Bowl hopes.

Mrs. Campbell agreed to accept Palm's guilty plea to the driving a boat while intoxicated charge.

Three jurors asked to be excused, one for emotional health reasons.

Dearborn does not often consider Henry Miller as a writer; for her, he is more a laboratory specimen on a Lost Generation mounting board.

Corbett, a gentle soul with a game-show-host grin, is one of the founding instructors of English 572.

He walked as uneasily as a young New York cop on a crack-plagued Queens block.

Foes of abortion in effect support compulsory pregnancies for 13-year-old rape victims.

Look again at the last two examples. Your writer's ear should tell you that "a crack-plagued block in Queens" sounds better than "a crack-plagued Queens block." The sentence about abortion was a clumsy sentence to begin with, but it could have been much improved merely by changing it to read, "13-year-old victims of rape." Instead of that weak, two-syllabled, short-voweled "victims," we now have the strong, monosyllabled, long-voweled *rape*.

In 1968 a couple of professors made a study of the reapportionment of state legislatures. They were especially eager to see the election of minority members. They wrote:

Without a fair opportunity to elect representatives, freedom of political association yields no policy fruits.

Technically speaking, nothing is wrong with that sentence, but it can be improved with a little tinkering. The trouble with *policy fruits* is that an innocent noun, *policy,* has been press-ganged into

service as an adjective. Let us try the little prepositional dog
trick:

> Without a fair opportunity to elect representatives, freedom
> of political association yields no fruits of policy.

Let us tinker once more. We have achieved a measure of parallelism by balancing *of association* with *of policy.* We need something to
balance *political.* Suppose we insert *governmental.* The sentence
now reads,

> Without a fair opportunity to elect representatives, freedom
> of political association yields no fruits of governmental policy.

The ear winces at *governmental.* It has the sound of civics teachers
at tea. Perhaps *public* would be better, in part because of the
alliterative effect:

> Without a fair opportunity to elect representatives, freedom
> of political association yields no fruits of public policy.

There! Not a great sentence, but in the academic context, not a
bad one either.

I don't mean to inveigh against the use of nouns as adjectives
in every case. Nothing is wrong with *street musician* or *five-course
dinner.* It would be silly to insist upon *crossing for deer* instead of
deer crossing. It's the piling on that's bad. A reporter covering the
Senate a few years ago insisted upon calling a piece of pending
legislation the "Bentsen 25 percent tariff surcharge bill." We can
do better.

Watch where you put those prepositions.

Some people who write, but know little about *writing,* insist that
prose composition is governed by certain ancient and inflexible
rules. I will give you four of them: Never end a sentence with a
preposition. Never split an infinitive. Never begin a sentence with
a conjunction. Never use sentence fragments. Good writers will
ignore all four of these commands, but good writers also will
acknowledge that the supposed "rules" have a core of sensible
substance.

Take the first one. A long time ago, a woman reportedly reproached Winston Churchill for violating the rule against ending a sentence with a preposition.

"Madam," Churchill is said to have said, "that is the kind of nonsense up with which I will not put."

Bully for Winnie! Granted, "the kind of nonsense I will not put up with" is clumsy. The two prepositions, *up* and *with,* bump heads in a tailgate collision at the end. Anyhow, we ought to note that some prepositions that appear to be prepositions, such as the *up* in *put up,* are not prepositions at all. They are indispensable parts of the verbs with which they are coupled. "How many jars of pickles did mother put up?" "How many hitters did Clemens strike out?" "Tomorrow the cavalry will move on." "We should ask the tourists to come in."

What appears to be a sentence-ending preposition may be an adverb: "Jane is somewhere about." It may be an idiom: "At his death Mozart was down and out." And sometimes it is best to leave an honest preposition at the end: "She spoke hesitantly, almost stuttering, as if the thoughts and words were a new language she was not quite familiar with." An editor could not improve that sentence by making it read, "as if the thoughts and words were a new language with which she was not quite familiar." Charles Osgood once wrote that, "Young Palestinians think of the past as something they should be willing to die for." The sentence would be wrecked by prissily emending it to read, "something for which they should be willing to die."

A sensible observation—not a rule, just an observation—is that most of the time it is indeed better to put a preposition where it usually belongs, before its object, rather than at the end of a sentence, where it hangs on like a guest who won't go home. When a reporter abandons the traditional Latinist placement, we get this sentence from the AP in Moscow: "There were no reported casualties in Moscow, which the military clearly was in control of." Yuuuck! Better: "There were no reported casualties in Moscow, where the military clearly was in control."

On this general subject, let us beware of piling up prepositions. A copy editor on the Las Vegas Sun drafted this infelicitous headline: "Graduates of technical school not finding jobs they're in it for." A headline writer in Terre Haute was having a bad day: "Artist hangs inflated image of himself up." A feature writer recalled a woman "who remembers the dresses that some of her aprons were made from the leftovers of."

Split if you damn well please.

None of the supposed rules of English composition is phonier than the rule against a split infinitive. It is no rule at all, yet as recently as 1981, when Professor Richard Tobin put the question to newspaper editors, 90 percent of them stoutly declared that splits are "abhorrent." In 1985 the Joint Chiefs of Staff issued an order: "Split infinitives are not to be used in OJCS correspondence."

This is nonsense, but like the supposed rule on the placement of prepositions, at bottom the rule is sound. God put the elements of English verbs together. Without good reason, let no writer rip the parts asunder.

Our first aim, as writers, is to turn out prose that is clear. A secondary aim is to turn out prose that is graceful. Syntactic sergeants of the Old Guard miss the second target. They seem not to understand that the placement of adverbs in infinitive constructions is a judgment call. The decision lies wholly within the writer's ear.

This was from The Wall Street Journal: "Mr. Savas explained that privatization has long been a proven way to efficiently deliver services." My ear would have told me, "to deliver services efficiently." This is from The Washington Post: "Von Raab insists that he is trying to quietly work out a compromise." I would have recast it to read, "is trying quietly to work out a compromise." My thought is that it is the trying that is quiet, rather than the working out that is quiet.

This is from The New York Times: "One thing all the experts agreed about is that Mr. Bush cannot afford to simply defend the status quo." My ear would move the *simply*, so that the sentence would read, ". . . cannot afford simply to defend the status quo."

At least half the time, I submit, it is better to split an infinitive than to paste it poorly together. This is from The New York Times:

> Coming two days after President Bush disclosed that the
> United States was prepared to quickly recognize Ukraine's
> independence, the decision by Mr. Yeltsin dramatized the
> difficulty . . .

I would leave that *quickly* right where it is. Nothing whatever
would be gained by shifting it.

> Mandela had previously refused to formally renounce the
> armed struggle of the guerrilla wing.

Only a contortionist would change the sentence to read, "Mandela had previously refused formally to renounce . . ." Still worse:
"Mandela had previously refused to renounce the armed struggle of the guerrilla wing formally."

My ear surely is not infallible in these matters. Your ear may
respond to other rhythms entirely. All I can ask, as a coach, is that
if you feel impelled to separate the parts of a verb, read the
suspect sentence aloud. If the split infinitive falls trippingly from
the tongue, okay, split the thing! If not, the best answer is quietly
to put it back together.

Keep your elements parallel.

Let us suppose that we have returned from the grocery store, and
now we are putting things away. We put eggs here, cheese there,
soft drinks somewhere else. But unless our attention has wandered badly, we do not put pork chops in a bin with the grapefruit.

This same sense of tidiness ought to guide us in prose composition. We should cultivate the art of parallelism, which is the art of
keeping fruit in the fruit bin and drinks with the drinks.

This is how not to do it, from a story in The Washington Post
about charges brought by the Securities and Exchange Commission against Drexel Burnham Lambert. The SEC charged the
defendants with engaging in a scheme that involved "illegal insider stock trading, rigging of corporate takeovers, stock price
manipulation, falsifying records, bullying clients and tax fraud."

The sentence was pork chops and grapefruit, participles and

nouns, all higgledy-piggledy. The writer gave us *trading* and *rigging*, then *manipulation*, then *falsifying* and *bullying*, and finally *tax fraud*.

For another example: A church bulletin set forth the purposes of the church. These are, "to worship God, to help the poor, and bringing families closer together." Admirable purposes, to be sure, but parallel infinitives would have helped: to worship, to help, to bring.

This is how one ought to do it, from that old master Edward Gibbon. He is speaking of Constantine's actions after the defeat of Maxentius: "The first time that Constantine honoured the Senate with his presence he recapitulated his own services and exploits in a modest oration, assured that illustrious order of his sincere regard, and promised to reestablish its ancient dignity and privileges." Gibbon lined up his verbs like centurions on review: *recapitulated, assured, promised*.

Gibbon discusses two of Constantine's laws, "the one for its importance, the other for its singularity; the former for its remarkable benevolence, the latter for its excessive severity." Notice, if you will, how *importance* balances *singularity*, and *remarkable benevolence* carries an equal weight with *excessive severity*.

In the fall of 1988 *U.S. News & World Report* editorialized on the difficulties in bringing Lieutenant Colonel Oliver North to trial: "The problems are at once simple in their inception and Gordian in resolution." The sentence was okay, but it lost its equilibrium and fell off at the end. The insertion of a single word would have helped: "simple in their inception and Gordian in *their* resolution."

Here is another example. The Chicago Sun-Times carried a story about outfielder Andre Dawson when Dawson was playing with the Cubs. At San Diego, Dawson "was booed, jeered, taunted, and the target of debris." The writer gave us three verbs and then—spoiling the sentence—a noun. The mind's eye expected another verb to match *booed, jeered,* and *taunted*. Bang! The eye blinked at *target*. The problem could have been corrected with a two-second emendation: Fans greeted Dawson with boos, jeers, taunts, and a shower of debris. Or, Dawson was booed, jeered, taunted, and made the target of debris.

The Christian Science Monitor, writing about baseball's all-star game, voiced a regret: "Unfortunately, the fans often vote from memory and based on sentiment." The sentence could have been rephrased: "Unfortunately, the fans' voting often is based upon memory and sentiment." Or, "Memory and sentiment often dominate the fans' voting." Or, "Some fans vote from memory and others vote on sentiment."

You will find an excellent discussion of parallelism in Wilson Follett's *Modern American Usage* under the heading of "matching parts." What is fatal to orderly prose composition, says Follett, "is to arouse an expectation of matched construction and then to frustrate it." The principle, he adds, "is the simple one that logically equal elements in a sentence had better be also rhetorically equal."

Let us match verbs to verbs, adverbs to adverbs, nouns to nouns, and thus keep grapefruit out of the meat bin. If Lincoln had spoken at Gettysburg of a government "of the people, by the people, and engaged in doing good works," the sentence would have gone as limp as last night's party balloon.

Watch the threshold conjunction.

The syntactical ailment known as *conjunctionitis* is more of an itch than an illness, but it's something to keep under control. The supposed rule forbids our beginning a sentence with an *and,* a *but,* or a *yet.* I thought about this on a Friday afternoon in 1992 when I was killing time in an airport lounge, reading the first section of the day's New York Times. Mercy me, I cried aloud, the Times is down with the *ands* and *buts!*

A.M. Rosenthal let us know that no other nation has quite the many problems that Israel confronts. "AND whatever their differences," Israeli leaders are clear-eyed about them. "BUT every time I visit I am seized" by a fresh understanding. Mr. Rabin hints that he will move Israeli troops. "AND, like Mr. Shamir, he sees Palestinian statehood as an unacceptable military danger . . . BUT where both men come together, is in how they see the world . . . BUT Mr. Rabin and Mr. Arens underline precisely the same long-range dangers for Israel."

On page one of the Times, *buts* came in from correspondents in Washington and San Francisco. Writers in China and Costa Rica had the rash. The Times's man at the United Nations reported that the U.S. is pressing for a tough embargo upon Serbia. "BUT Russia and China have appeared reluctant."

The day's biggest story had to do with Ross Perot's investment in land development. "YET harsh criticism has become . . . BUT Mr. Guajardo acknowledged . . . AND after Speaker Wright helped . . . BUT the biggest catch for the Perots . . . BUT despite the frequent clashes . . . BUT the younger Mr. Perot said . . . BUT the son persuaded the father . . . AND the family didn't have nineteen years to wait . . . BUT the most rancorous dispute continues . . . BUT Mr. Harris said the Perots . . ."

Now, there is no rule against beginning a sentence with a conjunction. Sometimes it's an effective device. But watch it. Nine times out of eleven, a sentence will be better without it.

Handle sentence fragments with care.

Another device to use with a deliberate touch is the sentence fragment. Old Guard grammarians, in the mold of Theodore Bernstein's Miss Thistlebottom, regard fragments as hobgoblins. Sometimes fragments prove to be real hobgoblins. Here is a splendid example, from *Newsweek* magazine, of how *not* to use this little gimmick:

> Say the name of Lee Wulff to any fly-fisherman and images start spilling out like attracters from an old fly box. A glimpse of the Royal Wulff, his buoyant dry fly, floating along the Madison River in Montana, daring the rainbows to strike. A memory of Wulff the bush pilot buzzing Labrador, the shadow of his wings producing silver flashes in dark river pools as spooked Atlantic salmon mistook him for a bird of prey. Wulff of the Catskills, lean as a cougar, padding up to the old Piper Cub he kept parked at the edge of a mowed field on the Beaverkill. And Wulff as the old man and the sea, craggy faced, hard as hickory, reeling in the humiliated marlin, sailfish and bluefin tuna he deceived with his flies.

Those weren't sentence fragments. They amounted to a whole archeological dig, with shards and bones competing for verbs to glue them back together.

Another Horrid Example comes from *U.S. News & World Report.* The editor-in-chief was grumbling about all the national shortcomings he could think of. (Of which he could think?) He was especially critical of the years of President Bush:

> During this period, we made fewer provisions for our future than at any time in our history, while middle-class Americans were kicked in the economic groin as their real incomes declined and their taxes went up. As soaring public and private debt loads strip mined the economy, denuding it of the savings it needs for investment capital. And as we suffered through the lowest growth rate and longest recession since the Depression.

Both of these specimens violate the first rule on fragments: Keep 'em short.

Watch for the telling details.

The novelist who has reason to describe a kitchen is not likely to begin with a recitation of dimensions—10 × 12 feet, with an eight-foot ceiling. Neither will we read that to the left of the door is a refrigerator, and to the right are cabinets next to a sink. A telling description is more likely to depend upon the telling details. Is the oven clean or dirty? Are there dishes in the sink? What notes or messages, if any, are fastened on the Kelvinator door? We will know more about this kitchen, and about the family around it, if we know that the cabinets have glass-paned doors, that the floor is covered with cracked linoleum, that a heavy iron skillet is on the stove. The trick here is to capture the small details that bring a scene to life.

Philip Larkin, the British poet, puts this gift of selective detail to effective use. In one poem he speaks of a farm woman who "carries a chipped pail to the chicken-run." He might have spoken of an old pail, a blue pail, a rusty pail, or a gallon pail, and we would have seen nothing special. A *chipped* pail is perfect.

Larkin speaks of neurotics who drag their feet "clay-thick with misery." He had looked intently at wet clay. He speaks of an unhurried day when "your mind lay open like a drawer of knives." He had looked at a drawer of knives. In one of his finest poems, Larkin takes a slow train to the city. He sits between *felt-hatted* mums. With that little detail, the passenger car comes to life.

It is generally better to be specific than to be general. In one of her novels, Lee Smith mentions Velveeta cheese. She speaks of Ladyfingers. Her automobiles have names: Buick, Olds, Packard. Margaret Gordon Williamson, the Memphis poet, wrote of "the battered dinner-silver on a train," and the dining car magically appeared.

Reporters—and poets too, for that matter—must be admonished not to fake the significant details. The whole effect depends upon absolute accuracy of observation. If a child has a hole in his sneakers, okay, remark the hole, but if there isn't a hole don't give him one.

Go easy on the adjectives.

Once upon a time, so the story goes, a young woman became attracted to the art of flower arrangement. She fared poorly in competitions, and at last asked a judge for advice. The judge gave her three envelopes, to be opened one at a time when she next tried her hand.

The message in the first envelope read, "Take out half of your flowers and rearrange the rest." She did so. The second message read, "Take out half of your flowers and rearrange the rest." She did so. The third message was the same. She followed instructions and won the blue ribbon.

This advice of the flower judge is sound advice for writers. I thought about it when a teacher in a Maryland junior high school sent me fifteen sentences written by her ninth-grade students.

She plucked the sentences from stories the students had written. Among them:

> Mesmerizing the already dazed driver, the ruthless pair of uniform windshield wipers marched methodically back and forth across the dappled field of glass.

> The many aisles of the run-down movie theater seemed to whisper of past audiences that once flocked to the now desolate cinema.

> Gliding smoothly, glaciers of butter slid over and down the sides of the hot, flaky, golden biscuits.

> Down the slope of the forest of moguls, the graceful skier slithered to the hot cocoa awaiting him below.

> Seemingly effortlessly, the long, supple fingers glided swiftly across the piano's keyboard, each phalange dancing with a life of its own.

> Under the full moon, silver-haired wraiths flitted about among the ivy-covered gravestones in the dark, musty cemetery, a favorite haunt of ancient memories.

The teacher asked me for criticism. What to say? One begins by praising these 15-year-olds for their spelling, commending them for their effort, and urging them to keep at it. What else could I say? I told them to take out half the flowers and rearrange the rest.

Beware the lure of Fine Writing! Remember the advice of Dr. Samuel Johnson: "Read over your composition," said the irascible sage, "and wherever you meet with a passage which you think is particularly fine, *strike it out!*"

The temptation to spread one's wings is especially strong among fledgling writers. The Maryland students were not content with hot biscuits; their biscuits were *hot, flaky, golden* biscuits. The skier must be graceful, the cocoa must be hot. It is not enough to speak of wipers sweeping across a windshield; these are a "ruthless pair of uniform wipers marching methodically back and forth across the dappled field of glass." Too many flowers.

In descriptive writing, the trick is always to leave something to the imagination of the reader. Not everything needs to be spelled out. If a gentleman is kissing a lady on her lips, it truly is not necessary to explain that her lips are red and her teeth are pearly white. This may reasonably be assumed. The English language provides a palette of many colors. We ought not to use all of them all at one time.

Unpack the portmanteau sentence.

Experienced travelers are masters of the art of packing a bag. They pack no more than they need for the trip; they put socks here and underwear there and toiletries somewhere else. When they have finished, the bag closes nicely; everything is neatly in its place, and no ties, hose, or bra straps are hanging out. Sentences should be as tidy.

Terrible things happen to untidy writers. This portmanteau sentence comes from the Las Vegas Sun.

> A stray bullet struck Christina Ayala on Thursday night while standing on a second-floor fire escape overlooking the gun battle between blacks and Dominicans nearby, said Police Capt. James Crean.

This is from the UPI, about a newly crowned Miss America:

> Smartly dressed in a blue wool long-sleeve black dress trimmed with black, black shoes, pearl and gold bracelets and her rhinestone crown, Akin said she was politically conservative, although she said issues of abortion and premarital sex should be left to the individual, and declared her support for sanctions against the South African government.

This is from the Anderson (S.C.) Independent-Mail, reporting the dedication of a dam near Calhoun Falls:

> During a speech from the grandstand by Sen. Sam Nunn, D. Ga., a jeep drove alongside the crowd carrying a prone man apparently suffering from the heat on a stretcher in the back to the powerhouse.

Newsday covered a bank robbery by a woman:

The woman held seven employees and five customers at bay with the automatic weapon while her partner vaulted the counter and collected the cash from three teller stations and a safe in a white plastic shopping bag.

The St. Charles (La.) Chronicle missed a great chance at an interview of historic dimensions:

Christ Community Church will address one of the most sensitive and personal issues of life—sexuality—including what God says about sex at the 10:30 worship service on Sunday.

A reporter for the Portland Oregonian packed a full bag:

Dr. Miguel Garcia, the first doctor to examine Linder's body in Bocay after the 8 a.m. Tuesday attack, told members of Witness for Peace that his examination has showed that Linder and a Nicaraguan were killed by shrapnel from hand grenades and that a second Nicaraguan was killed by rifle wounds, said Ed Griffin-Nolan, press secretary for the group, which is based in North Carolina, opposes aid to the Contras and seeks to document atrocities in the conflict.

The usually impeccable *New Yorker* provided this melange:

From the late twenties until just after the second World War, the Nicholas Brothers, or Nicholas Kids, as they were sometimes called—they were only about five and twelve when they became famous—starred regularly in vaudeville and at the Cotton Club, occasionally in the movies, and even on radio, where their tapping was broadcast, without apology, as percussion solo.

You get the idea. It truly is not necessary to pack *everything* into a single sentence. When your portmanteau won't hold anything more, metaphorically speaking, get another suitcase.

Handle metaphors as if they would break.

Metaphors are high wires for writers. One misstep and oops! Into the net below. The risk is worth taking, for an occasional crisp metaphor can revive a limp piece of copy. Two hazards await the adventurer. One is the mixaphor. The other is the metabore.

For the record, as parliamentarians say, a metaphor is a rhetorical device by which an actual image is transferred to an illustrative image. "The hot coffee of the House," said Thomas Jefferson, "is cooled in the saucer of the Senate." Mr. Jefferson had all the elements of that metaphor consistently in place. His sentence was short, and his image was familiar to everyone.

Not all metaphors turn out so happily. The Wall Street Journal once quoted a Vermont engineer who was concerned about new forms of energy. "If you get too much out of step with the mainstream, it will backfire." The Miami Herald quoted a creditor of an insolvent electronics firm. "They owe us $18.6 million," said a spokeswoman, "but in their circumstances they're probably just pulling every plug they can to keep themselves above water."

In Florida, the Vero Beach Press-Journal reported a plea-bargaining deal in a rape case. The defendant's attorney didn't like it, "but given the attitude of the normal jury on this type of crime, I feel we would be paddling upstream behind the eight ball." In North Carolina, a state agency unhappily accepted responsibility for locating an unpopular waste treatment plant. "I think we are talking about a fairly big bullet to swallow."

An advertising executive took a gloomy view of the stock market. "If a crash dictates belt tightening, most often it is advertising that is the first to feel the axe." In 1987 *Newsweek* reported a trivial spat between the White House and the State Department. Secretary George Shultz was out of favor at the time. In order to slap his wrist for disloyalty, the White House refused to pay for some air travel. "The mice at the White House were gored," said an aide to Shultz, "so they're sniping back." The same threadbare allusion appeared in Norfolk, Va., where a bankruptcy court cracked down on corporation executives who had been bleeding the company. "Except that their goose has been gored, they do not feel or appreciate the huge harm done to others."

These are memorable mixaphors:

If you try to take the whole enchilada, you get lost in the woodwork.

At 41 years old and a judge for less than a year, Ginsburg has left few fingerprints to provide administration critics a toehold of opposition.

Mike Tyson has come 360 degrees around, and that's the triangle of life.

State threw a curve at this Furman offense that was expected to be green about the edges.

It is not easy to stick your head out on a limb.

For any editor worth his or her salt, when a Trojan horse like that is laid at your doorstep, you begin to think somebody has an axe to grind.

Conservatives would rather go down in flames than accept a half loaf.

The trouble with most of these mixaphors is that the writers began with a cliché—the half a loaf, the Trojan horse, the gored ox, the eight ball, the tightened belt, the outstuck neck. Instead of creating a striking image, they ended with a blot.

When a skilled writer goes to work with fresh material, it's a different matter. Edmund Burke was a master of the metaphor. In his best known work, *Reflections on the Revolution in France,* he remarked that the bloody revolution in France carried a warning to England to look after its own social abuses: "Whenever our neighbor's house is on fire, it cannot be amiss for the engines to play a little water on our own." A British preacher questioned the validity of the crown because kings are not popularly elected. Burke said the minister's theory was "pickled in the juice of pulpit eloquence."

The metabore is an Energizer bunny. It keeps going, and going, and going. Some writers can get away with an extended metaphor, without its turning into a metabore, but it's a risky business. Burke got away with a long metaphor in his *Reflections.*

Because half a dozen grasshoppers under a fern make the field ring with their importunate chink, whilst thousands of great cattle, reposing beneath the shadow of the British oak, chew the cud and are silent, pray do not imagine that those who make the noise are the only inhabitants of the field; that, of course, they are many in number; or that, after all, they are other than the little, shriveled, meager, hopping, though loud and troublesome, insects of the hour.

Not many writers can successfully emulate Burke. When most of us get carried away, we wind up with something like this:

Let us select from the tool house of prose composition the two-edged axe of metaphor, but let us beware that the two edges may cut in ways we don't intend. Skillfully employed, the axe adds a sharp bite to one's prose, but the tool must be constantly honed. Ineptly handled, the metaphor can reduce the solid oak of a sentence to kindling.

And so on. And so on, until the log turns to splinters.

Never let your metaphors run on, and never, ever, without the most compelling reason, sail off on a metaphorical sea. This was from the business page of a weekly in Manhattan:

Although plans to build a Long John Silver restaurant in Jamestown's Brooklyn Square have been treading water this summer, company officials hope to be moving full steam ahead soon. A spokesman said plans call for the restaurant to set sail this winter.

That was bilge.

Try your hand at similes also.

A simile is a first cousin to the metaphor, but similes rely upon direct instead of indirect comparison. A fighter plane climbed *like* a homesick angel. The locker room smelled *like* the inside of a motorman's glove. Some inspired writer, hitting upon a beautiful simile, remembered the grace of "Jackie Gleason getting out of a Porsche." A writer for *Minnesota Monthly* watched as historic buildings were boarded up. "The sight powerfully focuses one's attention. It is like watching an undertaker close the lid of the casket."

In the Song of Songs which is Solomon's, similes tumble over one another like children at play: "My beloved is like a roe or a young hart . . . Thy teeth are like a flock of sheep that are even shorn . . . Thy lips are like a thread of scarlet . . . His eyes are as the eyes of doves . . . His belly is as bright as ivory, his legs are as pillars of marble . . ." Most critics read the Song of Solomon, with all its similes, as one extended metaphor, or even two extended metaphors, but let it pass.

In 1991 I conducted a simile contest through my "Writer's Art" column. The idea was to create similes for *serene, rough, slippery,* and *graceful.* My guess was that maybe three hundred to four hundred entries would come in. To my astonishment, 2,493 readers submitted entries, and because almost all of them provided at least one simile for each word, I ended by looking at more than ten thousand similes.

Most of them were awful. Well, not really *awful,* for they were blessed by the enthusiasm of their creators, but most of the similes were either trite, or labored, or inapt. Hundreds of readers sought a prize for *slippery as a banana peel* or *graceful as a swan.* They loved *slippery as soap,* and they loved its variations: *slippery as a sliver of soap in a Southern sorority house.* My fellow judges looked at *serene as a nun at prayer* until we could look no more.

The prize for *slippery* went to a reader from Canby, Ore., for, *The old cardsharp was as slippery as the new deck of cards he was dealing.* This won honorable mention: *The salesman's handshake was as slippery as a groom's new shoes.*

Two other entries had the same ideas. "The dealer was as slippery as the new deck of cards being cut," and, "With the ball, Kenny Anderson is as slippery as the bottom of cheap dress shoes." The judges chose the Oregon entry for a couple of reasons. There was a nice touch of repetition in the *s*-sounds: *sharp . . . was . . . slippery . . . as . . . cards . . . was.* The winner also had an anapest in her favor: as the NEW deck of CARDS he was DEALing. The judges concurred that other *slippery* entries would have been better off with something as succinct as, "Given the ball, Kenny Anderson is as slippery as new shoes," but nobody followed the brevity rule.

In the *serene* division, first prize went to a gentleman in South Carolina who drew upon recent corruption in the state legislature. He submitted, "While scandals rocked the legislature, the speaker appeared as serene as last year's winner at this year's beauty pageant." It was a little wordy, but the judges ranked it ahead of, "as serene as Whistler's mother," which they suspected had been used before. My own favorite was, "as serene as a snowman's smile," but the other judges talked me down.

The first prize for *rough* went to a contestant who wrote of an old fellow's hand, "as rough as a rip-sawed board." Just behind was an old horse trainer, "as rough as a farrier's rasp." The competition for *graceful* resulted in a tie. One reader remembered her grandmother's hands, "as graceful as a fall of ancient, unstarched lace." The grand prize winner combined metaphor and simile:

> Spring breeze is wind with its sleeves rolled up, skipping daffodil to daffodil like graceful snips of garden shears.

We may learn more from the losers than from the winners. Many entries failed for sheer want of plausibility. From Las Vegas came, "as slippery as a greased guppy." The alliteration was fine, but why should a guppy be greased? "As slippery as an eel in a Vaseline factory." What's an eel doing in a Vaseline factory?

Good similes should be compact, no bigger than a Volkswagen beetle. Hundreds of entries were stretch limousines: "He sat at his bench in front of the lathe, as serene as a Buddhist monk holding his beggar's cup in downtown Tokyo." And, "Her mind was as serene as the view illuminated by a full moon on a warm, cloudless September night from the shore of Lake Louise." And, "She ignored life's obstacles, cruising through her time as serene as an elderly out-of-state motorist sightseeing from the fast lane of the interstate, oblivious to all stares and curses."

We also learned from, "The weeping willow extends its limbs toward heaven, arching gracefully like the slender neck of a swan." And, "Her artless prose appeared careless and unstudied, yet was graceful as the meticulously crafted curves of a three-hundred-year-old Stradivarius." Too much, too much!

Similes must be in good taste—or at least they should fit into the context of a piece of writing. It was startling to find a hundred entries based on the slipperiness of snot. Gracious! One of the entries for *serene* involved a nurse in a burn ward.

Every word of a good simile has to be in the right key. From Topeka, Kans., came: "On hot afternoons, blinds drawn, she slept in the nude. I used to watch her gentle breathing, thinking that nothing is as graceful as the breasts of a snoozing woman." Snoozing? *Snoozing!* Aaargh!

Effective similes must rely upon reasonably familiar images. A gentleman in Portland, Ore., submitted, "Lines, graceful as gracillimus, were painted on the walls." He explained in a footnote that gracillimus is an ornamental grass. Another contestant wrote of something as serene as a Brancusian arc. Maybe so, maybe so.

Many entries failed because their authors tried too hard for alliteration. From Michigan came a princess "as serene as a calico cat on a cushion of cotton candy," a revolting image. Others failed because the writers had not looked intently at their comparisons. Lincoln on the penny is not serene; he's sad. Hockey players in a penalty box are seldom serene. Neither are whispering lovers likely to be serene. A student in a South Carolina high school submitted, "A passionate kiss is as serene as a moonlit night." Kevin M., I thought, has more to learn than the writing art.

Learn from the experts. John le Carré, in *A Small Town in Germany,* demonstrated his mastery of the art. Here he is talking about St. James's park in London: "Along the lake, girls lay like cut flowers in the unnatural heat of a Sunday afternoon in May." One incident involves a tedious formal dinner at which a talkative guest takes too much burgundy aboard. His adoring young wife continues to cast him adoring glances, but the remaining guests are silently expiring of boredom. "Behind them two Hungarian servants moved like nurses along the beds." The guest of honor endures the tedium: "His white hands were folded like napkins beside his plate." The adoring young wife commits a conversational gaffe. The table falls suddenly silent. "Once more the conversation lay like a fallen kite."

I cannot make the point too often, for it lies at the very essence of the writing art. Le Carré brought off those beautiful similes because he had looked *intently* at cut flowers, folded napkins, fallen kites, and nurses on their rounds. He had put the images in the pantry of his mind. They were there when he wanted them.

Novelist Ross Macdonald had the gift. In *The Way Some People Die,* he wrote of a man with "a belly large and pendulous, shaped like a tear about to fall." He described a cheap nightclub: "It had more decorations than a briefcase general."

Another writer of mysteries, Robert Parker, created a great character in his private detective Spenser. At one point Spenser goes uncomfortably to a black-tie dinner. "I felt like a weed at a flower show." Another guest "had on black and white saddle shoes and looked as happy as a hound in a doggie sweater." Parker describes the exit of a sultry photographer's model: "She got up off the couch without any visible effort, like a snake leaving a rock." He provides a cameo of a homosexual man who comes into a bar "in a sort of shuffling quickstep, his head still, his eyes looking left and right, like a kid about to soap a window . . . There was a hunched quality to him, like a dog that's just wet on the rug."

Superb similes turn up in all kinds of places. In the Seattle Times, John Hinterberger reviewed a book called *White Trash Cooking.* He reveled in recipes for alligator tail and roast 'possum. With this book, "a terrible and delicious equalizer has bumbled into food fashion, with all the effect and undeniability of a wet hound at a lawn party."

In the Los Angeles Daily News, Joe Jares took a sardonic look at the glitzy trappings of the Rose Bowl. "Connoisseurs of excess will be happier than sadists in a thumbscrew factory."

In *The New Yorker,* David Updike wrote of an old Sicilian woman who greeted a guest from the United States: "'Americano, si?' she said once, smiling up at Michael, rolling the word around in her mouth like a grape, to see how it tasted."

In *People* magazine, Brad Darrach looked at comedian Robin Williams: "nose like a tired mouse, tiny mad eyes as blue as antifreeze." In *Waiting for Childhood,* S.L. Eliot gave us a woman to remember: "She had a way of coming into a room as though she were obliging it." Leslie Hanscom of Newsday interviewed Jackie Collins, author of many steamy novels. "Read her latest, *Lucky,* and you, too, can have a mind like the grease trap of an army mess hall." Joan Kropf of the AP did a feature story on agronomists Cecil and Mary Compton: "The Comptons, a pithy pair who fit together as neatly as two halves of an apple, are fruit identification experts." *Two halves of an apple!* I wish I had thought of that.

Tom Callahan of *Time* magazine watched Yogi Berra: "Looking as he has always looked, like a taxicab with doors open, Berra took his leave after sixteen years with an old Yankee grace." Another *Time* writer, Jay Cocks, wrote about Princess Stephanie of Monaco when she came to New York: "Rumors started to fly like sand gnats."

In The Washington Post, Stephanie Mansfield interviewed actor Rex Harrison, and found him in a contemptuous humor. Contemptuous of what? Of *pop stars.* "He spits out the words like olive pits."

Sometimes—not often, but sometimes—similes come easily. More often they come hard. I will tell a true story on myself.

During the 1984 presidential campaign I was traveling with Walter Mondale. I watched his meeting with a group of women volunteers. Under the standard protocol for such occasions, he was required to buss a few of the ladies on the cheek. Watching this ritual, I was struck by an irreverent thought: *Mondale looks like a stepladder.*

Back at the typewriter I struggled to fashion the image into a workable paragraph or two.

> Mondale in private is a warm and easygoing man. In public he tends to cool off. He is visibly uncomfortable with some of the social graces expected of a politician who is working a crowd. Put to the test of bussing a lady on the cheek, he stands as stiff as a stepladder, and he seems not to know what to do with his hands . . .

It wasn't right. Perhaps I could lighten the thing:

> Walter Mondale is a man of many talents, but he never will make it as a kisser. Attending a reception at his Washington headquarters, he undertook to buss a woman volunteer, but he approached her like a stepladder kissing a lamp pole.

No good. Try again:

Watching Walter Mondale buss a lady is like watching a six-foot stepladder unfold.

No rhythm. No cadence. No zing. No nothing.

Imagine a stepladder. Imagine Walter Mondale bussing an elderly woman volunteer. You get the picture. The nominee stiffly unfolds, angles over, completes the buss, and folds back up.

Worse and worse.

The Democratic nominee, a dignified fellow in public, is visibly uncomfortable with some of the social amenities expected of a politician. Confronting a friendly female face— a face expecting a kiss—he goes at the task with all the jerky grace of a six-foot folding ladder. Stiff and angular, he completes the ritual buss, drops his hands, and retreats. Parade rest.

The hell with it. I still believe there was a simile in there somewhere, but I never found it. Maybe I should have used a deck chair: "Walter Mondale gets to his feet like an unfolding deck chair." Maybe I need to look more intently at stepladders. We want our similes wrapped as snugly in a sentence as a pimiento in an olive, but sentences resist the embrace. Keep trying.

Try your hand at humor.

Writing humor is the most difficult of the prose arts. Almost any writer, given a little tutelage, can turn out a readable report on the month's foreign trade. Every reasonably literate writer can review a book, describe a parade, cover a ball game. The craft of "writing funny" is another matter. When a funny piece falls flat, it falls flatter than a crepe suzette. The miserable author has no place to hide. His failure lies on a platter and sulks. Nobody laughs. In the silence someone coughs. These are the pits.

But when a funny piece comes off, it flies as close to heaven as a writer is likely to fly here on earth. I cannot tell you the secret of writing funny, for I don't know it. To attempt an analysis of humor, in Pope's phrase, is to break a butterfly upon a wheel. I can recommend only that writers saturate themselves in the juices of Mark Twain, that they have a go at Ring Lardner, and that they study such late twentieth-century humorists as Dave Barry, Art Buchwald, Calvin Trillin, Erma Bombeck, and Russell Baker. They rely upon wild exaggerations, flights of ditsy fantasy, and quiet musing upon the lunacy that affects humankind and Congress.

Does a writer have a gift for the pun? If so, let it be cultivated. A reporter for the Associated Press did a feature about a pet crow named Blacky. Almost everyone in the neighborhood loved Blacky, but some parents complained: Their children had been frightened by close encounters of the bird kind.

Sportswriter Shirley Povich noted that boxer Larry Holmes had put on excess weight; he had ballooned to 254 pounds, a vast waistland. In the Indianapolis Star, sportswriter Bob Collins noted the punishments that had been imposed upon several colleges for breaking the rules: In the division of recruiting, he said, they were tried and found wanton.

In *Time* magazine, Jack Kroll reviewed a performance of *Hamlet* at the Public Theater in New York. He found it disappointing. The actors weren't exactly acting; they were reciting. Their innards were not shaken by powerful emotion. Kroll concluded with a paragraph of pure beauty:

> But *Hamlet* is Hamlet. It may be that to reach the depths of the most multifarious role in world theater, an actor today must take extraordinary steps, sign out of the flesh-pots of Broadway and Hollywood for a year, take off in search of himself, think, read, meet new people, challenge his preconceptions not just about theater but about life. You can't make a Hamlet without breaking eggs.

This word of caution: It's tough to write humor, and it's even tougher to write satire. Good satire must be done with a deadpan sobriety that is fearfully difficult to sustain. In the writing of satire a writer is called upon not to be funny, but to be witty, and true wit is rare. Give it a shot, but if nobody laughs at your best efforts, go back to something less demanding, like a scholarly biography of an overlooked king.

Try some other little dog tricks.

A writer's individualistic style, to repeat, comes from within. It is
the intrinsic product of education, experience, vocabulary, a whole
way of life. In this sense, style cannot be changed at bottom—but
it can be decorated atop. These are among the trimmings:

ALLITERATION. This little trick needs a label: Handle with
care. Alliteration is garlic in a writer's sauce; too much quickly
becomes Too Much! The device has been around for centuries,
in every language on every continent. It is the stuff of tongue-
twisters: She sells sea shells by the sea shore. Peter Piper picked a
peck of pickled peppers. Ideally, alliteration should be barely
tasted. Used blatantly, the device overwhelms the spaghetti.

In the presidential campaign of 1884, which pitted Democrat
Grover Cleveland against Republican James G. Blaine, the electoral vote of New York became crucial. Blaine was well in the
lead, or so it was thought, when on Wednesday, October 29, the
Rev. S.D. Burchard made a fatal blunder. During a speech in
Manhattan he referred to the Democrats as the party of "rum,
Romanism, and rebellion." The alliteration was flawless, but his
timing was terrible. Over the ensuing weekend Catholic voters,
smarting under the slur, deserted Blaine. On Tuesday Cleveland
carried New York by barely one thousand votes, but this gave him
thirty-six electoral votes and the White House too.

Spiro Agnew, who served for a time as President Nixon's vice
president, had a way of denouncing the press. We were "natter-
ing nabobs of negativism." The silly alliteration constituted an
offense worse than the tax evasion that turned him out of office.

At the Democratic convention of 1992, Hillary Clinton, wife of
the party's nominee, attacked the Republicans for politics of
"denial, division, and diversion." Senator Bill Bradley of New
Jersey belabored the foe. For too long, he said, American leadership "has waffled and wiggled and wavered." The senator was so
enamored of that piece of garlic that he chewed on it five times
in two minutes.

Senator Bradley was not the first to use doubleyas in combat.
In 1964 Republican Representative Clare Booth Luce said the
Democrats would waver, waffle, and weasel on their moral plat-

form. Bradley confessed that he thought of using *weasel* himself. He also thought of saying the Bush administration had *waffled, wimbled, and wambled.* In any event, the speech flopped.

At the Republicans' 1992 convention in Houston, President Bush got in on the alliteration act. He said that "freedom's fight is not finished," and he painted the House of Representatives as a party of "PACs, perks, privileges, partnership, and paralysis." It seemed a bit much, but that is the trouble with alliteration. A little bit gets to be a big bit before you know it.

ALLUSION. Let us have a show of hands. David and Goliath. Donald Duck. John D. Rockefeller. Caesar's wife. Watergate. Auschwitz. Diomedes. Oedipus. John Bunyan. Elmer Gantry. Robespierre. Seward's Folly. Willie Horton. How many of our readers will get the allusion without an explanation?

The most apt and striking allusions are useless if the writer tosses them to uninformed readers. *Know your audience!* My pessimistic guess is that by early in the twenty-first century, most classical, literary, cultural and historical allusions will be lost on most readers. The allusions that survive will be allusions to comic strip characters, rock stars, and athletes. In the Bible Belt of the South, many Old Testament allusions will be widely understood—Lot's wife, Balaam's ass, Job's patience, Jericho's walls—but as religion progressively is put in quarantine, lest the public schools be infected, these allusions also will diminish in value.

The prospect is bleak. There was a time when the legends of Greek mythology were part of every child's inheritance. These we learned from elementary readers. No more. In some areas Christian fundamentalists have driven Greek gods out of the classroom. The zealots of diversification and political correctness have chased away the Great Books that once formed the core of a curriculum. There isn't room for everything. Do many of today's high school seniors meet David Copperfield, Sancho Panza, or the Wife of Bath? Do they ride with Phileas Fogg? The old tapestries ravel and fade.

Beyond the high school level, of course, the writer or public speaker finds a more fertile field for allusion. Within particular fields of interest, a writer who writes for a specialized magazine may confidently allude to *Marbury* v. *Madison,* or to Bach's Coffee Cantata, or to the Long Count. New and lively allusions come along in politics and the arts. If we have lost Hetty Green we have gained Leona Helmsley. Croesus is gone, but we still have Daddy Warbucks.

ANTITHESIS. This little tricker is among the loveliest flowers in the garden of syntax. *American Heritage* defines the device as a figure of speech in which sharply contrasting ideas are juxtaposed in a balanced or parallel phrase or grammatical structure. Don't let that definition throw you. The antithesis is as much fun as a square dance.

The trick is to begin with a contrasting idea: Mikhail Gorbachev was more popular abroad than he was at home. That simple indicative sentence is admirably clear—no one can complain of its structure—but it has no pizzazz. By fiddling around, we may pack the idea into a sentence in which one comment balances the other: During his last year in office, Gorbachev won London's praise, but Moscow's disdain. His ovations abroad could not silence catcalls at home. World leaders saw in Gorbachev the achievements of a statesman; his own people saw the failures of a bum.

Macaulay used antithesis to great effect. He spoke of George II, who "had neither the qualities which make dullness respectable, nor the qualities which make libertinism attractive." In commenting upon a history of the popes, Macaulay recalled a period in which "the whole zeal of the Catholics was directed against the Protestants, while almost the whole zeal of the Protestants was directed against each other."

The master of antithesis was Gilbert Keith Chesterton, the British critic, essayist, novelist, poet, journalist, and author of the Father Brown detective stories. In an essay on Robert Louis Stevenson, Chesterton recalled Stevenson's essential gaiety: "As most men have triumphantly maintained a level of sobriety, he triumphantly maintained a level of exhilaration. He discovered the new asceticism of cheerfulness, which will prove a hundred times harder than the old asceticism of despair."

Chesterton got off a lovely line in an essay on Thackeray. *Vanity Fair* tells the story of two young women, Amelia Sedley and Becky

Sharpe. Amelia, says Chesterton, suffers throughout the novel "from that first water-colour sketch of the two schoolgirls, in which Amelia is given all the water and Rebecca all the colour." In another essay, he remarks that Dickens "thought less of poverty because he had known it, and thought less of money because he had earned it." In still another essay he contrasts Browning and Tennyson. It was Browning who had a passion about ideas, Tennyson who had ideas about passion. As for *Alice in Wonderland*, it has all the charm of a soap bubble blown from a pipe of poetry, but "it has been robbed by educationists of much of the lightness of the bubble, and retained only the horrible healthiness of the soap."

Some of Chesterton's epigrams require a little straightening out, and I have often wondered, reading his rhinestone paragraphs, if there isn't less there than meets the eye. He was a master of antithesis, but sometimes antithesis mastered him. One trouble with writing epigrams is that epigrams often sacrifice the gravity of judgment to the spontaneity of wit. It is remarkably easy to get on this syntactical teeter-totter, but it is very hard to get off.

REPETITION. Many writers suffer from a small failing that can easily be corrected. They will not repeat an antecedent word. For them repetition is a hobgoblin. It scares them away from clarity.

Let us exorcise the specter. It is true that when words go bump-bump-bump, the effect is unpleasant, but clarity counts for more than euphony. In any piece of writing that involves several names, a writer should not hesitate to say "Susan" once, and "Susan" twice, and "Susan" yet again if this helps to identify the references and to keep the speakers straight. We ought never to be uncertain about who or what a referent refers to.

The best text I can offer on the value of repetition lies in Genesis I. The translators of the King James Bible knew what they were doing. They didn't run away from repetition. Look:

> And God said, Let there be light: and there was light. And God saw the light, that it was good: and God divided the light from the darkness. And God called the light Day, and

the darkness he called Night. And the evening and the morning were the first day.

And God said, Let there be a firmament in the midst of
the waters, and let it divide the waters from the waters. And
God made the firmament, and divided the waters which
were under the firmament from the waters which were above
the firmament: and it was so . . .

To rewrite those perfect verses, in order to avoid the repetition of
light, darkness, firmament, and *waters,* would be to destroy the beauty
of the verses altogether. Repetition may be clumsy at times, but
more often than not repetition will prove a useful device.

THE ECHO EFFECT. Here is a trick that works every time. If
your composition is a short piece, running to no more than 750
to 1,000 words, take a key phrase that appears at the beginning,
and use it once more at the end. If the phrase can be employed
gracefully in the middle, so much the better.

Joe Murray, a senior writer for the Cox Newspapers, went to
England for a summer course of study at Oxford. This is how his
story began:

CHARLBURY, England—I came a long way to this charming village of 2,500, tucked away somewhere in the English
countryside. I came by plane, by train, and by car. I came by
mistake.

Murray had expected to spend the night in the city of Oxford,
but hotels there were exorbitantly expensive. He consulted a
travel agent who found a Best Western near the city. A Best
Western sounded good, so he set out in a taxi to find the motel. It
was fifteen miles away; the cab cost $55; and the Best Western
turned out to be a hotel of only fourteen rooms, dating from
before 1700. Murray bumped his head twice as he lugged his bag
up the staircase. A bad beginning.

But he began to unwind. As the only guest in the hotel, Murray
got superlative service. He went for a walk, visited the local pubs,
admired the stone cottages, listened to the evening bells. He found
the village of Charlbury entrancing. This was his last paragraph:

> I came here by mistake. It won't happen again. Next time, I'll come here on purpose.

There was the echo effect, the last paragraph echoing the first, and it completed a charming piece.

In a fascinating little book published by National Review Books in 1992, Linda Bridges and William F. Rickenbacker provided a glossary of rhetorical terms. Writers and speakers often make use of *anadiplosis,* in which a clause begins with the last word of the preceding clause:

> The tyrant falls before the oligarch, the oligarch is swept aside by democracy, democracy brings liberty, liberty brings license, license brings anarchy, and anarchy invites the tyrant.

Another device is the *anastrophe,* the inversion of normal word order: "Blessed are the meek, for they shall . . ." Bridges and Rickenbacker explain such other devices as *epanelepsis, epistrophe, polyptoton, auxesis,* and *erotema,* and I commend all of them to you. Their guidance will be especially valuable to any writer whose job is to write speeches.

Edit your copy! Edit your copy!

This is the admonition that packs the most meaning. After a first draft has been completed, and after a second and third draft as well, the final task is at hand. This is to edit copy as if the writer had never seen or heard of the copy before. It is always a good idea to read a piece aloud, especially if one is attempting to bring off a pretty piece. The ear will catch wrong notes that the eye may miss.

We must read for accuracy: Are all the facts right? We must read for spelling, of course, and for errors in punctuation. Are all the quotations closed? We must read for consistency in style; we cannot abbreviate *avenue* to *ave.* on page 10 and spell it out on page 13. Do we have Twentieth Century at one point, twentieth century at another, and 20th century at still another? Could the piece be improved by recasting a sentence from passive to active voice? Are we certain that an unfamiliar word means what we think it means? Look it up! Dammit, *look it up!*

John Bremner of the University of Kansas will be remembered affectionately by every writer who was lucky enough to know him. Both literally and figuratively, he was a giant of a man. He stood six feet two and weighed an eighth of a ton, and when he began bellowing about a slovenly job of editing, he seemed twice that size. In his class on copy editing, he gave devilish tests. You may wish to take one of them (and do not avoid any grammatical issues by rephrasing or rewriting).

1. Volkswagon is only having trouble with one of there new models.

2. The grand marshal gave his councel to whoever sought it.

3. Only one of the people who work in the lab is a vetinarian.

4. He claimed he knows a star athlete who will sign with the school.

5. He felt bad due to the unhygenic accomodations.

6. He looks like he could pitch real good.

7. Traveling acrost the U.S., it's vastness effected her.

8. Like I said, he should be like I and do like I do.

9. He wanted to know if the criteria is valid.

10. Joe told his wife Alice he likes his mistress better than her.

11. The hero was presented with an historic award by the Congressman.

12. This is different than and hopefully more preferable over that.

13. Its easy to see the difference between she and I.

14. We must try and keep up with the Jones.

15. What kind of a woman could like those kind of men.

16. The principle reason for Lopez' dismissal was because he behaved weird.

17. Neither her nor him know how to play the ukalele.

18. Have you got a recipe for a clam chowder soup which won't make me nauseous.

The most glaring errors will leap at once to the eye, but beware: The art of copy editing is in part the art of correcting the little things, the errant comma, the Greek plural, the wrong date, the misplaced apostrophe. You will find the answers at the end of this chapter.

Now and then, try for the top.

In my world, the newspaper world, most of our writing is pedestrian writing. Not much can be done to elevate a report on the city budget. It is the nature of the piece. All that a city editor asks—most of the time—is that a reporter's copy be accurate and that it be turned in well before deadline.

Occasionally an opportunity arises to get away from humdrum coverage. Sportswriters and editorial writers hatch a sentence that takes wings. A feature writer polishes an interview until it gleams. By luck, or skill, or divine inspiration we hit upon the kindling phrase that ignites a vivid passage. When it happens, all the daily tedium is offset by a sense of accomplishment. At last *we have written one good sentence.*

Sometimes a single word can lift a piece above the mundane level. Marjorie Williams of The Washington Post covered a hearing before the House Banking Committee. The venerable Clark Clifford had testified eloquently and at length about the role he had *not* played in a corrupted bank. He left some members unimpressed. This was a paragraph far down in her story:

"It pains me to say this," said Rep. Toby Roth (R-Wis.), painlessly, "but others may believe your story, but I must say I don't believe a word of it."

Stand back and admire that deadpan adverb, *painlessly.* Marjorie Williams dropped it into the sentence as smoothly as she might have dropped an olive into a martini.

Opportunities to go for the Good Stuff lie in movie reviews and book reviews. Andrew Ferguson of The Wall Street Journal turned out a gem in a review in 1991 of Kitty Kelley's biography of Nancy Reagan. He began in friendly fashion by saying that as a biographer, Ms. Kelley has the ethics of a sewer rat. Then he threw moderation to the winds.

> Her efforts were studded with unavoidable ironies. There's something odd about excoriating Reaganite greed after being paid $4 million to retail unverifiable allegations about private lives. And Kitty's breathless revelation that a 70-year-old man dyed his hair only draws unwanted attention to her own coif, which has been redone to resemble a spray of electrical wiring. Her voluptuous accounts of Nancy's physical refurbishings are likewise hard to credit. Old Man Time's chariot has clearly dealt a few mean brushbacks to the once perky and petite Ms. Kelley too, who looks like an ice cream cone trying not to melt.

In a very different vein, Steve Duin of the Portland Oregonian wrote a piece in 1988 to mark Thanksgiving Day. He recalled a morning in early November when he had been awakened by a cry from his infant daughter Christina. She had wearied of sleeping alone and was calling for room service.

> She was waiting at crib's edge, reaching first for me and then for the bottle of warm milk in my bathrobe pocket. In a few moments we were all wrapped up in one another in the rocking chair, coasting in the darkness.

I cannot read those two sentences without being moved to the edge of tears. Duin said he felt a little embarrassed to go public with such emotions.

> When Christina calls for me to come and rock the night away, the comfort we take in each other is, I trust, familiar to most fathers and daughters, and sounds pretty maudlin

to everyone else. Don't worry: I'm not inviting anyone to share the moment. There's only enough warm milk for one, and enough mystery for two.

There was a writer at work. He was writing not for the ages, but for the next morning's Oregonian.

Good writing turns up constantly in the daily press. In the Cleveland Plain Dealer Alfred Lubrano thought about Prohibitionists in the presence of booze: "They're as uptight as Nixon on a nude beach." Rheta Grimsley Johnson of Scripps Howard wrote a nostalgic piece about her childhood, when children found summertime joy in running through a sprinkler on a suburban lawn: "This was a simpler time, a world before wet slides and videos and elaborate theme parks that tie you up and strap you down."

Mike Harden of the Columbus (Ohio) Dispatch wrote a highly personal column in December 1991. It demonstrates what a skilled writer can achieve by the devices of restraint and slow development. His story takes shape as steadily as the countryside appears in a dissolving mist. I invited readers to send me examples of the Good Stuff. Believe me, this is the good stuff.

A shared love and a medical necessity throw us together on a chaotic Monday morning. Our 17-year-old Annie has begun the week with a nasty cough and a fever that frightens both of us.

Operational necessity dictates that we split nursing duties. Suzanne volunteers to chauffeur Annie to the doctor. I will make the pharmacy run and the chicken soup.

In the doctor's office, Annie clutches her mother's hand and leans on her shoulder. She thinks she might faint. She feels as if she is dying. The relentless bark of the cough ceases only when she loses the breath to do it.

Acute bronchitis, the doctor pronounces upon inspecting the X-ray—nearly pneumonia. It is clear he is weighing the prospect of putting her in the hospital, although he doesn't say as much. He decides to watch it first for 24 hours.

Her mother and I sit at the dining room table sipping coffee, ears trained to the back bedroom, from which the coughing finally gives way to slumber.

"Do you know what today is?" she quizzes me when we are finally able to think of something other than the fever thermometer.

I shake my head.

"Twenty-three years it would have been," she tells me. "This is our anniversary."

"My God, that's right," I acknowledge. Twenty-three years ago we had pledged "I do" in a Navy chapel in Washington, D.C.

"Fraternizing with an enlisted man," her superior officers had sniffed when they learned we had been dating. Nothing good could come of it, they warned. The Catholic chaplain seemed twice as skeptical. Not only was I a non-com, I was a non-Catholic as well.

A moment of awkward silence follows my inability to recall the significance of the date. She defuses it with laughter.

There was precious little of that six years ago when it all ended.

"I'll make some Jell-O for her," she tells me. "Doctor wants to get that temperature down."

We were both children of parents who might have divorced—perhaps even should have—but didn't.

How curiously we now look back on our time together.

"Don't you think of those years as wasted?" I have been asked.

"I think children can help you overcome it," I have claimed. They are the proverbial phoenix rising from the nuptial ashes, the treasure you didn't know was hidden in the mattress until you ripped the marriage bed apart.

"I can stay here and keep an eye on her if you have to write a column," Suzanne offers.

"No," I tell her. "You're needed back at work. I'll keep you posted this afternoon. I think once she is able to sleep, and once the antibiotic takes hold, her temperature will come down."

"You know I love you both, don't you?" she asks.

I nod.

Friends of mine have told me about divorced couples who—years after domestic relations court has made final what religion thought permanent—salivate over the possibility of running over their former mate in a parking lot.

It is not hate but apathy that is the opposite of love.

"Tell John I said hello," I tell her as she leaves.

"Tell Debra," she replies.

There is a quiet in the room from which, for several hours, nothing but a nagging hack could be heard.

In our own ways, we try to make peace with our past. Sometimes it takes analysis. Sometimes it simply takes time. Sometimes, as the Bible reminds us, it is a child who leads us.

"Don't forget," Suzanne reminds me, "give her 500 milligrams of the antibiotic at 8 p.m."

"I know," I tell her.

In a room at the end of the hallway there burns a candle that has lighted a friendship I once thought impossible.

Divorce has taught both of us how to act as if we just might have celebrated 23 years together on December 9.

I won't spoil Mike Harden's beautiful piece by critical pathology. See for yourself how he brought it off.

Magazine writers have greater opportunities, of course, than writers who are confined by tradition to a newspaper's limitations. Lance Morrow's essays for *Time* magazine set standards for all of us in the business. He knew how to fashion similes from everyday life. He had some thoughts about slang: "It needs to be new. Its life is brief, intense, and slightly disreputable, like adolescence." He looked closely at comic actress Mary Tyler Moore, who used to do "a fine, slow turn, her indignation developing like a Polaroid." Morrow looked at a new subdivision; the developer had left "a single sapling that gives no more shade than a swizzle stick."

A neglected field lies untilled in the obituary piece. No one in the country does these better than William F. Buckley, Jr., the father of *National Review.* Instinctively and deliberately he follows a maxim I laid down some years ago: If you would move your readers to tears, do not let them see you cry. The trick is to stand back a little, to play the role of the chorus in Attic drama, to comment with objectivity barely touched by sentiment. In the same way, good cooks use lemon juice in making apple pie.

The actor David Niven was among Bill Buckley's close friends. In an obituary piece he recalled one evening . . .

> There were four at dinner that night at a restaurant in Monaco, and Rainier was, well, in a grumpy mood. Whatever it is that princes are trained to do to overcome royal distemper was not being done proficiently early on that evening, and this David Niven diagnosed with the speed of an X-ray machine and, like the physician, David Niven knew his duty, and he did it.
>
> It required about twenty minutes for the therapy totally to take hold. It began with a tale of David's initial encounter with a lady of pleasure, when he was fifteen. It traveled through disparate episodes in Hollywood, Bangkok, Camp David; involving Errol Flynn, Tyrone Power, his cook and ski teacher. His own naturally high spirits were engaged, but he was ministering primarily to the needy, and the neediest of all in this world are those who suffer not from hunger but from melancholy. David Niven had only the one fear throughout his working life, which was that he might bore somebody, someday. Or that he might fail to stimulate whomever he was talking to. And he had the physician's eye for who, in the room full of people, most needed attention. If ever there was a man who winked at the homely girl, it was Niven.

I never met David Niven, but I read Bill's obituary essay, and I knew him.

Go for the Good Stuff! Keep your similes short and your metaphors consistent. Play with words: Toss them, feel their weight, rearrange them, see how they fall. Put clarity first. Always put clarity first. But know that after clarity has been achieved, the fun begins.

Answers to John Bremner's Quiz

1. Volkswagen is having trouble with only one of its new models.

2. The grand marshal gave his counsel to whoever sought it.

3. Only one of the people who work in the laboratory is a veterinarian.

4. He said he knew a star athlete who would sign with the school.

5. He felt bad because of the unhygienic accommodations.

6. He looks as if he can pitch well.

7. Traveling across the United States, she was affected by its vastness.

8. He should be like me and do as I do.

9. He wanted to know whether the criterion was valid.

10. Joe told his wife, Alice, that he liked his mistress more than her.

11. The hero received an award from the congressman.

12. This is different from and preferable to that.

13. It's easy to see the difference between her and me.

14. We must try to keep up with the Joneses.

15. What kind of woman could like that kind of man?

16. The principal reason for Lopez's dismissal was that he behaved weirdly.

17. Neither she nor he knows how to play the ukulele.

18. Do you have a recipe for clam chowder that won't make me nauseated?

If you fared poorly, be consoled: A group of editors, attending a seminar of the American Press Association, averaged only 3.2 perfectly correct answers out of the eighteen examples.

5 Tools of a Writer's Trade

Anyone who sets out to compile a definitive bibliography of books about writing will die with the work half done. The major publishing houses produce a hundred titles a year. Smaller houses add to the unending flow. Most of the books are serious works of reference. Some are books for the guest room.

In the listing that follows, I have included only those works to which I regularly refer. Other professional writers would recommend other books. I have added a few titles for the fun of it. There is no such thing as a really *bad* book about language, but some are better than others.

General dictionaries

For everyday use, it is one, two, three and take your choice among the *American Heritage Dictionary*, Second College Edition (1982), *Webster's Ninth New Collegiate Dictionary*, Merriam-Webster (1983), and the *Random House Webster's College Dictionary* (1991). I like the notes on usage in *AH*, and I like the etymological notes in *Webster's Ninth*. (In the spring of 1993, just as this book was going to press, Webster's published the tenth edition of its *Collegiate Dictionary*. I haven't lived with it long enough to get a feel of it.) I like the typeface and definitions in *Random House*. All three are top-notch works. When it first appeared, the *Random House* turned off some critics by including such faddy entries as *womyn*, but the editors did it only to irritate me and to please their publicity people. It is an excellent desk dictionary.

In 1992, while I was finishing this book, American Heritage produced the Third Edition of its basic big dictionary. It was a case of love at first cite. The *AH3d* is too heavy to be a desk dictionary, and at 200,000 entries, it is not heavy enough to compete with *Webster's III*. But the usage notes are delightful, the typeface is clean and easy, the illustrations often are helpful, and I commend it warmly.

The granddaddy of dictionaries is the *Merriam-Webster Third International* (1976). It is wholly descriptive, which means that you will get little help from grandpa on preferred or proper usage. The editors implicitly take the view that questions must be asked: Preferred by whom? What is "proper"? What is improper? Says who? Not us.

The *Random House Unabridged* (1987) is not quite as comprehensive as *Webster's III,* but in the nonce phrase it is user-friendly. Sometimes I go to the *Oxford American Dictionary* (1980). It is delightfully prescriptive in a polite British way: "Careful writers do not use *contact* as a verb." Occasionally I will back-check a usage or a spelling in the *Merriam-Webster Second International* (1952). Back then, *gay* meant "merry, bright, lively," and that was all it meant. O tempora, O mores!

The great-grandfather of dictionaries is the *Oxford English Dictionary,* cited around the world as the *OED.* In its classic format, the work costs a fortune, weighs a ton, and takes up as much room as Rhode Island, but it will give you examples of English usage from the time of pithecanthropus. Four supplementary volumes have become available. I bought them, just to have them, but I haven't found much occasion to use them. The *OED's* two-volume micro edition comes with a fine magnifying glass. It serves nicely for purposes of research.

Specialized dictionaries

A writer should have at least one dictionary of quotations. I regularly use half a dozen. The Old Reliable is Bartlett's *Familiar Quotations.* Its sixteenth edition (Little, Brown, 1992) suffered from the selective bias of its liberal editors, but it remains reasonably comprehensive. Just as reliable is the *Oxford Dictionary of Quotations,* Third Edition (Oxford, 1979), which has the added advantage of providing the full Latin and Greek texts of selected passages. A recent addition to the ranks is the *Macmillan Dictionary of Quotations* (1989). I love it. An old favorite is H.L. Mencken's *New Dictionary of Quotations* (Knopf, 1962).

These are other good and useful resources: *Respectfully Quoted,* published by the Library of Congress in 1989; *Dictionary of Quotations,* collected by Bergen Evans (Bonanza Books, 1963); *Webster's New World Dictionary of Quotable Definitions,* Second Edition (Webster's New World, 1988); and the *New International Dictionary of Quotations,* selected by Hugh Rawson and Margaret Miner (Dutton, 1986).

Everyman's *Dictionary of Shakespearean Quotations* (Dutton, 1953) is a miserable work, abominably indexed, but it is the only one of its kind and it has a way of coming in handy. A writer should have on a nearby shelf the complete works of Shakespeare. A good, compact edition comes from Oxford.

I frequently refer to the *Barnhart Dictionary of Etymology* (H.W. Wilson, 1988), just for the fun of learning where our words are rooted.

A writer will benefit from a convenient authority on slang, if only to learn what not to print. The best of several excellent resources is the *Dictionary of American Slang,* Second Supplemental Edition, compiled by Wentworth and Flexner (Crowell, 1975). A bit more up to date is *A New Dictionary of American Slang,* edited by Robert L. Chapman (Harper & Row, 1986). An excellent work in convenient format is *The Thesaurus of Slang,* by Esther Lewin and Albert E. Lewin (Facts on File, 1988).

Even if verse is not a writer's forte, a rhyming dictionary is fun to have around. I like Willard Espy's *Words to Rhyme With* (Facts on File, 1986), though the format takes some getting used to. For everyday use, try to find the *New Rhyming Dictionary and Poets' Handbook,* by Burges Johnson (Harper & Brothers, 1957). In 1990 Doubleday published a revised edition of Clement Wood's *The Complete Rhyming Dictionary.* It offers some useful instruction in the art of versification, and it has some rhymes not to be found in Espy or Johnson, but the arrangement by vowel sounds is an infernal nuisance.

Writers who work in specialized fields will of course want their own dictionaries of art, music, medicine, science, law, and the like. These I leave to you.

Other useful dictionaries

William and Mary Morris, the indefatigable duo, in 1977 produced the *Morris Dictionary of Words and Phrases* (Harper & Row), a first-rate work. In the same field, and also highly rated, is the more comprehensive *Brewer's Dictionary of Phrase and Fable*, revised by Ivor Evans (Harper & Row, 1970). Still more comprehensive is the *Facts on File Encyclopedia of Word and Phrase Origins*, edited by Robert Hendrickson (1987). Each of them has entries not to be found in one of the others.

Let me recommend Webber and Feinsilber's *Grand Allusions* (Farragut, 1990), Laurence Urdang's *Numerical Allusions* (Facts on File, 1986), the Urdang-Ruffner *Allusions—Cultural, Literary, Biblical and Historical*, Second Edition (Gale, 1986), and the *Facts on File Dictionary of Classical, Biblical, & Literary Allusions* (1987). If an allusion isn't in one of these, it isn't worth alluding to.

If a writer is determined to use foreign words and phrases, defying my earnest remonstrances, he should search for a copy of the *Dictionary of Foreign Terms*, Second Edition, revised and updated by Charles Berlitz, published by Crowell in 1975. The book is hard to come by, and it omits many phrases that ought to be included, but it's *sui generis* (in a class by itself). A lightweight backup is Tad Tuleja's *Foreignisms* (Macmillan, 1989). Most of the familiar foreign terms will be found in the big dictionaries. *American Heritage* runs them in alphabetically. The *Random House Unabridged* provides good little dictionaries of French, Spanish, Italian, and German in an appendix.

Reference works on usage

Oxford published the first edition of Fowler's *Modern English Usage* in 1926. Age has not diminished its charm nor undermined its authority. It is still wonderfully pleasant reading. *Modern Ameri-*

can Usage, by Wilson Follett (Hill & Wang, 1966) is another classic work. It provides an excellent short appendix on punctuation.

The preeminent, indispensable work in the field is the *Webster's Dictionary of English Usage* (1989). I doubt that a day passes in my office—certainly no week ever passes—without a dip into this sometimes infuriating, always authoritative, altogether delightful work. I recommend it without qualification.

The *Harper Dictionary of Contemporary Usage* (Harper & Row, 1975) is another splendidly provocative and stimulating work. For pleasant browsing and solid authority, let me add *Words on Words* (Columbia University Press, 1980), by the late John Bremner. In 1985 Richard Tobin, a first-rate editor, published *Tobin's English Usage* (R.J. Berg, Indianapolis). It is a slim but excellent little book.

A writer will benefit from any book bearing the byline of Theodore Bernstein, the late, great copy editor of The New York Times. Try his *Miss Thistlebottom's Hobgoblins* (Farrar, Straus, 1971). Bernstein's *Reverse Dictionary* (Times Books, 1988) is another useful title.

As word maven, William Safire of The New York Times ranks at the top of the list. Every year or so he brings out a collection of his Sunday columns and daily correspondence. Published by Times Books, the Safire papers are splendidly indexed, highly opinionated, and generally stimulating.

Thesauri

In 1992 the field of thesauri suddenly became crowded. Within a span of eight months, three excellent volumes appeared.

Because I greatly admire the work of lexicographer Laurence Urdang, I give first mention to his *Oxford Thesaurus* (American Edition), published by Oxford University Press. It offers a fine selection of illustrative sentences, and it's easy to use.

Another excellent thesaurus is *Roget's 21st Century in Dictionary Form,* edited by Barbara Ann Kipfer, published by Dell. I like its format. It offers 450,000 synonyms and appears to be as comprehensive as one might ask.

Another thesaurus bearing the sainted name of Roget is *The Original Roget's International Thesaurus,* Fifth Edition, edited by Robert L. Chapman and published by Harper-Collins. For users unfamiliar with the format, it may prove a little on the complicated side, but it's worth the trouble.

The Synonym Finder, edited by Laurence Urdang, published by Rodale Press in 1978, remains my own first choice. Another old friend, still highly reliable, is Funk & Wagnall's *Standard Handbook of Synonyms, Antonyms, and Prepositions,* edited by James C. Fernald in 1947. If you come across a copy of either one of these works, grab it.

Grammar

I have yet to find a friendly book on grammar. The masterwork is Professor George Curme's classic two-volume tome on grammar and syntax, republished by Verbatim in 1977. It is too scholarly for me, but it covers just about everything. Another work of major scholarship, clean over my head, is James D. McCawley's two-volume work, *The Syntactic Phenomena of English* (University of Chicago Press, 1988). I mention it because Professor McCawley has a nice way of throwing change-ups and curveballs in the midst of his hardball instruction.

A few years ago Writer's Digest published *Pinckert's Practical Grammar,* and described it as a "lively unintimidating guide." Every time I recur to it, I wish the work were not quite so lively. *Elements of English Grammar,* by Harold Van Winkle, was published by EMGI-Evans Marketing Group in Tampa in 1990. It is a handsome textbook, and appears to be simply arranged. Maybe it is the book I have been waiting for, but its advice on gerunds leaves me a little uneasy.

Style (literary)

In this field, one little book leads all the rest. It is *The Elements of Style,* by E.B. White, enlarging upon an earlier work by Will Strunk

(Macmillan, 1959). This is a classic. No writer's library should be without it.

William Zinsser's *On Writing Well,* Third Edition (Harper & Row, 1980) is a fine work. *The Art of Persuasion* by Linda Bridges and William F. Rickenbacker (National Review, 1992) is a first-rate compilation of rhetorical devices. Let me be immodest and mention *The Writer's Art,* by me.

Style *(nuts and bolts)*

The Chicago Manual of Style, Thirteenth Edition (University of Chicago Press, 1982) is of primary value to those engaged in writing books, but its rules are useful for everyday purposes also.

The New York Times Manual of Style and Usage is authoritative. The Associated Press's *Stylebook* sets forth the rules that most newspapers live by. The U.S. News *Stylebook for Writers and Editors* is another good one. I am especially fond of the *Los Angeles Times Stylebook,* in part because of its sound advice on the comma: "Use a comma when it makes sense and when it makes the sentence clearer to the reader." That says it all.

Books *for fun*

I had intended to stop with reference works, but it is not required that writers be serious all the time. As Christmas gift possibilities:

The Dictionary of Misinformation, by Tom Burnam (Crowell, 1975).

The Grand Panjandrum, by J.N. Hook (Macmillan, 1980). His tests of word mastery are good fun.

The Miracle of Language, by Richard Lederer (Pocket Books, 1991). Watch for Lederer's byline. He has written half a dozen books on language, all of them beguiling.

A Pleasury of Witticisms and Word Play, by Antony B. Lake (Bramhall House, 1975).

A Pleasure in Words, by Eugene T. Maleska (Simon & Schuster, 1981). The crossword puzzle editor of The New York Times is charmingly erudite in this one.

The Joy of Lex, by Gyles Brandreth (Morrow, 1980).

The Mother Tongue, by Bill Bryson (Morrow, 1990). Any book by Bryson is a good buy.

The Joys of Yiddish, by Leo Rosten (Simon & Schuster, 1982).

The Ear is Human, by me (Andrews, McMeel & Parker, 1985), a handbook of a hundred homophones.

6 My Crotchets and Your Crotchets

In the spring of 1982, just feeling my oats, I established a Court of Peeves, Crotchets & Irks. It seemed a good way to deal with hundreds of letters that began, "My pet peeve is . . ." Besides, the idea appealed to my latent ambition to sit in the sitz bath of the bench and be sycophantly laved: *May it please the court* and *If your honor please.* Here I could grant petitions and overrule objections and play a magisterial role. Injunction denied! Objection overruled! I could learn from the peeves and the irks, and I could trot out my own little crotchets for inspection.

Presiding over this altogether unauthorized forum proved to be a world of fun. Readers filed complaints about all kinds of literary offenses I had never dreamed of. Could a contraption formed of flashing lights and Ping-Pong balls be properly called a *statue?* No! Would the court enter injunctions against *legendary, bottom line,* and *user-friendly?* So entered! The court ruled against *snuck* as the past tense of *to sneak.* The court pronounced sentence upon the manhandling of *quality,* as in a *quality* performance and a *quality* car. As prosecutor, judge, and jury, I disposed fearlessly of a docket that grew more crowded all the time. To be sure, some plaintiffs disagreed strongly with the court's opinions. No matter. From my edicts there could be no appeal! When I ope my lips let no dog bark!

What the court learned from all these mock proceedings is that great numbers of the American people care fiercely about the English language. They hate to see it abused, either in writing or in speech. They shudder at patent errors in grammar. They are irked—keenly irked—by, "She sent the invitation to George and I." They are peeved by "five times less" and "ten times thinner." Errors in punctuation offend them. They inquire of the court, "Why can't people spell?" Why don't writers know the difference between *affect* and *effect?* Why do the artists who draw comic strips make so many blunders? To such interrogatories the court replies cheerfully that, though prose be out of joint, fortunately I was born to set it right.

A

In *The Writer's Art* (1986) I condemned the redundant *a.m. in the morning* and pronounced anathema on those who speak of an artist's *abstracts.* The Court of Peeves, Crotchets & Irks distinguished *adapt* from *adopt* and warned against the misuse of *admonish.* Mr. Justice Kilpatrick had something to say about *aggravate* and *irritate.* The Court ringingly denounced the syntactic corruption that has stolen *alibi* and converted it to mean *excuse.* These prior decisions, all reported in *The Writer's Art,* covered *all due respect, all-important, all-time record,* and the reckless use of *alleged.* The Court distinguished *alternatively* from *alternately* and *apparent* from *evident.* The learned justice dealt temperately with *arbitrate* and *mediate,* exiled the abominable verb *to author,* and flawlessly fielded other such pop-ups and bunts. For these prior rulings, please see (and preferably buy) *The Writer's Art,* Andrews and McMeel, Kansas City.

a and an

Writers are a quarrelsome lot. At the drop of a serial comma we will fight about any old point of usage, but none of our controversies kicks up passions more flaming than the passions that are aroused by *a* and *an.* It is amazing. The words surely are not words well calculated to give offense, yet people who gaze with indifferent eye upon *arguably* or *a fun thing* will go into conniptions at an errant article adjective.

The Court of Peeves, Crotchets & Irks is forever getting petitions asking for a hard and fast rule on *a* and *an.* The court responds with the kind of easy ambiguity for which the U.S. Supreme Court is so widely known. There *is* no hard and fast rule on *a* and *an*. There is not even a soft and loping rule. The usage depends mainly on the writer's ear.

The Buffalo News says that Poland's Lech Walesa became "a electrician." Headline in the Los Angeles Times: "Lowly Catfish Earns a Haute Image." Contrariwise, a book about Jesus by Michael Grant carries a subtitle, *An Historian's Review of the Gospels.* A columnist in the Philadelphia Daily News finds "an hilarious story."

What goes on? Every schoolboy knows the general rule: We should use *a* before all words beginning with consonants and *an* before all words beginning with vowels, but slavish obedience to that rule will get you into this sort of thing: "Willie McGee hit a RBI single on an 1–2 pitch from Roger McDowell." Try reading that sentence aloud, and you will say "an RBI single" and "a 1–2 pitch." This is because a working rule turns not upon the presence of an initial consonant or vowel, but on *the sound of the word to be modified.*

Thus our ears tell us that RBI really is "ar-bee-eye." The count on McGee was "won-too." We hear *yew-nique* and *Yew-nited Nations.* A columnist in *Business Week* searches for "an S&L worth buying."

Our inconstant ears hear some things differently. It is the aspirated *h* that causes bloodshed. The rule in American English is that there is practically no such thing as a dropped "aitch." William and Mary Morris, whose authority merits respect, say that only five words with a silent aitch remain in American English: *heir, honest, hour, honor, herb,* and their derivatives. To that list I might add *humble,* but it's a close call.

My ear doesn't hear an aspirated aitch in such combinations as *an hysterical bystander* and *an hilarious comedy.* I hear elisions, as if the words were *anysterical* and *anilarious.* To further confound matters, my ear tells me to write of *a history* of England; then it tells me to praise *an historical novel* and to read *an historian's review.*

The desirable thing is to be consistent. If you write about *an L.A. policeman* in the first paragraph, don't turn the officer into *a L.A. policeman* later on.

above

In the sense of being on top of something, *above* is an indispensable preposition: The dish towel is above the sink. Lieutenant-colonels are above majors. In other applications *above* will not work as well. It is all very well to speak of "the above examples of the unaspirated aitch . . ." if the examples are indeed *above*. But suppose the examples are on a preceding page. In these constructions, *foregoing* nearly always works better.

Unless there is some compelling reason to use *above* as a noun, I would avoid it. Something is unhappily stilted in, "By referring to the above, you are likely to be thoroughly confused." The same observation applies to *same* as a noun. I know that the *Book of Common Prayer* speaks of the death and resurrection of Jesus and offers most hearty thanks "for the innumerable benefits procured unto us by the same," but the construction still sounds legalistic and awkward.

In some parts of the South (and in other parts of the country, for all I know), you may hear *above* in a curiously Victorian way: "It must be above a month since I saw Uncle Jed." The unfamiliar construction creates one of those infinitesimal hesitations that mar the flow of a sentence. I would recommend, "It must be more than a month . . ."

absent

William and Mary Morris, editors of *Harper Dictionary of Contemporary Usage,* put a question to their panel of critics. Would they use *absent* in the sense of *without* in this sentence: "Absent new evidence to the contrary, the verdict must be judged correct."

The twenty-eight panelists jumped all over the sentence. "Awful," said Whitney Balliett. "Certainly not," said Willard Espy. "Silly," said John K. Hutchens. "Horrible," said Elizabeth Janeway. "Pedantic," said Herman Wouk.

Not so fast, say I. In most constructions, *without* would indeed be preferable to *absent*. We certainly would not write that, "Absent her makeup, the actress is not much to look at." But there are times when *absent* works just fine. Columnist William Raspberry, writing in The Washington Post at the time of the confirmation of Justice Clarence Thomas, found it useful. "On what basis," he inquired, "should Thomas have been denied the seat that, absent the accusation, would have been his?" Here he was using *absent* in the sense of "if it weren't for." It is a tragedy, Raspberry continued, that two splendid lives have been tarnished "and that, absent some dramatic confession, they cannot be restored." Here he was using *absent* in the sense of "without," but here again *absent* worked well.

absolute words

Controversy continues over the number and nature of a few adjectives that often are regarded as absolute words, i.e., words that cannot properly be intensified or compared. Dear old *unique* perhaps has been sufficiently belabored, but for the record: A thing cannot be more unique, or rather unique, or pretty unique, or very unique, or the most unique. If something is unique, that's it. The same observation applies to *dead, fatal,* and *lethal.* "Shot Kills Intruder Dead." "Woman Dies of Fatal Wound." Cyanide cannot be more lethal or less lethal. It is lethal, period.

Some newspapers maintain a list of absolute words. Ordinarily such glossaries include *complete, dead, equal, essential, eternal, fatal, final, indispensable, lethal, naked, nude, total, unanimous, unique, universal, valid,* and *virgin.* These are good enough as starters, but I am reminded of that cantankerous old colonel made immortal by Ward Dorrance. The gentleman set out to write a book called *Preeminent Sons of Bitches of Boone County, Mo.,* but every time he wiped his pen dry he thought of one more entry, without whom the edition would be less than definitive.

The trouble with making such lists is that other words keep rolling in: *accurate, correct, empty, endless, illegitimate, inevitable, infallible, insoluble.* At one time I included *pregnant,* but popular usage has entrenched "a little bit pregnant" and "very pregnant."

Opinion remains divided on *perfect.* The Constitution speaks of creating a "more perfect union." In one of his plays, Sheridan remarked upon a "very perfect" gentleman. *The Reader's Digest* in 1990 spoke of the Hubble telescope as "the world's most perfect mirror." I don't believe something could be "rather perfect" or "a little bit perfect." Let the sense of the sentence be your guide.

Hundreds of mathematical and technical terms qualify as absolutes, but these rarely give trouble. Strictly speaking, an object can't be "very square" or "a little bit round," though I see no objection to "almost square" or "roughly triangular."

Perhaps the soundest advice is to think twice before using modifiers of degree. E.B. White scorned *rather, very, pretty,* and *a little bit.* In a lovely metaphor he called them "leeches that infest the pond of language, sucking the blood of words." If a given argument is valid, nothing is gained by making it *very* valid.

access (v)

Behold how the language changes, right before our eyes. When I wrote the first edition of *The Writer's Art* in 1984, none of the great unabridged dictionaries listed *access* as a verb. *Webster's III* never heard of it. Now every dictionary recognizes *access* in the sense of entering the innards of a computer. Another verb from the world of computers, *to scroll,* has flashed across the screen and into the language. Scores of such terms will be coming out of the mouths of babes in the twenty-first century. We may as well get used to them now.

acme

Let us have no fears for *acme.* It is secure in its meaning of the highest point of something: the acme of computers, the acme of chamber music. Even so, I submit that *acme* is a pretentious sort of word. It tries too hard.

Not that the familiar synonyms are much better. *Apogee* sounds like a sponge mop. *Capstone* is too heavy. What about *zenith?* Too fancy. *Vertex?* Sounds anatomical. *Apex?* Might be a detergent. We could get mountainously metaphorical and write of the peak or summit of a quarterback's career. Is there a haven in *culmination?* There comes a day when the word a writer wants just can't be found. It's the acme of frustration.

acronyms

In Charleston, S.C., a planning commission labored to produce a report on where the city should be going in 2000. It was a long report. The editor began with a helpful note: "These anachronisms are used in the following chart: LDV, P&UD, CDBG, BOA, BAR, COG . . ."

These weren't anachronisms, of course, though Charleston is full of those. They were acronyms and initialisms.

An acronym is a pronounceable word derived from the initials of a phrase: *loran* (long-range navigation), *sonar* (sound navigation ranging), *NOW* (National Organization for Women), *CORE* (Congress of Racial Equality). An initialism is a combination of letters: *FBI, CIA, NAACP.* Some manuals of style require periods, as in *U.N.* The abbreviation for "general issue" may be *GI* or *G.I.*

On first usage, do we spell these things out? Or do we go at once to the short forms? These are judgment calls. I see no reason to spell out such household initialisms as *NBC, ABC,* and *CBS.* Perhaps *CNN* also qualifies; maybe *HBO* does not. At The New York Times, the rule is that every combination must be spelled out the first time it is mentioned. Theodore Bernstein, the Times's great wordmaster, once explained why. "Every day of the world," he said, "someone is born who has yet to meet the NAACP and must be told what it is." Bernstein's rule is generally sound. If you are satisfied that all of your readers know what is meant by an *LBO,* an *l.c.d.,* or a *MIRV,* okay, never mind explaining that an LBO is a leveraged buyout, an l.c.d. is the lowest common denominator, and a MIRV is a multiple independently targeted vehicle. You're the writer, but remember that good writers treat their readers with respect.

actually

There is a respectable place in English composition for *actually,* but only when a writer wishes to emphasize a point of fact or reality. Those greens looks like spinach, but actually they are collards. He told his wife he was going to Memphis but actually he went to Paducah. In these constructions the *actually* is not redundant. It could be left out, but the rhythm and texture of the sentence would be damaged.

The usage that drives some parents bonkers is the prefatory *actually* or the teenager *actually*. "Actually, if you weren't so stubborn, we would have seen the play long ago." "I'm sure Roger loves me, actually." I doubt if the frilly *actually* ever turns up in writing, but it infects the high school jargon.

A.D. and B.C.

Let us take them one at a time. B.C. (before Christ) never causes a problem. It *always* follows both a century and a specific year: King Tut came to the throne in the fourteenth century B.C. Aristotle was born in 384 B.C.

The problem lies with A.D. (anno domini). It can go either fore or aft, depending upon one's ear and the editor's manual of style. At one time the custom was to put it before the year: In A.D. 1492, Columbus set sail for the Orient. A Mayan artifact dates from around A.D. 750. This is my own preference, but many other writers like to put A.D. after the year and especially after the century: The Carolingian dynasty reigned from the eighth century A.D.

The important point here is to be consistent, or at least reasonably consistent. Your ear will tell you where to put the A.D. In a formal work of history, I'd put A.D. before a date; in less formal writing, I might put it after. Before putting it anywhere, I'd wonder if it were necessary to use an abbreviation at all.

addicted

At one time, *addicted* carried no pejorative overtones. Without raising an eyebrow, we could profess an addiction to jazz, an addiction to crossword puzzles, an addiction to chocolate ice cream. Things have changed. I would reserve *addict* and *addiction* for harmful things. Smoking is more than a smelly habit; it is an addiction. A genuinely stupid person is a crack addict. In the same fashion, let us retire *shot in the arm* as a refreshing stimulant. Shots in the arm are not funny anymore.

adequate

This is a word in transition, as the *Random House College Dictionary* makes clear. The first definition is "fully sufficient." The second definition is "barely sufficient." My guess is that the word is slipping down the chute into a bin with other insults. If we say that a musician's performance was "adequate," we mean it was pretty sorry. An adequate meal is—well, adequate. There may be a better way to convey the belittling thought.

adult

It now appears that *adult,* like the departed *gay,* has become a victim of wordnapping. The word has been around a long time. It came out of the Latin *adultus,* meaning fully grown or mature. By the sixteenth century it was respectably settled in that comfortable sense.

Now *adult* carries a heavy load of sexual freight. A film designed for "adult audiences" is a film characterized by explicit or implicit intercourse. The word suggests pornography, mild or hot, and everyone understands *adult* in this sense. These days, when one drives by a neighborhood advertised as an "adult community," one wonders idly what lascivious games are going on behind those chaste venetian blinds.

affidavit

A few years ago I spent an afternoon reading a book about General William C. Westmoreland's libel suit against CBS. Every time the author spoke of a *sworn affidavit,* I flinched, and because he spoke at least fifty times of a *sworn affidavit,* I passed a painful afternoon.

I have said it a hundred times and may say it a hundred more: If an affidavit isn't sworn, it isn't an affidavit. The statement has to be made *under oath.* Otherwise a statement is only a statement, or a handout, or a press release. On a related question, it is redundant to speak of *sworn testimony* in court, for in court witnesses always are sworn. The testimony that is given before a legislative committee ordinarily is not sworn, but some chairmen require that witnesses in some investigative proceedings be put under oath.

allergic

The only thing wrong with *allergic,* in the nonmedical sense, is that the adjective has lost its fizz. Someone is allergic to Madonna. Someone else is allergic to exercise. In common parlance we may be allergic to piping bands, Cajun cooking, or the dribbles of Jackson Pollock. The usage is tired, banal, worn out. Let us give it back to the allergists.

all / not all

In North Carolina, a real estate developer made a positive statement: "All retired executives aren't ready for relaxation and golf." A Washington Post writer began a feature in the same confident vein: "All book parties are not alike." The editor of the Post's editorial page ventured a philosophical comment: "Everything about the old politics wasn't bad."

Hold on! Surely some retired executives are ready for relaxation and golf, and surely some book parties are like other book parties. The editor meant to say that not everything about the old politics was bad. Not all a coach's advice need be taken, but a warning to think about *all/not all* constructions is a warning to take to heart.

alright / all right

Let it be said loudly, firmly, without qualification or ambivalence, *alright* is not a word. I tell you, *it is not a word!* Alas, sigh, it is a word, and I advance no grounds beyond pure prejudice for pronouncing anathema upon it. There is no more reason to denounce *alright* than to denounce *almighty, already,* and *altogether,* but there is something about *alright* that just looks screwy. Use *all right.*

amend / emend

Here is a small distinction. I suppose we should preserve it, though I'm not sure quite why. Except for politicians and proofreaders, nobody greatly cares. *To amend* is to change; to emend is to correct. Thus the House may amend a bill, adding something to the bill or taking something out. Before it becomes a Public Law, the bill is further emended, in order to catch wrong numbering or typographical errors.

among / between

A cherished notion survives in some quarters—I used to cherish it myself, until I read *Webster's Dictionary of English Usage*—that *among* and *between* should be used according to a simple rule: Use *between* when we are describing the relationship of two persons or objects; use *among* for more than two.

In most applications the rule works well. "Christopher was born between Sean and Kevin." "The city of Charleston lies between the Ashley and Cooper rivers." And, "Among the great outfielders of history, DiMaggio and Williams are preeminent."

Beyond those easy examples lies a long list of exceptions. The North Atlantic Treaty is not a compact among the signatories, but between them, the theory being that each nation covenants separately with every other. The rule does not apply in such constructions as, "Between gardening, keeping house, carpooling the children, and paying bills, there's no time to make dessert." Somewhere in this compendium of crotchets, I make a stab

at distinguishing between such uncertain classifications as *kind,*
sort, and *type.* Off the record, and between us girls, a writer's ear is
a better guide than a pedant's rule.

and and but (to begin a sentence)

The supposed rule against beginning a sentence with *and* (or
with its conjunctive cousin *but*), is like many other "rules" of
prose composition: It is no rule at all. I discuss the matter and
supply Horrid Examples on pages 91–92. Let me emphasize one
admonition: Keep your *and* and *but* sentences short. And don't
use too many of them.

The device can be used effectively. Back in 1985 I wrote a
column about President Reagan's nomination of so many conservative Republicans to the federal bench. I pointed out that Presidents Lyndon Johnson and Jimmy Carter had nominated liberal
Democrats. This is the way the system historically has worked. All
presidents have tried to shape the court in their own philosophical image. I identified some of the Democrats who were com-
plaining so bitterly about the Reagan nominees, and I ended the
column with this observation:

"They should have elected Mondale. But they didn't."

Suppose we recast the cracker to make it read, "They should
have elected Mondale, but they didn't." The sparkle leaks out of
the sparkling water. Try another version: "They should have elected
Mondale. However, they did not." That is even flatter.

Carefully and sparingly employed, the beginning *and* will get
you away from semicolons and tedious serials. An initial *but* will
let you evade the mushy *however.* Come to think of it, a useful rule
would be never to start a sentence with *however* anyhow.

anniversary

An anniversary occasion draws its adjective from the Latin *anni-*
versarius, referring to something that returns annually. Thus it is
etymologically inaccurate, but probably pleasant, to speak of the

newlyweds' "six-month anniversary." The trouble is, there is no good word to designate such an occasion. A banker once advertised notes that bore interest *mensiversally*. The coinage is etymologically pure, but it never caught on.

anymore

In the sense of "nowadays," *anymore* scarcely raises an eyebrow anymore. The spelling may be either open or closed, two words or one, take your pick. The *Dictionary of American English* cites a usage from 1931: "People used to shop a lot in the morning, but any more the crowd comes in about 3 o'clock." *Webster's Dictionary of English Usage* cites a quote from Harry Truman: "It sometimes seems to me that all I do anymore is go to funerals."

Webster's III snubs *anymore* as dialectal, but more recent dictionaries accept it without a murmur. The adverb appears most frequently in negative contexts, as in, "Youngsters don't read much anymore." Yogi Berra is said to have said that "Toots Shor's is getting so crowded that nobody goes there any more." It often appears in positive contexts as well: "We mostly watch the Blue Jays anymore."

anxious / eager

I like the distinction. To be *anxious* about something is to be apprehensive, fearful, uneasy. On a bitter night, when the streets are covered with ice, we are anxious about the safety of a granddaughter. The word probably is rooted in the Latin *angere*, to choke or cause distress.

To be *eager* is something else. It stems from the old French word for keen or sharp, and it implies an edge of excitement, of impatient expectation or intense desire. We are eager to hear her key in the lock.

arbitrate

Small point to remember: It's redundant to speak of a "binding" arbitration. The whole idea of taking a dispute to formal arbitration is to be bound by the arbiter's decision. If it isn't binding, it isn't arbitration. It's just yakking.

arguably

Nonce words are words that come and go. *Arguably* is a word that can't go fast enough. *Newsweek* told us at one time that the deficit is "arguably the nation's worst problem." A director of Sotheby's remarked of a certain painting by Jasper Johns that it is "arguably the finest Johns remaining in private hands today." *The Washington Monthly,* reviewing a book about J. Edgar Hoover, observed portentously that "Hoover will remain arguably the most challenging and significant subject of American political biography of the twentieth century." USA Today let us know that the trial of William Kennedy Smith in 1992 "is arguably the most closely watched rape trial in the nation's history." San Francisco's Joe Montana is arguably the greatest quarterback who ever trod the field. Pavarotti is arguably a greater tenor than Caruso. The AK-47 rifle, reported The New York Times, is "arguably one of the best known products of the Soviet Union." And so on. In my book it is no longer subject to argument: *Arguably* is an inane excrescence. Away with it!

assure / ensure / insure

In a technical sense not much of anything, except for the Atlantic Ocean, separates *ensure* from *insure.* An insurance company in England ensures against loss; American companies insure against loss.

To *assure* is something else entirely; assurance has nothing to do with insurance. The verb should be used only in the sense of imparting confidence, informing someone positively, giving comfort on a doubtful matter. "The president assured suspicious Republicans that he would not renege on his tax pledge." "The police chief assured worried residents that the danger was past."

Few writers will have trouble with *ensure* and *insure* in real-world application. The uses of *ensure* are many; beyond the pages of an insurance policy, the uses of *insure* are few. My impression is that *insure* requires the elements of risk and financial compensation. These are not required for *to ensure.* By political horse-trading, a president could ensure enough votes to pass a bill. One might ensure the return of a lost dog by promising an attractive reward. In 1992, speaking of Haiti, a spokesman for the State Department wanted "to ensure that those who have a well-founded fear of persecution . . . are interviewed carefully."

as to

Some English constructions are just plain awkward, and *as to* is one of them. In his 1987 book about the Supreme Court—an excellent book for nonlawyers—Chief Justice William Rehnquist got stuck on *as to.* He recalled that in 1947 Harry Truman had not yet committed himself "as to whether he would be a candidate." Justice Robert Jackson's clerks at one point had no indication "as to his feeling." He spoke of uncertainty "as to the result the decisional process was producing." Rumors once began to circulate "as to who should be appointed." There are better, more direct ways of getting into these expressions, but *in regard to* isn't much better.

author

Most authors do not *author* books, they *write* them. The only people who author books are little old ladies who write little old vanity press books of little old poems.

a while / awhile

Two words or one word? I am a two-word man myself, but my passions are not furiously engaged on this one. There may be constructions in which the compressed *awhile* is acceptable—plenty of such citations may be found in the works of respectable authors—but my eye likes: "Please stay a while" and "We sat on the veranda for a while." It takes a while to edit a manuscript. I can't see that *awhile* gains anything but one unit of space. Meanwhile it offends the tetchy reader.

B
bad / badly

The Morrises' panel on usage took a look at *feel bad* and *feel badly* and copped out. Some of the panelists stuck with classic grammarians: They might have felt bad, not badly, about Buffalo's loss in the Superbowl. To feel badly, said Isaac Asimov, "is the mark of an inept dirty old man." Mostly the panelists ducked. Said Robert Cromie: "I avoid the issue by saying, 'I feel lousy.'"

You will find an extended discussion of the controversy in *Webster's Dictionary of English Usage.* Maybe you will get something out of it. I didn't get much. The editors conclude that respectable usage shows the camps about evenly divided. They scoff at the notion that if I say, "I feel badly," I mean only that my fingers are numb, or callused, or mittened—that I am having problems with my sense of touch.

My own inclination is to go with, "I feel bad," when it is a physical condition to be described. The meaning is clear and unmistakable: I am sick, or depressed; I felt bad when I woke up. I still feel bad. I would use the same construction for other copulative verbs such as *smell.* If you smell badly, perhaps your nose is stopped up. If the dog smells bad, give the poor mutt a bath.

When the condition to be described is emotional, there's nothing wrong with *badly.* One feels badly about a divorce in the family. Old folks feel keenly, not keen, about a bill to tax total benefits from Social Security. We seldom look fond; we look fondly. We do not feel deep; we feel deeply. To feel strong is one thing; to feel strongly is obviously something else. Like so many choices of usage, this is finally a question of the writer's ear.

basically

Before the Court of Peeves, Crotchets & Irks, Bill Mabe of Wichita, Kans., offered an excellent motion. He moved for a permanent injunction against *basically*. In evidence he offered:

> There was just basically the skeleton inside the building . . . making him basically say uncle . . . Basically, he'd lay down his life for me . . . He said that he, basically, was looking for a woman over thirty . . . They just basically acted like they knew us . . . The area around the corner is where basically her aunt did her soliciting.

Enough! Enough! Injunction granted!

beauteous

I thought *beauteous* had been interred with Queen Elizabeth I, but it turned up in 1991 in a review of a garden show. The reporter found it a *beauteous* display. My own irreverent thought is that the only contemporary use for *beauteous* is in nonsense verse:

> Paris thought Helen a damsel most beauteous,
> Especially in her remarkable gluteus.

We can safely let this one go.

beget

People magazine in 1991 summed up the plot of *Little Man Tate*, directed by actress Jodie Foster. "She also stars as the mother who can't quite comprehend just what she begat." The mother in this movie didn't beget anyone. Women don't beget. Only men beget. Thus Adam begat Seth, and Seth begat Enos, and Enos begat Cainan, and Cainan begat Mahalaleel, and Mahalaleel begat Jared, and Jared begat Enoch, and when Enoch was sixty-five he begat Methuselah who died at 969 years of age. All these gentlemen begat additional sons and daughters, but the daughters never made it to Genesis 5.

begs the question

Someone who *begs the question* isn't asking for a question, or prompting a question. To beg a question is to evade an issue by getting ahead of onself. Suppose that a young man from a prominent family is charged with raping a young woman in Palm Beach. A friend of the woman asks what punishment should be imposed upon the defendant, thus begging the question of the defendant's guilt.

behoove

Yes, *behoove* is beloved—but only by editorial writers of the Old School. Ordinarily it is Congress that is behooved, as in, "It behooves the Senate swiftly to adopt a cloture motion and get on with the bill." Politicians often are ill-behooved, as in, "It ill behooves the president to complain of excessive spending when he has sponsored so much of it." I raise no passionate objection to the verb, but it usually indicates a stodgy mind at work.

believe / think

In informal writing, one verb is as good as the other. In the split-hair division of logomachy, we are told to use *believe* for matters of emotion, *think* for matters of intellect. Thus, I believe my granddaughter loves me, and I think she is neglecting her spelling.

Watch out for, "I don't think," as in, "I don't think abortion is right." Who cares what we *don't* think? This may be okay in casual speech, but it looks odd in writing. Better to write, "I believe . . ."

blackmail / extortion

The crimes are similar, but there is a distinction dear to the hearts of lawyers. The crime of extortion almost always involves money or property. The victim is coerced into paying up. Blackmail also may be used to extort money, but a person may be blackmailed by threats of exposure or damage to reputation.

blatant / flagrant

There's a nice distinction between *blatant* and *flagrant,* but the distinction is more to be sensed than defined. Something that is blatant is deliberately public. A woman may wear her jewelry blatantly, just to show off. During a political campaign, a demagogue may blatantly appeal for votes. A teacher may show blatant favoritism. The whole idea is that something is done openly, perhaps brazenly, with no attempt at concealing the act. A blatant thing is not necessarily an evil or unlawful thing. The act may do no more than offend someone's sense of good taste.

By subtle contrast, something that is *flagrant* is always offensive in itself: a flagrant violation of duty, a flagrant evasion of taxes. In the famous hearings of 1991 on the confirmation of Justice Clarence Thomas, one side or the other was telling a flagrant lie—a lie that had the trappings of perjury.

In sum, a great many of life's irritations may be *blatant*—willfully conspicuous, out in the open, blinds up, top down. But not all blatant acts are also flagrant acts.

blond / blonde

To be absolutely politically correct, one should never spell it *blonde.* In the lexicon of feminine liberation, Hillary Clinton and Robert Redford are blonds. If the dictates of P.C. weigh lightly upon your writing hand, you may wish to reserve *blonde* for females and use *blond* for males and Scandinavian furniture.

boat / ship

The oversimplified rule is that a boat is any vessel small enough to be carried aboard a ship. The rule works for lifeboats and motorboats, but it runs into an exception at sailboats, which come in sizes small, medium, and bankrupting. Naval officers visibly flinch when a destroyer is referred to as a boat. It is permissible to call a non-nuclear submarine a boat, but a nuclear sub is a ship.

bombshell

This spavined old noun should be put out to pasture. It lost all its zing when Hollywood's last blonde bombshell breathed her last sexily sibilant breath. Her come-hither had gone thither. The metaphorical uses of *bombshell,* in the sense of a surprising event, expired long ago. Apart from its banality, *bombshell* suffers from the further objection that the word has no metaphorical meaning. It isn't a bombshell that suddenly explodes. It's the bomb inside it.

bottom line

This is another one for the glue factory. There is a place in bookkeeping and accounting for *bottom line,* but as an all-purpose synonym for result, outcome, or consequence there's not much profit in the tiresome borrowing. And not much originality, either.

boycott / embargo

The quick and easy distinction is that a boycott is a private action; an embargo is an act of government.

Boycott is of interest. The noun and verb owe their origin to Captain Charles Boycott (1832–97), an English land agent who gained notoriety for his harsh treatment of Irish tenant farmers. His petty tyranny aroused such animosity that local villagers organized a campaign to have no dealings with him. The practice spread, and *boycott* swiftly gained lexicographical standing.

Barnhart finds derivatives of *boycott* around the globe: In France, *boycotter,* in German, *boykottieren,* in Russian, *boikotirovat,* in Spanish, *boicotear,* and in Polish, *bojkotowac.* It's a *boikotto* in Japan. This tells you more about *boycott* than you really wanted to know.

An embargo is something else. Government may undertake to impose a general embargo, halting all trade; more likely it may attempt a selective embargo, for example, an embargo on shipments of arms. By extension the word has slipped into journalism, where a widespread custom is to give reporters an advance text of a speech or press release "under embargo."

bring / take

This is another of those distinctions that once were thought to be clear but now are pretty well blurred. When rules of construction were simpler, *to bring* meant to convey someone or some thing *toward* the place from which the action is regarded, e.g., lady is in the hammock, gentleman is in the kitchen. "Honey," she calls, "would you *bring* me a long gin and tonic?"

In theory, *bring* is the opposite of *to take,* which is to convey someone or some thing *away* from the point of view. We bring food to the table, and we take the dirty dishes away.

The rule does not always work. Suppose a picnic is in prospect. "What will you bring in your car?" "I will take the big basket in mine." "Will you remember to bring a flashlight?" "Let Clarence take the fishing tackle." In most instances the more appropriate verb will suggest itself. In other instances it seems to make no difference.

A much neglected alternative is *fetch.* Jack and Jill fetched the pail of water. Old Mother Hubbard fetched her poor dog a bone. Antique sideboards fetch a high price; a Labrador fetches game. A boxer fetches a blow to his opponent. Barnhart traces the verb to the Old English *feccan* about 1000, in the sense of "bring to." Gradually *to fetch* came to mean, "to catch one's attention." By 1880 the adjective *fetching* had evolved. *To fetch* has meaning for sailors, but not for me.

C

calculated risk

This is one of many facile phrases, easily manufactured, that ought to be sent back to the factory for a second inspection. In its proper place, *calculated risk* serves a useful purpose, but its place lies with actuaries, stockbrokers, and senior military officers. All kinds of factors enter into their calculations—age, earnings, air support—and they do indeed *calculate* the risk that may be involved in flying, buying, or taking on the Iraqis.

caliber

In the world of weaponry, *caliber* has a precise meaning. The meaning may be meaningless to almost everyone, but here it is anyhow: *Caliber* is the diameter of the bore of a rifled firearm, measured metrically from land to land. A .22 caliber rifle is slightly larger than two-tenths of a millimeter; a .357 Magnum would be a handgun whose barrel has a diameter of more than one-third of a millimeter.

Shotguns do not come in calibers. They come in gauges. This too is a measure of the internal diameter of a barrel, equal to the number of lead bullets of such diameter required to make one pound. The British spelling is *calibre*. And thank you, National Rifle Association.

can / may

Some years ago, when I was living in the Blue Ridge Mountains, I offered a ride to an old countryman. "Can I give you a lift?" I asked. "You can and you may," he said. His formal education stopped at the fourth grade, but this was one point of usage that stuck in his mind.

Nothing useful remains of the old distinction between *can* and *may*. It is time to scrap a rule that once was a grammarian's darling. Miss Thistlebottom, the creation of Theodore Bernstein, would have fallen into the flutters if one of her eager pupils had asked, "Can I help you?" instead of "May I help you?" In ordinary, everyday usage, not a dime's worth of difference separates the two modal auxiliaries.

The Thistlebottom rule required *can* for what is possible and *may* for what is permissible. The rule led to much ambivalence. Thus, *the witness can testify* is clear enough. It tells us that the witness is physically able to take the stand. But *the witness may continue* leaves us in doubt. Are we talking permission? Or are we talking probability?

Canada goose

It is not an issue that is likely to come up every day, but I include it here out of nostalgic sentiment. Selective Service classified me

4-F for asthma in World War II, unfit for military duty, so I spent the war years as brigade leader of a fireguard in Henrico County, Va. It was not hard duty. We would have extinguished any fires the Nazis started in Glen Allen district of Henrico County, Va. between eight and eleven o'clock on Wednesday evenings.

With all the able-bodied reporters off to war, all kinds of duties fell upon the stay-at-homes. It will give you a fair measure of those desperate times to learn that when the outdoors editor reported to his infantry division, I became—yes, yes!—the outdoors editor in his stead. In my whole life I had never caught a fish much larger than a bluegill bream. I had never shot a deer, a dove, a quail, a groundhog or a rabbit, and I certainly had never shot a goose.

"Every man a tiger!" cried the managing editor. He arranged for me to spend three hours of a bleak December morning, sitting on my frozen stern in a duck blind, while other stay-at-homes made war upon geese. I returned to write a column about the slaying of *Canadian* geese. Taking my ignorance into account, I thought it a pretty good piece. My description of the Canadian goose was especially vivid.

The paper was blessed at the time with a great slot man on the copy desk. He read my epic account with a stoic's eye, and then waggled a finger for me to approach. He pointed his copy pencil at an offending line.

"*Canada* goose," said Mr. Bell.

The dictionaries tolerantly list *Canadian* goose as a variant, but be not deceived. That handsome brant is a *Canada* goose. I never hunted any kind of goose again.

cannot help but

This fumbling, bumbling, clumsy circumlocution serves no useful purpose. It cannot be read gracefully. It conveys no immediate meaning. "'I cannot help but admire Mrs. Thatcher,' said a Liberal M.P." What is one to make of that? The presumption is that the author would rather not admire Mrs. Thatcher. He admires the Iron Lady because he cannot help it. Why can't the

poor fish help it? "I cannot but defend the president." Out with
it, man! If we can't say something straightforwardly, let us not say
it curved-backwardly.

careen / career / carom

In the sense of "to lean a ship on its side," *careen* goes back to the
1600s. Out of "leaning" came the image of lurching or swaying.
A car that is *careening* down the street is weaving from lane to
lane. A car that is *careering*, by contrast, is a car that is speeding.
Time magazine in 1988 described a motorcade "that careered
through Baghdad at 80 m.p.h." To *carom*, which comes out of
billiards and lives eternally in crossword puzzles, is to bounce off
something.

From this threesome I would save *careen* and *carom*, and abandon *career* in favor of "race" or "speed." To say that Lyndon
Johnson used to career across Texas leaves a fleeting thought
that we're talking about his history of employment.

care less (couldn't)

A reverse spin sometimes affects phrases of the clearest meaning.
Everyone understands what is meant by "a cold glass of beer,"
though it is the beer that is cold and not the glass that is cold. So
many people have pointed to the confusion of "A mind is a
terrible thing to waste" that the United Negro College Fund has
a form letter by way of response.

This is another backspin lob: *The senator could care less about the
president's criticism.* This clearly implies that the senator cares in
some degree, however slight—say, four on a caring scale of ten—
but he could care *less*. His care score might drop to two. But this
is not what the senator's press secretary meant to say. She meant
to say that the senator could *not* care less. That is, the senator
cares not at all; and if he cares not at all—if his degree of caring is
zero—*he could not care less.* In any event, the phrase is hackneyed.
Let us search for a fresher way to express disdain.

cement

The Court of Peeves, Crotchets & Irks has reversed itself on this one. At one time the court pronounced it positively wrong to write of a *cement sidewalk* or of *pouring cement*. Cement is one ingredient in *concrete*. A person who walked on a cement sidewalk would be shuffling through a clay and limestone powder.

Courts ought to overrule their opinions now and then. In this instance, popular usage effectively and permissibly has overtaken the Code of Building Materials. It would sound odd to speak of a "cement foundation" of a substantial building, but no great violence is done by referring to a cement floor in one's basement.

Metaphorically, we may speak of manners as the "cement of civilization," but a politician's views are not "set in cement." We say they are "set in concrete." But not for long.

to chair (a meeting)

Every respectable dictionary now sanctions *chair* in the sense of "to preside over a meeting." The verb serves a useful purpose: *The committee meeting will be chaired by the senior senator* is an acceptable, if passive, alternative to *The senior senator will preside over the meeting*. If we can table a motion, we ought to be able to chair a meeting. The verb nevertheless grates on the sensitive ear.

charisma

Words have something in common with machinery. After a time they wear out. They lose their novelty; they surrender precision to sloppiness. Such a word is *charisma*. It is rooted in a Greek word for grace or favor. When it appeared in the mid-nineteenth century its meaning was pretty well confined to a theological context. A person with charisma had been specially endowed with divine grace; a charismatic was one who could heal by the laying on of hands.

A century passed, and *charisma* was born again. It acquired a meaning of charming leadership. John F. Kennedy had charisma.

So did Martin Luther King, Jr. Soon things got out of hand. The editors of Webster's *Dictionary of English Usage* found whole cities with charisma. The aerospace and defense industries were said to have charisma. Persons born under the sign of Libra were thought to have charisma. Actors and actresses blossomed with charisma. Tennis player Bjorn Borg had charisma. All God's chillun got charisma.

It's time to retire *charisma* for another century. It is about to be overtaken by *persona* anyhow.

cheap

Watch this one. Whatever its connotation may have been at one time, *cheap* now means far more than merely "inexpensive." It has come to mean tawdry, shoddy, contemptible, stingy, inferior in every way. The politician or writer who takes a "cheap shot" deserves a rebuke.

Chicano

Be careful with this one, too. At one time the noun had the narrowly defined meaning of a Mexican man who worked as an agricultural laborer. Over much of the Southwest, Chicano crews came seasonally to harvest fruit and vegetable crops. Then the word took on a politically serrated edge, and some political factions found it offensive. When in doubt, use "Mexican" or the generic "Hispanic."

Chief Justice

Webster's usually reliable *Dictionary of English Usage* flunked on this one. The editors looked at *Chief Justice of the Supreme Court.* Then they looked at *Chief Justice of the United States.* Finally they concluded inconclusively that, "We find both terms in good use."

Heaven knows where the editors looked, for only one title is in good use today. William Rehnquist, like Burger, Warren, Vinson, Stone, and other eminences, is *not* Chief Justice of the Supreme Court. He is Chief Justice of the United States. This has been the chief's title since Congress passed the Judiciary Act of 1866.

The Constitution speaks only of a "Chief Justice." The basic Judiciary Act of 1789 was as laconic. Chief Justices Jay, Rutledge, Ellsworth, Marshall, Taney, Chase, and Waite were commissioned under the title of "Chief Justice of the Supreme Court of the United States." The nomenclature officially changed with the act of 1866. Even so, several statutes thereafter were passed in which the chief was the "Chief Justice of the Supreme Court." The last of these was in 1911, and since then the usage has been fixed. Any lawyer who would speak in a brief or in oral argument of the "Chief Justice of the Supreme Court" is asking for a stony glare from the bench.

claim

Pause for a moment before putting *claim* to use as a verb. We may properly claim a hat, a title, an inheritance, or a staked tract of land. Nothing is wrong with saying that a certain problem "claims our attention," but let us avoid the feckless use of *claim* in the sense of to assert, to say, to believe, or to maintain.

"He claimed his check was in the mail." . . . "She claimed her husband was unfaithful." . . . "Coach Gibbs claimed repeatedly that the Giants were holding." These are clumsy abuses of the verb. When we have a verb with a nice narrow meaning, we ought to hold on to it.

clandestine

Bruce Springsteen and Julianne Phillips were wed in 1985. The wire services described it as a "clandestine ceremony." I commented at the time that *clandestine* implies something more than privacy or secrecy; it implies something illicit. For this observation, the editors of *Webster's Dictionary of English Usage* severely rapped my knuckles. Their view is that *clandestine* carries only a connotation of "fear of discovery."

Well, horsefeathers. Any act that is performed in secrecy is performed with some fear of discovery, but we would not say that a teenager kept a "clandestine diary." If a man and a woman meet for some clandestine purpose they are up to no good.

cohort

In 1984 a pair of pranksters managed to release a jar of live cockroaches in the White House. The Miami Herald identified the daring duo as activist Suzette Rowe "along with cohort Lynn Gillespie."

Yes, some permissive lexicographers sanction a singular *cohort*, in the sense of a colleague or companion or comrade, but those who were weaned on the Gallic Wars must protest the corruption of a colorful word. Lynn Gillespie, all by herself, couldn't possibly have been a cohort.

In the beginning, *cohort* had a splendidly precise meaning. It identified a company of three hundred to five hundred infantrymen who formed one-tenth of a Roman legion. Given that root, no one reasonably could object to the contemporary meaning of "a band of followers," but to be a cohort there must be a band of some sort. A cohort is like a troop or a platoon. We would not write that, "The scoutmaster and his troop got in the front seat." "The sergeant and his platoon rode the two chestnut geldings." No way.

collective nouns

The question comes along as regularly as the phases of the moon: Is a couple *is*? Or are a couple *are*? Like many another collective noun, it all depends.

It depends upon how you are thinking of the couple (or the

pair, or the brace, or the family, faculty, congregation, team, or whatever). Do you see the couple as a single unit?

Then the noun takes a singular verb: The couple *has* taken a house in Poughkeepsie. Are you thinking of two individuals? Then you will need a plural verb: The couple *have* given custody of their children to the grandparents. (It is beside the point, but in informal usage, *couple* can mean "a few." When a defendant in traffic court says he has had "only a couple of beers," he has had at least five.)

This same ambivalent rule applies to collective nouns generally. More often than not, collectives will be treated in the singular: "His family is scattered over the South." But it is equally acceptable to write, "His family remain in Alabama and Tennessee to this day."

Our British cousins treat many collectives quite differently. In their jurisprudence, the jury *have* reached their verdict. In Parliament, the committee *have* reported a piece of legislation. Their tradition affected the U.S. Constitution of 1787: The House of Representatives chooses *their* Speaker.

I seem to advise, with distressing frequency, that a writer should let his ear be the guide. The advice applies to many collective nouns. Read an uncertain sentence aloud. If it sounds right, it probably is. If it sounds wrong, rewrite it.

compose / comprise

These are trickers. The traditional rule may be stated simply: The whole comprises the parts, and the parts compose the whole. Thus, the British Empire once comprised a number of colonies. Fifty states compose the American union. The editors of *American Heritage* comment that the distinction is getting blurred. No useful purpose is served by a nit-picking insistence upon correctly responding to Miss Thistlebottom's Friday quiz. Whether one writes that, "The American Bar Association comprises several sections," or, "Several sections comprise the Bar Association," the meaning is clear. Where lexicological distinctions truly matter, we should cling stubbornly to them. This one doesn't truly matter.

concept

This chickweed word has taken root in a hundred gardens. We are overrun with political concepts, industrial concepts, educational concepts, post-Soviet concepts, any old kind of concept one can think of. The art community, whatever that is, has wildly embraced the gauzy noun, with the result that conceptual art has become the rage. If your intention is to write arty, write of idealized concepts intricately interwoven into the contemporary zeitgeist. Yahoo!

contact

The battle over *to contact,* in the sense of "to get in touch with," ended long ago. In formal writing, the idiom lacks a coat and tie. "President Lincoln contacted General Grant before the siege at Chattanooga" seems a little casual. In everyday communication the use of *to contact* is so well entrenched that the matter doesn't merit a quibble.

convince / persuade

Let us cling to this distinction. To *persuade* is one thing; to *convince* is something more. *Persuade* takes an infinitive: We persuade someone *to do* something. *Convince* should never take an infinitive: We convince someone *that* he should do something.

These are Horrid Examples: "Twenty years ago a New York ad man convinced a skeptical chicken farmer named Frank Perdue to do his own television commercials." . . . "Army life convinced him to take a new look at his future." . . . "The court ruled against a leukemia victim who is trying to convince a woman to donate bone marrow." . . . "She recently convinced her lover to take her to Monte Carlo."

No, no, no! The ad man persuaded Perdue. The persuasion was so effective that in time the ad man convinced Perdue that he should do his own commercials. The rigors of army life first persuaded and then convinced. Persuasion is foreplay. Conviction is the real thing.

D
dais / lectern / podium

The terms constantly are confused, but there is no reason for confusion. A *dais* is a large platform, capable of holding more distinguished guests than are truly distinguished. A *lectern* is a piece of furniture designed to hold a speaker's notes. Some lecterns are small, slant-topped pieces that go on top of a desk or table; most lecterns are floor-level affairs. A *podium* is a small platform intended for single occupancy, as by an orchestra conductor.

My impression is that *podium* is going through a sea change. At the national political conventions, the orators now are said to be speaking "from the podium." From a little-bitty four-by-four thing to stand on, *podium* has grown to the size of a Hollywood stage.

dam (a tinker's)

First off, it's not a tinker's *damn*. Tinkers may not have ranked high on the social scale, but there's no reason to suppose that a tinker's curse is any more meaningless than a sailor's damn, a plumber's damn, or anyone else's damn. The hackneyed phrase is, "as worthless as a tinker's dam." In the days when tinkers repaired pots, the tinker often used a pellet of bread to dam the molten solder. The pellet then was discarded. Them days is gone forever. Find a new simile for cheap or commonplace.

daylight saving time

The thing to remember here is that it is not *savings*. It is *saving*. The Associated Press and *American Heritage* hyphenate the term:

daylight-saving time. Webster's leaves out the hyphen. *Random House* obligingly says to hyphenate or not, as you please. The better choice: no hyphen.

days (long)

The Court of Peeves, Crotchets & Irks once scorned the whole notion of someone's spending "thirty *long* years" in the Army or "ten *long* days" in remorseful thought. The court's idea was to take these things literally. Was a long day a day of twenty-six hours? Were there five quarts in a full gallon, six thousand feet in a long mile?

The court owes some deference to the doctrine of *stare decisis,* but deference to precedential opinions can be overdone. It is a universal experience to labor through a day or a week that surely seems interminable. The woman who devotes nine months to bearing a child has a right to speak of *nine long months* without suffering the court's injunction. Use the idiomatic stretcher if you must, but it's not a device to use very often.

decimate

Let's stop quarreling about *to decimate.* Some purists insist that the verb should be preserved as if it were an early Roman band instrument: It should be employed only when precisely one-tenth of something has been destroyed. This is pointless pedantry. The verb reasonably may be applied to any form of destruction that is substantial but not total. The football team that has been decimated by injuries has lost three or four of its eleven-man offense. To complain that a hungry fox has decimated a hen house is to complain that the fox made off with four or five from a flock of thirty.

Some years ago the United Nations reported hard times in Ethiopia. There had been "a decimation of livestock ranging between 40 and 90 percent in the Sahel." The word ought not to be abused in this cavalier fashion. Let us use it precisely, or let us use it generally, but let us not fall in between.

decision

Except in the context of prizefighting, where Louis decisioned Walcott and Tunney decisioned Dempsey, the verb is a barbarism. A committee cannot decision to fire the manager. The committee simply decides.

descendants / ancestors

When the cold war was still hot, Queen Elizabeth received an invitation to visit Moscow. Prime Minister Margaret Thatcher said no. The Associated Press reported that the very idea "sent a shudder through royal-watching circles, where it was quickly noted that the Russian royal family, murdered by Bolsheviks in the Russian revolution, were the queen's ancestors."

Well, Tsar Nicholas wasn't the queen's ancestor. He was the queen's distant relative. The more familiar boner lies in confusing *ancestors* and *descendants*. Thus The Wall Street Journal noted that Earth Prizes had been developed "by an ancestor of the fellow who created the Nobel prize." The Saginaw News in 1986 headlined a story from North Carolina: "Ancestors of former slaves gather to learn of past." The Cleveland Plain Dealer reported that thousands of spectators annually attend an outdoor drama built around the life of Tecumseh. The great Shawnee leader must marvel "at the homage being paid to his memory by these ancestors of his mortal enemies." Come on! These were descendants of slaves and descendants of white settlers.

dialogue

Latin and Greek roots combine to produce *dialogue,* which once meant the alternating statements of two persons. "You did!" "I did not!" "You did!" That was *dialogue,* but the word long ago lost that narrow constriction. It now embraces almost any kind of discussion, conversation, colloquy or debate in which two *or more* persons engage.

There is a verb, *to dialogue,* that has been around since the early

1700s, but it ought to be returned to Queen Anne for decent inter-ment. In today's polluted atmosphere, "the principals dialogued with the school board" has the sickly smell of academic jargon.

different than / from

You will find exhausting discussions of this issue in every book on usage ever written, and you are likely to be more confused than ever when you finish your research. The oversimplified but rea-sonably useful rule is to use *different than* when you want a follow-ing clause: Today's well-educated political reporters are different than they used to be in Mr. Dooley's day. But, Dukakis in 1988 was not much different from Mondale in 1984. Your ear should tell you the right combination.

dilemma

Dilemma is a word that once had a sharp edge. Let us hone it back to its narrow meaning. A dilemma is a choice between two equally unsatisfactory alternatives. When voters are offered no more than a choice between Candidate A, who is an airhead, and Candidate B, who is a blowhard, the voters confront a dilemma. Other words may be drafted to convey the idea of a general puzzlement or a difficult choice.

While we're on the topic, let us bury *horns of a dilemma* in the graveyard of hackneyed phrases. The phrase came out of a meta-phor involving a bull. The bull has two horns. The matador may be gored by either horn. Thus the fellow who is royally pitched was caught on the horns of a dilemma. Surely we can find a better image if we try.

disinterested

The distinction between *disinterested* and *uninterested* is so mani-festly clear that no writer should have a problem with it. Evidently many writers do have a problem, for *Webster's Dictionary of English Usage* devotes more than four columns to a disquisition on the topic.

A reporter for *U.S. News* had a problem in writing in 1988 about the public's midsummer apathy toward the presidential election: The public "could be even more disinterested as the Olympic games preempt prime-time TV." Kurt Russell, the long-time co-vivant of actress Goldie Hawn, said the couple is disinterested in marriage. He meant they were not interested, that is, they were uninterested in getting married.

Note the distinction. If we have to go into court, we want a disinterested judge and a disinterested jury. At the ballpark we want a disinterested umpire. On the football field we want a disinterested referee. The idea is to have decisions made by persons who have no bias one way or another.

distaff side

This is another word that should have been killed off long ago. When spinning wheels were in common use, everyone knew that a distaff is the rod or staff from which the flax is drawn. By synecdochical extension, *distaff* came to mean "female" or "woman's." It was an awkward extension two hundred years ago, and it has not improved with references to "the distaff side" of a tennis tournament, or a store's "distaff line" of clothes for spring. It is arch, coy, or patronizing, or simply irritating to refer to "a distaff jockey." If the element of gender is important, use "woman jockey" and be done with it.

ditsy

In the spring of 1986 USA Today reviewed a movie, *No Small Affair.* We learned that actress Ann Wedgeworth played "the hero's ditzy mother." A year later the adjective achieved respectability in Robert L. Chapman's *Dictionary of American Slang.* It appears that the preferred spelling is *ditsy.* It means "vapid and frivolous, silly;

airheaded." It may be a combining form of dizzy and dotty. Anyhow, it fills a need that evidently is not wholly filled by flaky, bubbleheaded, or far out.

doubtless

No significant difference is involved in a choice among *doubtless,* *no doubt,* and *undoubtedly.* Each of them expresses about the same degree of certainty. "Senator Smoot doubtless will reintroduce his bill on pornography. The ACLU undoubtedly will oppose him. No doubt the controversy will enliven Senate debate." The choice is largely a matter of the cadence of a sentence.

drapes / draperies

The Court of Peeves, Crotchets & Irks gets positively magisterial on this one. *Drape* has a specific meaning, both as a noun and as a verb, and the meaning has nothing to do with drapery. One may drape a suit, drape a corpse, or drape a patient for surgery. An artist drapes a model. A tall fellow may drape his legs over the arm of a chair. But the long, heavy pieces of fabric adorning a window are not drapes. Dammit, they are *draperies.* It will contribute to domestic tranquillity if we will keep the distinction constantly in mind.

For the record, living room curtains are something less formal than draperies. A window shade rolls up and down. A blind, as in venetian blind, may be almost anything intended to keep out the light.

due to

In his sixth survey of contemporary American usage, Richard Tobin of Indiana University asked about *due to,* as in, "The game was canceled due to rain." Three-fourths of the responding editors said they would change *due to* to *because of.* An alternative that I have come to employ when my ear winces at either *due to* or *because of* is *owing to,* as in, "Owing to a heavy rain, the game was stopped before the Cubs could bat in the bottom of the fourth."

The trouble with *due to* is that it creates a millisecond of doubt whether *due* conveys a sense of time or whether it conveys a sense of causality. It may mean "scheduled," as in, "The plane is due to arrive at 5 o'clock." Or it may mean "because of," as in, "Due to the plane's late arrival, he missed the dinner meeting." It's better to stick with plain old "because."

E
each is

There is no such thing as a plural *each,* but now and then some absent-minded writer will come up with, "Each of the soloists are masters of the piano." Yeccch! This ear-jarring collision probably is owing to the reasoning that if "soloists" is plural, it must take a plural verb, therefore, etc. But "soloists" isn't the subject. *Each* is the subject, and *each* is.

each other

Some dictionaries of usage, showing more tolerance than they have any business showing, will tell you that *each other* and *one another* may be used interchangeably. Piffle! It is this kind of permissive fungus that rots the language. Use *each other* when you have two: "Jefferson and Madison often visited each other." Use *one another* when you have more than two: "Members of the faculty visited one another during the holidays."

early on

Why does the idiomatic *early on* offend so many language lovers? The Court of Peeves, Crotchets & Irks hears regularly from plaintiffs who find the adverbial construction annoying. What is the matter with, "Early on, she showed a talent for music"? It is the functional equivalent of "early in life" or "in her formative years."

The phrase has a nice, easy informality about it. Complaints dismissed!

else

The argument over *somebody else's* and *somebody's else* should have gone out with the hoop skirt, but some crotchety fellows continue to defend the indefensible. This is strange. If we learn that somebody's else is in the bedroom, we are bound to wonder, first, what is an else, and second, what on earth is an else doing in the bedroom? Granted, there is no explanation that logically could justify *somebody else's*, but who ever said English is logical?

encounter

Some years ago, in an altogether audacious moment, I defined *encounter* as meaning only "to meet as an adversary or enemy; to engage in conflict with; to run into a complication." The editors of *Webster's Dictionary of English Usage* gave me the "we wonder" form of reprimand, a civilized rebuke with a parliamentary air about it: "We wonder why Kilpatrick is so ready to abandon its 'meet with' sense, which the *OED* shows to have been in use since the 14th century."

Well, Kilpatrick has no passionate feelings on the matter, but why *not* confine *encounter* to its adversarial meaning? What's wrong with that? English provides abundant verbs that mean to run into, to happen across, to meet with, to experience. By using the generic verbs we may preserve *encounter* for times when we need it—when we encounter a tough problem, encounter a really insolent waiter, or encounter an ill-tempered terrier. My thought is to hold on to the narrow meanings, to cherish the key words that fit in one lock only.

engine / motor

All motors are engines but not all engines are motors. In ordinary observation, large things run on engines: airplanes, for example, and steamships. An engine has higher social status than a motor; engines belong to better clubs and cost more money. Small things run on motors: electric fans, mopeds, lawn mowers. The technical distinction is that an engine is a machine for converting thermal energy into mechanical power, but this distinction no longer carries much authority. A Mercedes has an engine. The tin lizzie had a motor.

enormity

In 1981 Professor Richard Tobin asked about *enormity* in his annual survey of usage. His test sentence was, "The enormity of the crowd created a massive traffic jam." The responding editors overwhelmingly rejected this usage.

In 1986 the Senate Finance Committee voted to reverse a position it had taken firmly only a few months before. A Washington columnist was staggered by this turn of events. "To understand the enormity of what occurred," said the pundit, "you must understand that over the years . . ."

On the West Coast, a 49-year-old Tacoma accountant launched a magazine called *40+*, intended for women over forty. Two test issues were big hits. Subscriptions came rolling in. She forecast a circulation of two hundred thousand in another few months. "I am reeling from the enormity of it all," she said.

In the spring of 1988, firefighters at the Seattle-Tacoma International Airport did a superlative job of extinguishing a fire aboard an inbound passenger plane. Letters of thanks and congratulations poured in. The chief was astonished. "Nothing he'd seen quite prepared Smith for the enormity of the public response."

In Charleston, S.C., a book reviewer praised James Reston's memoir of a long life as a newsman, but the reviewer was staggered by "the enormity of the project."

None of these things was an enormity. In precise usage, *enormity* carries a connotation of wickedness or evil. Scotty Reston's memoir was a large undertaking, but it was not an enormity. If our purpose is to describe something as very large, any thesaurus will provide a dozen choices. Let us save *enormity* for high crimes and use something else for misdemeanors.

enthuse

This is a word that wears spats. It has a perfumed hanky in its coat. It says *ta-ta* and *ciao,* and it calls everyone dahling. In short, a sissy word. Kill it. Women who enthuse remain at the tender age of sixteen and seven months. Let us be enthusiastic, or excited, or full of applause, but in a grown-up world let us never enthuse about anything.

envy / jealousy

Here is a distinction quite worth preserving. I envy what is yours. I am jealous of what is mine. In an article about Pittsburgh beer, a brewer said, "Breweries all over the world are jealous of our yeast." No, sir. It is the brewer who is jealous. His competitors are envious. In a more romantic vein, the young man who is engaged to some delectable creature gets jealous when another lad pays attention to his girl. The other lad, in turn, may envy the young man's red Ferrari.

epitome

Uncounted generations have grown to old age in the confident belief that the epitome of something is the very best of something. In November 1991 *Newsweek* used the noun in that sense: "Formal French restaurants that once represented the epitome of fine dining in America are almost extinct."

That isn't what *epitome* means at all. An epitome is no more than a typical or ideal example of something. *Newsweek* got it right in the same article. France is worried about the creeping Americanization of French eating habits, "epitomized by the raging popularity of McDonald's in Paris."

In a related sense, an epitome could be the embodiment of something: Hubert Humphrey was the epitome of neoliberalism. George Raft was the epitome of movie gangsters. For "the very best," try *acme, pinnacle,* or *peak.*

erstwhile

Try this one on your pianola: "Capitalism's Grand Vizier, Donald Trump, erstwhile collector of professional football teams, glitzy casinos, and gold-plated urban palaces, on Monday announced his latest addition to the global Monopoly board: the world's tallest building."

The trouble with that bouncy sentence lies in *erstwhile.* The point of the story was that Trump was continuing to collect these things. All that is meant by *erstwhile* is "in the past" or "former." At the time the item appeared, Trump wasn't erst at all. He was very much with us, late and soon.

Erstwhile is one of those words affected by academics and editorial writers. When they hire *erstwhile* they are putting on the dog. Others use *erstwhile* as a put-on word, a play-pretend word, a comic pretension by people who think they are funny. In the same silly cluster is *quondam,* which means the same thing: former. If you want to get truly into knickers and old sleeve-sprung jackets, you may say that Jimmy Carter is a *whilom* president. People will look at you oddly, and well they may. All three words— *erstwhile, quondam,* and *whilom*—are words beloved only by second raters and other losers. Purge them.

esquire

When knighthood was in flower, an esquire was a kind of caddie. He carried the knight's shield, as well as the knight's woods and irons. He advised him on the distance to the dragon. As the centuries passed, and knighthood withered, upwardly mobile Britishers affected to call themselves squires. The pump jockey at a gasoline station might not have qualified for an *Esq.* after his name, but otherwise any male over the age of eighteen could be so addressed. In England the custom continues, but feebly.

In American usage, *esquire* has become the exclusive property of lawyers, both male and female, but these are generally bush-league lawyers. Their letterheads are printed, not engraved, and all their shoes need heels. Use *esquire* in addresses if courtesy demands, but do not address a letter to Mrs. Portia Pettifogger, Esq. The proper form is simply Portia Pettifogger, Esq. The salutation is Dear Pettifogger. On more intimate acquaintance, you may call her Portia darling.

et al.

Et al. is the familiar abbreviation for the Latin *et alia,* or *et alii,* and others. Do not use it to mean "and so forth," and do not bastardize the Latin by fashioning an English plural of "et als." That means more than one guy named Albert.

-eth endings

If you are absolutely determined to write in biblical English, or in quasi-Shakespearean English, I pray thee, or prithee, butcher ye not the ancient tongue. The Indianapolis News once carried a headline: "Oh, let the snow falleth." The Wall Street Journal, similarly winsome, fell into, "Defenders of the Civil Rights Bill Doth Protest Too Much." Dear Abby commented that, "He who seeks the knowledge of the number of ribs hath man and woman had best look upon the X-rays of both. Then let him go forth and compareth." Urrrkk!

The *-eth* suffix properly belongeth only to the third-perthon singular prethent indicative. The writer who useth the ending wrongly looketh pretty damn foolish.

everyone had 'his,' dammit

In the autumn of 1991 Judge Alex Kozinski looked back at the tumultuous Senate hearings on Justice Clarence Thomas. He commended the chairman "for ending the proceedings before everyone forgot why they were there." Bingo! The sentence may be cited as a rare event: Here *everyone* required a plural referent. "Everyone in the crowd gave themselves up to merriment" would provide another example, but you won't find many.

In good solid, traditional English, everyone has *his* book, everyone blows *his* nose, and everybody goes *his* way. Some years ago, in an absent-minded moment, columnist Erma Bombeck laid down a rule: "Anyone over the age of six should never bare their navels," which prompted readers to ask how many navels we are talking about. It is not often that we meet a person with more than one.

The Court of Peeves, Crotchets & Irks receives more complaints about *everyone/their* than any other abuse of the rules of prose composition. Horrid examples sprout everywhere. I have discussed some of these in Chapter Four, dealing with sexist phrases.

The Federal Aviation Administration urged male pilots and flight attendants not to grow beards, because the combination of beard and oxygen mask "could result in *that individual* being impaired in the performance of *their* assigned safety-related duties."

In Roanoke, Va., a funeral home asked a bothersome question: "Why should *anyone* plan *their* own funeral?"

The Wall Street Journal instructed us in the matter of federal deposit insurance. Up to $100,000 "*no one* loses any of *their* principal or interest" if the institution goes under.

President Reagan was alarmed that *an American citizen,* anywhere in the world, might be deprived of *their* constitutional rights.

A Florida clergyman, writing in the Stuart News, managed to foul up a proverb. Speaking of the Bakkers, Jim and Tammy, the reverend gentleman declared that "*no one* can have *their* cake and eat it too."

The Seattle Post-Intelligencer carried a feature story on the hazards of applying for a job: "If *a candidate* is caught misrepresenting *themselves,* it is tough to recommend that person . . ."

The Miami Herald interviewed a marriage counselor on the matter of infidelity. "It seems to me," the gentleman said, "*the uninvolved spouse* always knows when *their mate* is not as emotionally available as they used to be."

Enough! Some of these horrors, though very few of them, may be attributed to ignorance. No one ever taught these writers that such words as *everyone, everybody, anybody, nobody, no one,* and *each*—not to mention half a million nouns in their singular form—must take a singular referent in antecedal constructions.

Nearly all of the gaffes, I submit, are the ghastly product of intellectual cowardice. Writers have been so cowed by feminist bullies that they dast not write of a mixed audience, "Everyone kept his head." They opt for, "Everyone kept their heads," as if we were talking of geeks on a midway. How many navels? How many heads?

Fear overcomes even the normally fearless. A few years ago Professor John Kenneth Galbraith published *The Anatomy of Power.* The gentleman was then a professor emeritus of economics at Harvard, a man of great wit and sagacity, who succeeded in writing readably about the dismal science he taught. He also qualified as a morocco-bound, hand-tooled, gilt-edged liberal, a man acutely aware of the sensitivity of many females to the male nuances of the English language.

Galbraith tried to keep the faith. He began by speaking of circumstances in which "the individual refrains from speaking his or her mind." Very well. On page 14 he was still politically correct, but only parenthetically: "Compensatory power offers the individual a reward or payment sufficiently advantageous or agreeable so that he (or she) forgoes pursuit . . ." He stuck with *he or she* to page 40.

At about that point the professor gave up. I can hear him saying, "Ah, the hell with it." Whereupon, on page 42, he returned to English: "The individual who has access to the instruments of power has a natural attraction for those who wish to share his influence, live in his shadow. It would not be seemly to tell him that his access . . ."

Another of my favorite liberals, Supreme Court Justice William Brennan, took a charming route. On the theory that what is sauce for the goose is sauce for the gander, Brennan used to sprinkle his opinions with feminine referents. It was startling.

Midway in *Shapero* v. *Kentucky Bar Association,* a case that dealt with lawyers who use direct mail to solicit clients, the reader stumbled headlong over: "An inaccurately targeted letter could lead the recipient to believe she has a legal problem that she does not actually have."

In *Florida* v. *Riley,* a case involving surveillance by helicopter, Brennan wondered if an expectation of privacy could be defeated "if a single member of the public should conceivably position herself to see into the area in question." In *Maryland* v. *Buie,* Brennan said that a police officer may frisk a suspect "in order to protect herself from personal danger."

Justice John Paul Stevens liked Brennan's gallantry so much that in *Michigan* v. *Sitz* he got in the act: "From these statistics, it would seem to follow that someone who does not herself drive when legally intoxicated . . ." Stevens's heart wasn't in it. In June 1992 he concurred in the St. Paul, Minn., "hate speech" case. This was all in the same sentence:

> Threatening someone because of her race or religious beliefs may cause particularly severe trauma or touch off a riot, and threatening a high public official may cause substantial social disruption; such threats may be punished more severely than threats against someone based on, say, his support of a particular athletic team.

Those who knew Brennan, a fellow who was born with a twinkle in his eye, are bound to suspect that he did this only to annoy Chief Justice Rehnquist and other staid colleagues on the bench. That was a worthy purpose, but it was off-putting prose. The reader of Brennan's opinions was brought up short by the unexpected feminine referent. The train of thought ran off the track. The device may get a reader's attention by waking him up, but it seems a curious way to go about it.

No writer, I assume, wants unintentionally to offend his or her readers. The judicious use of *his or her* offers a way out. "An uninvolved spouse knows when his or her mate . . ." Keep in mind, though, that a little clutter of *her or him* goes quite a long way. The venerable Fowler had no patience with this formulation. "No one who can help it chooses it; it is correct, and is sometimes necessary, but it is so clumsy as to be ridiculous except where explicitness is urgent."

As I suggest in Chapter Four, a far smoother escape may be found in resort to plural constructions: All the children had their books . . . If candidates are caught misrepresenting themselves . . . American citizens cannot be denied their constitutional rights . . . Depositors will lose none of their capital.

If neither *he and she* nor a plural construction works, the best course is to damn the torpedoes and recur to English as it has been written for centuries. Only a handful of readers will be gravely and permanently offended.

exact same

Webster's Dictionary of English Usage insists that *exact same* is common in speech and is used by "educated speakers and writers." Rilly? Where were these educated speakers and writers educated? If *same* demands amplification, nothing is wrong with *exactly the same,* though *very same* also would serve the purpose; and nothing is wrong with saying that two things are *identical,* if indeed they are. The problem is that *exact* is not now, and never has been, an adverb. It's an adjective: *exact* copy, *exact* reproduction, *exact* boundary.

expertise

If *expertise* were a fish, it would be a trash fish—the kind of fish one cuts up for bait. The word dates from 1868, but age has not improved its character. Around 1886 a few writers tried *expertism,* but it never caught on. The nouns serve no purpose that is not better served by *knowledge, skill, talent,* or *know-how.*

F
fabulous

Once upon a time, which is how a fable begins, *fabulous* had the meaning of fabled, or legendary. That was a very long time ago, in a kingdom by the sea, where *fabulous* appeared about 1425. About 1609, Barnhart tells us, it took on the meaning of incredible. The day before yesterday, when teenagers seized upon it, dear old *fabulous* ceased to mean anything but gordy to the max, which is to say, extravagantly successful, altogether wonderful, as in, "Jason is a basically fabulous hunk."

facility

I cannot do better on this noun-of-all-work than to cite Bremner's *Words on Words*. He said:

> As a building, informally, a facility is an outhouse. As a building, formally, a *facility* is a flatulent word tacked on to anything from a concert hall to a prison. *Facilities* is a handy generic word for a collection of buildings and assembly rooms with different purposes, as in "The university will open all its facilities during homecoming." But call a gymnasium a gymnasium, not a recreational facility, and a school a school, not an educational facility.

farther / further

Old guidelines still govern the usage. Use *farther* for a distance that actually or metaphorically may be measured. Use *further* in matters of degree.

Thus, "It is farther from Houston to Chicago than it is from Houston to Charleston." "The candidates will move farther along the campaign trail after Super Tuesday." But, "Upon further examination, the bill appears to be a turkey." "Before we further amend the bill, we should hear additional witnesses."

fault (v)

The editors of *Webster's Dictionary of English Usage* have given their benediction to *fault* as a transitive verb. Their blessing ought to be sufficient for everyday use. Besides, they say, *fault* has been around since the middle of the sixteenth century. The *OED* cites from 1559, "Shall I fault the fates that so ordain?" A bit later we find, "The lion was faulted by the lioness that his breath stank." In 1791 a restaurant critic suggested that a patron "fault the poor flesh and quarrel with the fish." So go ahead and fault someone or something. No knowledgeable reader will fault you for it.

feasible

Nice distinctions separate that which is *feasible* from that which is *possible,* or *plausible,* or *probable.* Let us sort them out.

It sometimes appears these days that almost anything is *possible.* The scientists can do things on earth and in space that once would have been dismissed out of hand as "impossible!"

For seventy years political scientists agreed that the collapse of communism was *possible.* Indeed, a *plausible* case could be made for such an eventuality, but the academicians did not believe the collapse was *probable.* It was conceivable, but it was unlikely. All the same, if the right Soviet leader came along, dismemberment of the Soviet Union might be *feasible.* It was something that might be accomplished successfully.

Practicable goes beyond *feasible.* When we say that capitalism has become a *practicable* answer to some problems in the former Soviet Union, we have gone the whole route, from *possible* to *plausible,* from *plausible* to *probable,* from *probable* to *feasible,* from *feasible* to *practicable.* Behold, the walls came tumbling down.

fibula / tibia

The human lower leg has two bones. The big one is the tibia. The narrow one is not the fibia, as some ignoramuses suppose. In this regard I was once an ignoramus. The narrow bone is the fibula. Writers must be careful about anatomical terminology. For example, the big pelvis bone is known as the Ilium on one side and the Odyssey on the other.

first annual

On the face of it, a first annual convention is an impossibility. Something cannot be an annual event until at least a year has passed. The Morrises cite as "truly preposterous" an announcement of a school's "First Annual Traditional Christmas Play." There is something pretentious in advertising a "First Annual Hopscotch Contest." Modesty would suggest that the sponsors wait to see if the contest catches on. If so, a year hence they could promote the second annual event.

In a similar area, let us think twice about *first formed,* as in "First formed in 1982, the choir has regularly won awards ever since." Unless the choir has disbanded and then formed a second or third time, the *first* is redundant. The objection has less force in, "Rayburn first met Johnson when Johnson was a struggling schoolteacher." Here the clear implication is that some time elapsed between their first meeting and their subsequent meetings.

firstly

Nothing is grievously wrong with *firstly,* or even with *secondly* and *thirdly,* except that one ought to be consistent, and if one goes on long enough one will get to *fourteenthly,* which sounds damfoolishly. In formal writing, it is far better to say that the noun *fault* has fourteen meanings, and these are: (1), (2), (3), and so on. My own objection to *firstly* in speaking is that it is hard to say it without lithping and it comes out *firsthly.*

first three

An antiquarian plaintiff in the Court of Peeves insists that the proper phrase is not the *first three* but the *three first.* The dear fellow is persistent; he is persistently wrong. He insists that the court seems incapable of understanding "that if you speak of the 'first three' attempts to pass a bill, you are clearly implying that there was another set of three attempts, to be identified as the 'second three.'"

No, sir. If we are talking about horse racing, the first three across the line are win, place, and show. No one is going to write about a second three, for there may be only five horses in the race. But everyone has his own crotchets. *Three first* is his.

flak / flack

There's no reason to confuse the two nouns, but writers manage to confuse them anyhow. *Flak* is an acronym formed from the German *Fl(ieger)a(bwehr)k(anone)*, aircraft defense gun. Its shells scatter metal shards. A *flack* is a press agent who scatters flak metaphorically.

flaunt / flout

Flaunt and *flout* are wholly different words. Etymologically speaking, they are not even second cousins. They have never met. They have nothing in common except their beginning letters, yet even respectable writers confuse them.

To flaunt is to boast. To flout is to scorn. *Flaunt* is rooted in an Old Norse word meaning "to rush around." It means to brandish boldly or ostentatiously, to wave aloft, to display arrogantly. A rich woman flaunts her diamonds; the chairman of a congressional committee flaunts his authority.

Flout is something else. For reasons known only to etymologists, it comes from the Middle English *flauten,* to play a flute, but the verb has nothing to do with pretty music. It means to scorn, to trample underfoot, to treat with contemptuous disregard. The scofflaw who ignores a hundred parking tickets is flouting the law. The fellow who turns up at a formal dinner in black tie and tennis shoes is flouting convention. Tennis star John McEnroe used to flout the well-mannered traditions of his game.

In this regard, pay no attention to *Webster's Ninth New Collegiate,* for on this issue *Webster's* has it wrong and will only confuse you. *Webster's* says that *flaunt* means to treat contemptuously, which it does not, and offers bad examples to support its error. Louis Untermeyer is quoted as having said someone "flaunted the rules."

Oscar Lewis spoke of someone "flaunting the law." Marchette Chute spoke of developers "flaunting their authority." These writers bungled the verbs out of carelessness or ignorance. It happens to all of us who write for a living.

flotsam / jetsam

Only word mavens and admiralty lawyers are much concerned about the distinction between *flotsam* and *jetsam*, but it is nice to be precise when we can. This is the difference: Flotsam floats. Jetsam has been jettisoned. Thus, the debris that floats around after a shipwreck is properly flotsam. Before the wreck, the crew may have attempted to avoid the emergency by throwing stuff overboard— articles that would sink or eventually wash ashore. That's jetsam.

flounder / founder

These are two splendid verbs, useful in both literal and metaphorical ways, and we ought to treat them with respect. *To flounder*, says *Random House*, is to struggle clumsily, helplessly, or falteringly. An animal may flounder in mud. Figuratively, an unprepared student may flounder when called upon.

Founder is much more serious. A ship that founders is a gone ship. It has filled with water and sunk. A presidential candidate who loses badly—McGovern in 1972, Dukakis in 1988—sees his campaign founder. It's a sadly final experience.

fluke

A few years back, in Wilmette, Ill., an 11-year-old boy drowned in a swimming pool only four feet deep. A local newspaper called the death a "fluke accident." In the Chicago Sun-Times, a column of advice to the lovelorn dealt with this problem: A woman had invited a male co-worker to dinner. She got out the good china, polished the sterling, chilled a dry wine—and the fellow never showed up. What should she say to him? The advice: "Tell him you'll assume his display of bad character was either a fluke or a true representation of the sort of guy he is."

Hold on! A fluke is not an aberration or a momentary lapse. A fluke is an unexpected stroke of good luck. The boy's death clearly was not a fluke. Neither was the boorish conduct of the no-show guest a fluke. It was damned rudeness. The word comes out of billiards or pool. When a point is scored by accident, rather than by design, it's a fluke. A fluke is also an uninteresting flatfish of the flounder family.

foreword

It is astonishing—no other word will do—how many wannabe authors begin their wannabe books with a *forward*. Even a vanity publisher, for Pete's sake, sent me galleys that began with a *forward*.

The most reputable newspapers fall into error. It would be unkind to identify the prominent paper in Oregon whose writers had a terrible time with this in 1987. Maybe things are better now, but its critics spoke regularly of forwards to books that were being reviewed. Elsewhere, a naval analyst spoke of the forward to *Jane's Fighting Ships*. The New York Times reported a spat between economist Lester Thurow and Simon & Schuster. Thurow had written a forward to a certain scholarly work three years earlier. The forward was to be used only in the academic edition. Thurow had received for his forward a fee of $400.

Attention! That little introductory essay, usually written by someone other than the author, is a *foreword*.

for free

In September 1991, to the astonishment of almost everyone, consumer advocate Ralph Nader accepted an invitation from the Corvair Club to speak at the club's annual convention. *Fortune* magazine added to the amazement: "Nader spoke for free."

A few months later, *Newsweek* reported that panelists for the National Academy of Sciences often command consulting fees of

$350 an hour and up, but as NAS panelists, performing a public service, "they work for free."

Purists object, but their objections are unpersuasive. The idiomatic *for free* has found a niche and filled it precisely. The phrase is shorter than the stiff and formal, "Nader spoke without charge," and conveys a slightly different meaning: "Nader spoke for free" is a clear and vigorous expression. "Nader received no compensation for his appearance" may be proper, but it's feeble.

fortuitous

Professor Dick Tobin once put this sentence to his poll of editors: "It was fortuitous that the driver was wide awake." Most of the editors said they would recast the sentence to get *fortuitous* out of there. Good thing, too, because *fortuitous* carries a connotation that ought to be observed. It was not by accident that the driver was wide awake; it was just lucky that the driver was wide awake.

In its Third Edition, *American Heritage* gives us two definitions: (1) happening by accident or chance, which is the old definition, and (2) happening by a *fortunate* accident or chance, which is how the adjective is universally employed today. By the time the Fourth Edition appears, the second definition will have replaced the first.

free gift

Aaargh!

free complimentary gift

Aaargh! Aaargh!

fulsome

It always is a shock for a writer to discover that a familiar word doesn't mean what he thinks it means. So it is with *fulsome*. For a good many years I thought *fulsome* was a friendly word. Many others thought the same thing. In 1983 a Midwestern newspaper reported on astronaut Sally Ride: "Ms. Ride, appearing fresh and spirited despite her trail-blazing, six-day voyage, modestly accepted President Reagan's fulsome praise."

No, no, no! *Fulsome* does not mean abundant, or copious, or florid, or excessive. Its primary meaning is insincere, phony, offensively effusive. Members of the Senate engage in fulsome speech when they speak of an "able, distinguished, erudite, and dedicated" colleague. This is spatula speech, the kind of no-cal icing that may be piled upon a pound cake.

fun

It is too late in the day to complain about *fun* as an adjective. The *OED* cites *fun room* in 1846, *fun town* in 1908, *fun person* in 1959, and so down the hill. The bastard adjective has no place in serious writing, or even in serious journalism, but *a fun thing to do* manifestly fulfills a need not filled by *pleasant, enjoyable, delightful, joyous, amusing, diverting,* or *swell.* It's a teenager's adjective, when the teenager is not using *neat.*

G
gambit

Like many another word that once was precise—*parameter* and *replica* come instantly to mind—*gambit* has been effectively word-napped. It is now employed figuratively for almost any scheme, plan, plot, or ploy. Anna Quindlen of The New York Times, usually a careful writer, wrote a light column once about her hobby. This is the study of bats. She mused that Merlin Tuttle, an expert on bats, might use "I bet you think flying foxes echolocate" as "a conversational gambit." That's no gambit. That's just erudition swelling its chest.

Lovers of chess must suffer real pain when they see *gambit* abused. In its pristine meaning, before journalists messed it up, a gambit was defined as an opening move in which one or two pawns (or a minor piece) are put at risk in order to gain a position thought to be advantageous. If we are to use *gambit* metaphorically, we ought to preserve this element of risking something in exchange for something else. A negotiator for a labor union might try a gambit at the outset of bargaining: He would risk a small cut in pay in the hope of gaining doubled hospitalization benefits. We ought not to debase *gambit* by dragooning it into meaning something to pique our interest.

gamut / gantlet / gauntlet

Like old overalls, some words never die; they only fade away. These are fading. A *gamut* is a whole range of things—a spectrum, a piano keyboard, a complete set of Dickens. The most hackneyed of all gamuts is the alphabet, most brilliantly employed in Dorothy Parker's crack that Katharine Hepburn once ran the gamut of emotions from A to B.

Until the notorious brawl of the Tailhook Association in 1992, when drunken navy pilots made young women run a *gantlet,* no one had used the word in years. At one time miscreants were punished by ordering them to run between parallel lines of men wielding clubs. Less refined punishments later were devised.

As for *gauntlet,* it is literally a glove, figuratively a challenge. Not since the days of King Arthur has anyone done anything with a *gauntlet* except to throw the fool thing down.

gap

When a woman's skirt and blouse fail to meet, it is said that she is suffering from gaposis. A similar problem arises in public affairs. First there was the missile gap. Every year when the federal budget is under discussion, we find a revenue gap. When a poorly rated TV program is sandwiched between two more popular shows, we hear of a time gap. During the primary elections of 1992, The New York Times reported that Sen. Bob Kerrey suffered from a plan gap. The usage suffers from overuse. Time for a *gap* gap.

-gate

In the summer of 1972, a small band of overzealous and incompetent burglars broke into Democratic campaign headquarters in the Watergate complex in Washington, D.C. It soon transpired that the bunglers were in the pay of the Nixon presidential campaign. The incident led to the disgrace and abdication of the president, and it didn't do the language any good either. The affair sired the *-gate* suffix.

The appendage should have dried up and disappeared a long time ago, but it lingers on. When Jimmy Carter's brother Billy became involved with Libya, we had *Billygate*. After a while we had *Contragate* and *Irangate*. Various scandals, long since forgotten, gave us *Pentagate, Huttongate,* and *Milkengate*. The Bush campaign of 1988 produced *Hortongate*. In 1990, when wheeler-dealer Charles Keating embarrassed five senators, we read about *Keatinggate*. Keating was a part of *thriftgate*. House speaker Jim Wright was caught in *bookgate*. More than a hundred members of the House suffered painful publicity in *bankgate*.

This foolishness has to stop. A whole generation has grown up with only the vaguest notion of what *-gate* is all about. Knock it off, I say! The Watergate *-gate* is a great gate for closing.

gay

The editors of *Webster's Dictionary of English Usage* say that it is premature, to put it mildly, to bemoan the loss of the traditional senses of *gay*. These traditional senses "are still in regular use."

Sorry, dear friends. *Gay* is irretrievably gone. The twenty-first century will bring dictionaries that list as the first meaning of *gay:* homosexual. The writer who writes today of a "gay party" or a "gay festival" would be clearly understood in this sense. We will have to find some other word to describe something that is gay, merry, colorful, lighthearted and the like, but *gay* is no longer with us.

In a note on usage, *American Heritage* suggests that *gay* be used in a social, political, or cultural context, thus reserving *homosexual* for medical, legal, or psychological commentary.

gentlewoman

From time to time, the Court of Peeves, Crotchets & Irks receives complaints about *gentlewoman*. The plaintiffs find it a cumbersome term, indeed a nonsensical term, and they ask what is wrong "with that perfectly good word, *lady*."

The court rules against the plaintiffs, but the court rules reluctantly. Let us suppose we are writing about a public hearing on a local bond issue. A forceful speaker is "Mary Allen of Pawtucket." What is one to do at the second reference? We do not know if she is Miss Allen, Mrs. Allen, or Ms. (aaargh!) Allen. To use the surname alone is to sound a truculent note: "Allen offered a motion." Besides, another speaker at the hearing is George Allen of Newport.

"The lady offered a motion" smacks of a sarcastic gentility. "The Allen lady offered a motion" is impossible. "The woman offered a motion" has the air of a putdown. Under the circumstances, *spokeswoman* offers no relief, for Mary Allen is speaking only for herself. Lamely, the court falls back in favor of *gentlewoman*, which sounds like an excess of parliamentary speech, as if the writer had dwelled too long on Capitol Hill. If any reader has a better solution, let us have it.

gift

Among the more abominable verbs to creep back into English in recent years is *to gift*. The British gifted presents in the 1600s, but then good taste drove the verb into exile. American advertising writers rediscovered *to gift* in the 1960s, and it hangs on.

The Morrises submitted the usage to their panel. The vote was 95–6 against it. Barbara Tuchman called it horrible, Herman Wouk found it disgusting, Vermont Royster termed it pretentious, and Red Smith said he would accept it when he could write that he donationed generously and contributioned unselfishly.

gonfalon

When they weary of writing about "pennants," some sportswriters will resort to *gonfalons*. They ought to stick with pennants

For the record, a gonfalon is not a flag. It is a rectangular banner, suspended from a crosspiece, that is carried in parades. The Knights of Columbus make quite a show of them.

got

Some years ago Pennsylvania's state board for tourist promotion adopted a slogan: "You've got a friend in Pennsylvania." Word mavens jumped up and down on this friendly assertion. Dick Thornburgh, who was then governor, responded by arguing that "You've got a friend" is just plain friendlier than "You have a friend." Maybe so, but critics of *got* are not likely to be greatly appeased.

Many critics properly regard *got* as one of the two ugliest verbs in English. It is a belch of a word, a flatulent word; it has all the charm of a flyswatter's smack. The writer hasn't been born who could make anything euphonious out of "she got permission," or "He got the measles from his sister," or "we got dinner at the hotel." Barclay's International Bank used to tell its depositors, "You've got 5,300 branches to choose from." Kodak used to advertise, "If you've got the content, Kodak has you covered."

What's wrong with plain old *have?* "You have 5,300 branches" is just as clear as "you've got 5,300 branches," and surely it sounds more bankerly. In casual speech, yes, there is a place for the emphatic *got.* "I've *got* to catch that plane" carries more wallop than "I *have* to catch that plane" or "I *must* catch that plane." It would be captious to complain of *got* on Tinpan Alley. "I have you under my skin" would be a dead loser, and "I have a girl in Kalamazoo" would lose its zing. A good rule for writers would require us to pause whenever we fall into *got.* In serious writing, *got* grates.

gourmet / gourmand

The distinctions are as big as an archbishop's belly. A gourmet is a connoisseur, an authority, an accredited judge of food and wine. True gourmets are likely to be slender; they shudder at the thought of smoking cigarettes; they work at keeping up their credentials. In contrast, gourmands are like as not to be fat slobs, cigarette smokers who waddle at their work. They like fine food more than beanery food, but they eat heavily and heartily. A gourmand may be pleased to be called a gourmet, but a gourmet would have everyone know he is not a gourmand.

graduated

This is the rule, and it is a rule worth preserving: Students do not graduate. Institutions graduate. Let me run that by you again. In careful usage, we ought to write that Clarence Thomas *was graduated* from Yale Law, rather than, "Thomas graduated from Yale Law." (Heaven forfend that we should fall into the barbarous construction of, "Thomas graduated Yale Law.") A parallel rule applies to the armed forces. A retiring soldier does not discharge the army. The army discharges him. Back in civilian life, he was discharged, precisely as a student was graduated.

graffiti

One strand of spaghetti is a *spaghetto,* and one drawing or inscription on a wall is a *graffito.* Both Italian words have been so thoroughly Americanized that the plural *spaghetti* and *graffiti* are well entrenched as singular forms. The singular *spaghetto* can be dismissed—it hasn't been seen in a sentence in years—but *graffito* is still around. When a boy scrawls "Peter Loves Lucy" on a neighborhood wall, that's a graffito.

guest

The same objections to *gift* as a verb apply to *guest* as a verb. Early in 1992 the nation's biggest name-dropper had an announcement: "Richard Nixon guests with me on *Larry King Live* this

Wednesday night at 9 p.m. EST on CNN." (Let us pass over the redundant *9 p.m. Wednesday night*). It may seem capricious to say that *to host* is okay and *to guest* is ridiculous, but that's the situation. Eventually *to guest* may come into respectable use, but that time is not now.

H
had better

Nothing is wrong with *had better,* as in a father's saying to a young swain, "You had better have my daughter home by ten o'clock." The *OED* dates the idiom from 971, a vintage year. In British usage it's more often heard as *had best.*

In this construction is *better* a verb? As presiding justice of the Court of Peeves, Crotchets & Irks, I put the question to Laurence Urdang, the erudite lexicographer who publishes the quarterly *Verbatim.* He said, no, it's an "objective predicate adjective." He quoted the great grammarian George Curme as his authority.

What the protective father is saying is an elliptical kind of thing. The reader, or the young swain, must supply the words that are left out: "You will find it more advantageous [prudent, wise, diplomatic, physically safer] to have my daughter home by ten o'clock." It depends upon the father, and the swain, to interpret the parting admonition.

half-mast

In their Harper *Dictionary of Contemporary Usage,* the usually infallible Morrises say that either *half-mast* or *half-staff* is correct. They're wrong. As a symbol of mourning, a flag flown on land is at half-staff. A flag flown at sea is at half-mast. Seems logical.

hanged / hung

Pictures are hung. Criminals are hanged. You will find an interesting note on this trivial controversy in *Webster's Dictionary of*

English Usage. The editors concluded from their research that the use of *hung* in matters of capital punishment is "certainly not an error."

All right, it's not an "error," but it is stylistically much better to say that a rogue was *hanged.* The vigorous verb carries the bang of a trapdoor flying open. Something in the sound of *hang* evokes the sound of anger. By contrast, *hung* is putty soft.

Note of amplification: The rule does not apply in the matter of effigies. People may be *hung* in effigy, a ritual that is lusty but not life-threatening.

hare's breath

Come now! Let us get straight on a couple of easy ones. A newspaper in Vancouver, B.C., quoted a music producer on young talent. "Some people are just a hare's breath away from stardom." A spokesman for Blue Cross and Blue Shield commented in 1987 that "Cleveland is a hare's breath away from overtaking Detroit" as the nation's fourth most expensive city for hospital care. On another occasion, this time in Terre Haute, the Tribune Star quoted a leading citizen on the restoration of Deming Center. His committee had done well. "And we came within a hare's breath of doing the same thing with the Terre Haute House."

Gracious! Hares with halitosis? Fetch the mint-flavored Lagomorph mouthwash. The phrase is *hair's breadth.* The related phrase, for moments of horripilation, is *hair-raising.* First time I've had a chance to use *horripilation* since I found out what it meant.

And while we're on the subject, it's not *hair-brained.* It's *hare-brained.* A lagomorph (crossword puzzle word) may not have many brains, but a hair has none.

headquarter

Back in 1981 *American Heritage* asked its panel on usage about *to headquarter,* as in, "NATO is headquartered near Paris." Ninety percent of the panelists voted against it. It is doubtful that even a simple majority could be marshaled against the usage today. For reasons that defy rational explanation, *to headquarter* sounds orderly and *to office* smells of jargon. Prejudice, pure prejudice.

healthy / healthful

People do get mightily upset about the distinction between *healthy* and *healthful.* There is indeed a distinction, and careful writers may want to observe it. Something healthful is conducive to good health. Until the government rules otherwise, bran is healthful, fruits are healthful, sensible exercise is healthful. Cigarettes and booze are not healthful, junk sweets are not healthful, and so on.

Healthy has to do with enjoying or exhibiting good health and vigor: a healthy child, a healthy appetite, a healthy debate. *Webster's Dictionary of English Usage* casts a tolerant eye on the argument: "If you observe the Distinction between *healthful* and *healthy* you are absolutely correct, and in the minority. If you ignore the distinction you are absolutely correct, and in the majority." Stick with the minority on this one.

hectic

A yuppie word. It has lost the old zing. At one time *hectic* was a medical term having to do with fluctuating fever. From that honest root in both Latin and Greek, the word grew to cover a situation that was feverish, exciting, wildly confused. Now a *hectic* day at the office could mean a day in which the copier broke down. We ought to give *hectic* a rest and look for a fresher word.

hero / heroine

Martina Navratilova, for many years the superstar of tennis, went back to her native Czechoslovakia in 1986. A sports writer for The Washington Post went along for the ride, and was much moved.

Quite clearly, he said, "she still is a hero to the people of the country she left behind." A question arose: Wasn't she properly a heroine, not a hero?

Random House typically begins by defining *hero* as "a man" of distinguished courage or ability, but in the next breath extends the meaning to "any person" who has heroic qualities. That's fine, but *heroine* should not be abandoned. Let us reserve *heroine* exclusively for the leading female character in a bra-bursting paperback novel. Martina was properly identified: *hero*.

historic / historical

There's a big difference here. Things that are *historical* have specifically to do with history. Gore Vidal's *Burr* and *Lincoln* are historical novels. The Smithsonian Institution houses items of historical interest.

Historic is something else entirely. It deals with events that are memorable, important, famous. When Lincoln spoke at Gettysburg, it became an historic occasion. The trial of John Scopes in 1925 was an historic challenge to Darwinism. The Watergate scandal of 1972, in its sad way, was historic.

Unless Robert Byrd is speaking on the history of the Senate, you won't hear an historical speech in the Senate today. Come to think of it, you are unlikely to hear an historic speech either, but one may always hope.

hogwash, et al.

Not long after I began writing my column on language in 1981, a gentleman in Port Charlotte, Fla., took strong issue with one of my wise and sensible pronouncements. He termed the column *hogwash*.

It is a useful term of invective, traced by the *OED* to the Middle English *hoggyswasch*, meaning swill or slop. Intending to be helpful, I responded by suggesting kindly that *hogwash* was suffering from too frequent employment. If he wanted to give me another hiding in the future, he might elect an alternative term.

He might have called my column *balderdash!* It is a splendidly contemptuous ejaculation. It dates back to 1596 in the sense of "a jumbled mixture of liquors, such as buttermilk and beer," but by early in the seventeenth century the meaning had been extended to embrace "a senseless jumble of words."

Most of us, I suppose, would rather be accused of writing balderdash than of writing baloney, but *baloney* has its place in the vocabulary of invective. The word is variously spelled—*baloney, boloney, bologna*—and originally applied to an inferior prizefighter. In the days when bologna sausage was an inexpensive meat, the word carried a connotation of cheapness as well as inferiority. Al Smith gave currency to *baloney* first as mayor of New York and later as a presidential candidate.

Closely related to *baloney* is *buncombe,* from which we derive *bunco, bunk,* and *debunk.* The story is that early in the nineteenth century, a county in North Carolina was named for a hero of the Revolution, Colonel Edward Buncombe. Years passed. What is now the Eleventh District of North Carolina sent to the House of Representatives a tedious fellow, inclined to deliver speeches both long and dull. Whenever he arose to speak, his colleagues fled to the cloakrooms. Undaunted, he would say his remarks were not intended for them anyhow. They were addressed "to Buncombe." Senators still are full of buncombe.

My apoplectic adversary in Florida might have charged me with writing *bilge,* an excellent word. He could have said my sentiments were *poppycock,* though I cannot recommend this for publication in a family newspaper. You should look it up. Other terms of opprobrium spring to mind: *Rubbish! Trash! Garbage! Junk!* My own taste runs to the British *rubbish.* As a Reply Churlish it has just the right ring to it, especially if one rolls the initial *r.* I would reserve the American *trash!* for a Countercheck Quarrelsome. There is much to be said for *garbage!* It carries a kind of aromatic ambience, raising images of rotten vegetables, spoiled fruit, and tainted meat. Neither should we overlook *humbug, drivel,* or *hokum.* On appropriate occasions, nothing takes the place of *horsefeathers!*

Do I write *tripe?* Could be. Some years ago a genuinely artistic fellow accused me of writing *slumgullion.* On investigation it turned out that *slumgullion* once was the muddy residue that remained after panning for gold. By extension it became the product of the cook in the mining camp.

Ah, if only someone once again would charge me with turning out *slumgullion*! The best that pantywaist in Florida could do was to say he would like to punch me in the nose. Lawsy me! I will just say *phooey* right back at him. That comes from the Yiddish *pfui,* meaning in this context, any drooling idiot could do better than that.

hoi polloi

Some language mavens get grumpily aroused over the Greek *hoi polloi.* Their position is that *hoi* means *the* in Greek. Therefore we should not write of *the hoi polloi.* Well, yawn. Nobody but an affected ass, trying to show off, or trying to be funny, would write *hoi polloi* anyhow. If you are writing about the populace, or the citizenry, or the common people, say so in English.

hold (a meeting)

A Midwestern editor had a large crotchet about *to hold,* as in holding a meeting, or holding a conference, or holding a get-together. It seemed a curious crotchet. Meetings have been *held,* and councils have been *held,* since at least 1450. Editors get these things in their heads and will not let them go. Humor them. They deserve a little humoring.

-holic

Alcoholic came usefully into the language about 1890. If the *-holic* suffix had stopped there, you would hear no crotchety complaints from this quarter. The vile habit did not stop there. The passing years have given us the workaholic, the golfaholic, the speechaholic, and the stereoholic. We also have the shopaholic, the jazzaholic, and the teenaged phonaholic. Some college graduates become alumniholics.

Suggestion: Hold on to *alcoholic,* and scrap the rest.

home / house

It takes a heap o' livin' in a house, said Edgar Guest, t' make a house a home. The sentiment regularly is reinforced by critics of advertisements for real estate. Something about "home for sale" gets the adrenals pumping. It's a *house* for sale, they cry. Not until a house becomes a residence—not until people actually live in the house—may the house properly be termed a *home.*

The objection is frivolous. There are times when a given edifice is a house and times when it is a home. H.L. Mencken lived in a house on Hollins Street in Baltimore. It was his home for sixty years. In Washington we direct tourists to the house that Woodrow Wilson occupied after his term ended. Writers need only to think about the distinction. The right word will come naturally.

hopefully

For no discernible reason, the stupid *hopefully* came suddenly to life in the 1960s and developed into a full-blown fad by the mid-seventies. The stupid *hopefully,* as distinguished from the polite and proper *hopefully,* is the kind of *hopefully* that precedes a mundane sentence such as, "Hopefully, the sun will shine tomorrow." This is stupid, because the sun does not shine hopefully.

Hopefully, the child's feet will stop growing . . . Hopefully, the train will arrive on time . . . Hopefully, the market will go up . . . Hopefully, the printer will meet his deadline . . . Hopefully, the senator will stop talking soon. The stupidity of such sentences may be grasped by moving the gypsy adverb to its regular position. Do feet grow hopefully? Do trains arrive hopefully?

Bill Safire once attempted to defend the orphan *hopefully* by beginning a series of paragraphs with *angrily, coolly, fortunately,* and *doubtlessly.* It was a feeble attempt, for each of his exemplary adverbs served a legitimate purpose within the given sentence. Thus, no one could complain of "Traditionalists angrily hold that the word is an adverb . . . The language slob coolly replies . . . Fortunately we do not have to choose up sides . . . My decision doubtlessly will be attacked . . ."

My own impression, offered without a shred of evidence to support it, is that the rage for *hopefully* is on the wane. You will understand that I say that hopefully. We can always hope. That was what Clarence Darrow said to the Tennessee judge in the Scopes trial. The judge said he hoped Mr. Darrow did not mean to be in contempt. Darrow said the judge could always hope.

host

Okay, open the door and let it in. As a verb, that is. This represents either a change of heart or a dulling of the ear. In *The Writer's Art* I wavered about *to host*. An editor in Kansas had jumped me for writing that the schools of Jacksonville, Fla., will *host* an annual Academic Super Bowl. My friend raised such a commotion that I fled the arena, promising never to sin in this regard again. But my heart felt no remorse. After all, the *OED* traces *host* as a transitive verb to 1485. The delicate ear may be offended mightily by *to guest* and *to author* and *to office*, but, "New York will host the Democratic convention" should not offend anyone at all.

however

Douglas Southall Freeman, famed biographer of Lee and Washington, was a man of many crotchets. He may not have regarded the misplacement of *however* as a fundamental matter, but he felt strongly about it. His rule was unequivocal: In the sense of "on the other hand," *however* must never be used to begin a sentence. He didn't have much use for *however* anywhere else, come to think of it.

Part of his objection was that a springboard *however* could be momentarily misunderstood. If the speeding eye misses a significant comma, comprehension flickers: "However, the Weeks case has been interpreted . . ." is wholly different from, "However the Weeks case has been interpreted . . ." Freeman's main objection, was that he found the on-the-other-hand *however* a limp handshake.

I
ignorami

In my Early Mencken period, somewhere around 1944, I figured that if the Sage of Baltimore could invent words, I could too. Mencken invented *booboisie* and *ecdysiast*. My addition to the language, or so I supposed, was a plural form of *ignoramus,* to wit, *ignorami*.

It seemed a creation of surpassing beauty. It had the low growling sound of dog-Latin. It was far more euphonious than *ignoramuses*. To my regret, the publisher's cousin thought I was talking about the Japanese art of folding paper. Others took *ignorami* to be African gazelles. It still struck me as a brand new coinage of enduring value.

Alas, some years later I learned that the venerable Fowler had mentioned *ignorami* casually in 1926 as if the plausible plural had been around for quite some time. This was a comedown, or a comeuppance, either one. Writers with no imagination may stick with *ignoramuses* if they please, but the word has the slurpy sound of hippopotami in a wallow.

ilk

At one time *ilk* had the innocent meaning of "the same kind," or "the same sort." It was then possible to speak of Twain, Ade, Bierce, "and others of their ilk," meaning other masters of comic writing.

Innocence has vanished, and *ilk* now carries an unmistakably pejorative connotation. This is a curled lip word, useful in expressing contempt. "Saddam Hussein, Colonel Qaddafi, and others of their ilk." The term is too melodramatic for everyday use, but it comes in handy now and then.

It came in handy early in 1992 for a contributor to The Wall Street Journal. Writing about the brief campaign of Patrick Buchanan for the Republican nomination, the writer noted that

Buchanan had the support of activist Howard Phillips and columnist Joe Sobran. "In 1988, conservatives of their ilk supported
such ill-fated candidates as Jack Kemp and Pat Robertson." Nice
little spin there.

impact

The editors of *Webster's Dictionary of English Usage* devote three
columns to *impact* and wind up limply with this conclusion: "You
need not use this verb if you find it unappealing." There's nice
bold, knockdown linguistic leadership for you.

American Heritage, in an extended note on usage, acknowledges
the low esteem in which *to impact* has been held. Only one writer
in twenty approves, "The children at the army base heavily impacted local schools." But the dictionary's editors predict that in
time, opposition to *impact* will go the way of opposition to *contact.*
Maybe so, but it's a dismal prospect to think that we will continue
to read, "The president's budget sharply impacted the bond market." The usage is slovenly. The ear flinches and the hair curls.

Mind you, nothing is wrong with *impact* as a transitive verb in
the sense of "to compress" or "to bind together firmly." Thus,
"the steam roller impacted the soil." But everything is wrong
with, "A course in folk art will favorably impact the curriculum."

The noun *impact* carries such a dramatic wallop that I would
reserve it for dramatic events—the impact of a bullet or a batter-
ing ram. For everyday purposes, *influence* or *effect* or *pressure* will
work quite well.

Nothing kind can be said of the adverbial form. A flier came in
the mail in 1983 for an Atlanta publication, *Executive Air Guide.* It
offered a coupon saying, "I would like more information on how
Executive Air Guide can, impactfully, help to reach the corporate
decision maker." Yecch!

impeach

Never write that "Congress threatened to impeach the President,"
or that, "Many Senators willingly would impeach the district

judge." Only the House of Representatives can impeach. The Senate tries the impeachment after the House has done its job.

implement

The battle over *to implement* began about 1806 and ended before it got off to a good start. It is both pointless and useless to complain about the usage now. The most respectable writers see no fault in *implementing* an agreement. It is just as clear as "to give practical effect to," and it's much shorter.

imply / infer

These distinctive and quite different verbs ought not to puzzle writers, but evidently they do. Every commentator on English usage deals at length with the matter. To *infer* is to deduce; to *imply* is to insinuate. In ninety-nine cases out of one hundred, that is all there is to it.

Some years ago I wrote a column about the surgeon-general's report defining a relationship between smoking and cancer. I said the relationship had been inferred from statistics. An apoplectic reader inquired rhetorically, "How much did the tobacco companies pay you for that column?" Here he implied that I had been bribed; I inferred that he held me in low esteem. He insinuated, and from that snide insinuation I drew an inference. It was a sound inference if I ever drew one.

Rare instances come along in which this rule will not work. Bernstein provides an example. On the morning after a bibulous night before, husband puts ice pack on brow, wife comments on the therapy, and husband asks: "Are you inferring that I have this headache because I drank too much?" She could be either deducing or insinuating. It probably would depend on the tone of her voice.

important(ly)

The writer who is dead set on beginning a sentence with either *more important* or *more importantly* should go with *more important.*

One might do better with *of greater importance,* or some such phrase, but there is something about *more importantly* that is puffed up, pompous, and pretentious. It has the look of a pouter pigeon.

The Washington Times did a feature on an elderly golfer who played a respectable eighteen holes. The headline read, "A 78, but more importantly he played." One is minded to ask, "He played importantly?" A public opinion poll some years ago found substantial support for the Palestinians, but "more importantly" found the Palestine Liberation Organization still wedded to violence. A bulletin of Southern Oregon State College promoted a course in changing lifestyles "that will make you healthier, both now and even more importantly, in the future." Aaargh!

incredible / incredulous

In the summer of 1985, United Press International carried a story on the Wimbledon tennis tournament. The story spoke of Boris Becker's "incredulous feat" of winning the title at age 17. The same blooper turned up in the Baltimore News-American. It was "incredulous," wrote the sports editor, that Oakland and Baltimore should be playing in the championship match of the U.S. Football League. In Lake Forest, Ill., a poll of public opinion found most respondents were very satisfied with living there. "The numbers are incredulous," said the city manager, which was not what he meant at all.

The word they wanted was *incredible.* To be *incredulous* is to be skeptical, unbelieving. The adjective connotes a state of mind in which one is unwilling to accept something that purports to be palpably true. News of Becker's victory left some tennis fans *incredulous;* we couldn't believe it. But the victory itself was, in an exaggerated sense, *incredible*—fantastic, miraculous, stunning, extraordinary.

innumerable

Some years ago the Chicago Sun-Times called attention in its *Book Week* to a venerable librarian who had won "innumerable honorary doctorates and degrees." A reader objected that *innumerable* means incapable of being numbered. Would it have been better to speak of "numerous" degrees?

Strictly speaking, yes. In the sense of "a very great many," *innumerable, countless,* and *numberless* all mean the same thing. In Psalm 104:25 we read of the "great and wide sea, wherein are creeping things innumerable, both small and great beasts." Milton in *Il Penserosa* spoke of things "as thick and numberless as the gay motes that people the sunbeams."

The trouble is that neither *innumerable* nor *numberless* works with the elderly librarian. He might have racked up thirty-five or forty Chinese degrees, as Westbrook Pegler used to call them, but surely these honorifics were capable of being counted. Yet in the context of an admiring paragraph, *numerous* somehow smacks of denigration. It is as if we were indifferent to the degrees: They are not worth counting. If a reporter couldn't find out exactly how many degrees the old boy had won (twenty-two), or roughly how many (more than a score), the reporter could fall back on the gushy *countless.* In lapidary writing, as Dr. Johnson once observed, we are not upon our oaths.

insightful

Bah! Put it away with *meaningful.* They deserve each other.

intents and purposes (all)

You can be certain, without looking into the matter deeply, that *intents and purposes* is a phrase devised by lawyers. These were lawyers who examine every jot and tittle. The inflated phrase echoes the old question of a witness, "What is his reputation for truth and veracity?" If there is a significant difference between intents and purposes, it escapes me. It both escapes and eludes me. It escapes, eludes, *and* evades me. Each and every time I see *to all intents and purposes,* I am minded to search every nook and cranny for a less redundant phrase.

interface

In its place, which is the world of the computer, *interface* has a precise meaning. *Webster's Ninth New Collegiate* defines it as "the place at which independent systems meet and act on or communicate with each other." If we think of an interface as a common boundary, in the nature of a property line, the meaning becomes clear. Hardware and software interface. In this technical sense the verb is not easily replaced.

But the *Ninth* goes on to say "broadly," and when a lexicographer says "broadly," precision flies out the window. Broadly, we get "the high school–college interface." Thus corrupted, *interface* becomes a turkey word, like *paradigm* and *parameter,* much loved by pompous folks who want to wiggle their wattles, spread their tails and strut their stuff.

irregardless

Take my word for it: There is no such word. Yes, it is in the dictionaries, but *there is no such word.*

iron, wrought

Writers should keep in mind that many architectural elements that are described as *wrought iron* aren't. They are more likely cast iron. For the record, wrought iron is "a commercial form of iron that is tough, malleable, and relatively soft." Cast iron is "a commercial alloy of iron, carbon, and silicon that is cast in a mold and is hard, brittle, nonmalleable, and incapable of being hammer-welded."

ironic

A great many things that are said to be *ironic* are not ironic at all. They may be paradoxical, or incongruous, or inconsistent, but that is not what *irony* means. We must have a situation in which reality contrasts sharply with expectations.

It was ironic that President George Bush should have been defeated by the very "no new taxes" pledge that elected him. It is ironic (or ironical) that the government supports the tobacco farmer even as it condemns cigarettes. There was a certain irony in the career of Justice Clarence Thomas, who opposed the very programs of affirmative action from which he benefited.

Comments that are ironic are not far removed from comments that are sardonic. Both convey a sense of private laughter (or public scorn) at the inconsistencies of humankind. *Ironic* is too fine a word to waste on things that aren't.

J-K-L
jail / prison

Jails and prisons are equally to be avoided, but they are different institutions. A jail is a local structure, used for confinement of misdemeanants, felons found guilty of relatively minor offenses, and persons who have been arraigned and are awaiting trial. Sentences of less than one year ordinarily are served in jails. A prison (or penitentiary) is a state or federal institution, used for incarceration of persons who are sentenced to longer terms for more serious crimes.

The nomenclature is impressive. One who goes to jail may be sent to a *jug, can, pokey, clink, hoosegow, joint, lockup, coop, cooler, cage, calaboose, tank,* or *county hotel.* On the other hand, if one winds up in a *slam, slammer, stir, pen, big cage, big house, big joint, icebox, maxi, bastille, college, statesville,* or *up the river,* one has been sent to prison. Esther and Albert Lewin, editors of *The Thesaurus of Slang,* may now take a bow.

jerry-built / jury-rigged

A numismatic columnist for the Columbus (Ohio) Dispatch recalled a fire in the San Francisco Mint in 1906. The mint, he said, had a "jerry-rigged electrical system." No, sir.

A clear distinction separates *jury-rigged* from the unrelated adjective *jerry-built.* On a ship, something that is jury-rigged is a temporary contrivance, intended to serve until a proper replacement can be made. A structure that is jerry-built is a structure that has been put together with inferior materials and incompetent workmanship. It is a house built to sell but not to last.

Some etymologists speculate that *jerry-built* stems from the biblical Jericho, whose walls came tumbling down after the seven priests with their seven horns set up such an infernal racket for seven days. It seems unlikely. The scornful adjective dates from 1869.

jettison

The point to remember here is that *jettison* has a precise meaning at sea—a meaning that ought to be preserved in metaphorical or figurative phrases. To jettison something is to throw it overboard. Crewmen will jettison cargo in an emergency in order to lighten a ship or to stabilize it. The object is to save the ship. That which is jettisoned is jetsam.

A political analogy developed in the presidential campaign of 1972, when Democrat George McGovern felt he had to jettison his vice-presidential choice, Tom Eagleton. It had transpired that Eagleton long before had been treated for mental illness. McGovern thought that by throwing Eagleton to the sharks he would improve his own chances. Nothing could have improved McGovern's chances, and it was a sad thing to do to a fine man.

judgment

Webster's and *American Heritage* say it is acceptable to spell *judgment* as *judgement*. It isn't. *Random House* has it right. American spelling calls for *judgment* only. Let the British spell it their way.

kids

It may be permissible to *speak* of children as "kids," and in certain informal pieces it may be permissible to *write* of children as "kids," but the usage is clumsy, offensive, unappealing and generally inept. Use *children*.

Through their first year males and females alike are *infants*. At two they are *toddlers*. For a considerable period thereafter they are, redundantly, *little girls* and *little boys*. Girls are *girls* through the age of fourteen. At fifteen they become *young women*, a denomination they maintain to age twenty-five or thereabouts, after which they should be described in a second reference as *women*. Male children are *boys* through age fifteen. They qualify as *young men* through age nineteen, after which they may be identified as *men*.

kind / sort / type

In August of 1988 I raised a question that has puzzled me: What is the difference, if any, between *kind*, *type*, and *sort*? For my own part, I would write that Lee Iacocca is the *kind* of man who could sell anything; national party platforms are the *types* of baloney we should expect in election years; a department store sells all *sorts* of merchandise. But why would I make these choices? I don't know.

To pose this kind of question to writers is to throw a worm toward a hungry bass. Letters rolled in, among them a letter from lexicographer Laurence Urdang. He regards the words as "virtually interchangeable in most contexts." Most writers, he speculates, would choose, "He's not my kind of person" over, "He's not my type of person" or "He's not my sort of person," but it's a close call. Urdang added a couple of paragraphs that should be observed by every serious writer:

> *Kind* carries with it the 'contamination' from the other *kind*, meaning benevolent, which, I cannot help feeling, gives it a subliminal friendliness lacking in *sort* and *type*. Then, too, *sort* and *type* also appear as verbs in somewhat sterile surroundings.

> As I needn't tell you, these nuances are felt by some but not by others, and the careful choice among them would fall on deaf ears in most cases. Is *type* considered more learned because it looks more foreign? All these (and other matters, like your feeling about *type* if you are a compositor) have

some effect on word choice and connotation, a vastly complex subject.

kinds

William and Mary Morris put a question to their Harper's panel on usage: Would you sanction, *These kind of things are*? Members of the panel voted 87–13 against the construction. The wonder is that they didn't vote 100 percent against the construction. There is no way properly to combine the plural *these* with the singular *kind*. It's either, *This kind of thing is,* or, *These kinds of things are,* and there's an end to it.

The editors of *Webster's Dictionary of English Usage* firmly disagree. They regard the matter as "much more complex" than I think it is, and they carry on for four columns intended to mushify my conviction. They quote a long roster of eminent writers who fell into "those kind of objections" (Sir Philip Sidney, 1595) and "these sort of people" (Charles Dickens, 1843). They cite Shakespeare, Milton, and Jane Austen. They cite Swift, Pope, and Daniel Defoe.

Pfui! Nobody's perfect. Stick with *this kind* or *these kinds,* and you will sleep better at night.

knots

Unless you are well prepared to fend off an assault by every sailor who ever went to sea, do not write, please, that the frigate proceeded at *25 knots per hour.* Avast! Belay it! A nautical knot is a unit of speed equal to one nautical mile an hour. A nautical mile is 6,080.2 feet, eight hundred feet longer than an ordinary mile. To say that the frigate was proceeding at 25 knots per hour is to say that the vessel was proceeding at 25 knots per hour per hour.

kudos

In 1991 The New York Times reviewed James Reston's charming autobiography, *Deadline.* During his long career, Scotty Reston "interviewed more big shots and won more kudos from his fellows than just about anybody else in the business."

Well, pfui! And the *pfui* is directed not at Reston, who earned every honor bestowed upon him, but at *kudos*. Any writer who will treat awards as kudos is a writer who will treat umpires as arbiters. The trouble is that *kudos* is a pretentious word, smacking of house organs and high school journalism, and it ought to be retired altogether. If you must—absolutely must—use *kudos,* remember that the noun is singular. There is no such thing as one *kudo.*

lady

Except when putting a sign on a restroom or addressing an audience, *ladies* and *lady* should now be retired. The feminist movement (whatever that is) has done these ancient honorifics in. A reader in La Grande, Ore., fumed at the usage:

"The term *lady* has become mildly (or more) offensive to some of us. Though it used to be used or meant as a term of respect, I believe it is now appropriate only in the case of Lady and Lord Whittemore, or used as an address, 'Ladies and Gentlemen.' The use of *lady* where *woman* can be substituted is risking the wrath of many a feminist. Why? I suppose it remotely connotes respectability (or lack of promiscuity), and the feminist viewpoint would be, 'It is none of your damned business whether she is a lady or not a lady.'"

An older generation of writers will yield with reluctance and regret. Surely there is a useful distinction between *ladylike* and *womanly.* More than a slight nuance distinguishes the *saleslady* from the *saleswoman,* though both of these terms have become politically incorrect. In parliamentary speech, the custom has been to refer to the "gentlewoman from Colorado," or wherever, but one hears murmurs of discontent. Eventually we will refer simply to the "member from Colorado." The little grace notes get drowned out, one by one.

late, the

At what point does a recently deceased senator get to be "the late senator"? This is a judgment call. I submit, with no authority to support me, that twenty years is a reasonable period of lateness. In 1995 we might speak of "the late Professor Meritus," referring to a gentleman who died in 1975 or thereafter. By 1996 he would be plain old Professor Meritus.

A more familiar problem with *late* arises from a confusion of time and tense. The Indianapolis Star carried an obituary on a young man who had died in a fire. The surviving members of his family were identified: "Mrs. D. said her stepson is survived by his mother, his late father, his brother . . ." In Danville, Ill., "Mr. and Mrs. Gerald K. and the late Gwendolyn K. announced the engagement of their daughter . . ." In 1965 newspapers reported that "the late Lyndon Johnson signed the Voting Rights Act of 1965." A Dartmouth student turned in a term paper on ideological novelists: "In 1957 the late Ayn Rand wrote *Atlas Shrugged*."

Well, the Indiana youth's "late father" couldn't have been a survivor; the late Gwendolyn K. could not have announced an engagement. The thought of Ayn Rand and LBJ arising from their graves, pen in hand, gives one pause.

lay / lie

No verbs in the English language are as constantly confused as *lay* and *lie*. Every book about usage will give you a long disquisition on the subject.

The rule that will work in almost every instance is clear: *lay* takes an object; *lie* never does. Wilson Follett had another workable rule: What man does with his body is *lie, lay, lain*. What man does with objects is *lay, laid, laying*.

Thus hens, cartoonists, and comedians lay eggs. Masons lay bricks. A judge lays down the law. Governments lay taxes. The youngest daughter lays the table. By contrast, a patient lies in bed; an assassin lies in wait; the players were lying about the stage during the rehearsal.

Note: Ships lie at anchor. In the present tense, B'rer Rabbit, he lay low. An open book lays flat. In the past tense, the president's body laid in state. In the House and Senate, motions are made to lay a bill on the table.

A gentleman in Glendale Heights, Ill., sent me an old story. A mother and father were doing the supper dishes one crisp October evening when ma said to pa, "It's weather like this makes me think of our two daughters layin' up there in the cemetery."

"Yeah," says pa, "sometimes I almost wish they were daid."

Beware of the demonstrators, male and female, who reportedly were laying in the street. Let us surmise that they were merely lying in the street.

learning experience

Is there *any* experience that is not in some sense a *learning* experience? It seems unlikely. Let us scrap the banal phrase, and if an adjective is required, let us send out for useful experience, profitable experience, unpleasant experience, or a worthwhile, interesting, truly valuable experience.

legendary

There was a time, perhaps a legendary time, when *legend* and *legendary* had lovely meanings. Then we reserved them for the fictitious, the fabled, the unverifiable: the legendary deeds of King Arthur, the legend of Paul Bunyan.

No more. An orchard in Oregon wants us to "savor the legend" of its fabulous pears. A hotel in Singapore urges us to visit this "legendary island nation." At Caesar's in Atlantic City, Dame Joan Sutherland and Luciano Pavarotti appear as "two of the legendary voices of our time." RCA records advertises its "legendary artists." A tennis magazine recalls "Fred Perry the legend." A tool company says its locking pliers "live up to their legend." The New York Times, whose writers are devoted to *legendary*, describes the political spin doctor Frank Mankiewicz as a man with a "legendary reputation." George McGovern's reputation for ease with the media is legendary. In the Times, the very subways are "legendary as an underground maze of hostility and suspicion."

Enough! With the possible exception of the plug for Singapore, all these examples are examples of how the words ought

not to be used. Before we waste *a legend in her own time* on someone who is not now, and never truly will be a legend, let us turn
down the volume. The words are too fragile to bear the weight of
Oregon pears and locking pliers.

lend / loan

This battle is lost. Forget about it. Careful writers will hang on for
another generation, saying that banks *lend* money rather than
(ugh!) *loan* money, but no one will abide by their fussy example.
As a transitive verb, *loan* has been around since the time of Henry
VIII. A few years back the Knoxville News-Sentinel reported that
Knoxville "probably will lose any hope of recouping the $1 mil-
lion it loaned to the developers of the Sunsphere." Come now!
The city *lent* the money. If the city fathers never got it back, they
deserved it for *loaning* the money in the first place.

less / fewer

In theory, the rule is simple: Use *fewer* for things that can be counted;
use *less* for everything else. Thus, when we move from a large
house to a small apartment we have less space and fewer rooms.
Busy executives have less time for leisure, fewer hours for golf; less
cream pie, fewer calories; less reading, fewer books. And so on.

Trouble is, the rule collapses under the slightest strain. I once
wrote that Addison's little essays ran to 1,500 words "or less."
Readers jumped on the sentence, crying that I should have written, "1,500 words or fewer." I saw the essay as a whole, not as a
string of countable words, thus "1,500 words *or less.*"

As Theodore Bernstein observed, you can get into trouble by
applying the grammar school rule mechanistically, as in, "Not
many of these buildings are fewer than thirty years old." A useful
guideline may be found in the difference between exact numbers
and round numbers. With exact numbers, *fewer* usually works:
"No fewer than twenty-seven persons applied for the conductor's
job." With round numbers, try *less:* "Letters to the editor should

be held to two hundred words or less." In constructions involving time, *less* is almost always preferable: "Coe was determined to run the mile in 3:48 or less."

like (conjunction)

Once upon a time men ate with their greasy fingers, spit on the floor, and wiped their noses with their sleeves. After a while their spouses and daughters decided this was bad manners. Thus came Kleenex and the fork, and civilization was on its way.

So it has been with the use of *like* as a conjunction, as in, "His face looked like he had slept in it." Shakespeare used *like* in this fashion. So did other respectable writers. But in the nineteenth century the conjunctive *like* fell into disfavor. Tennyson, for one, thought it bad usage. Victorian grammarians agreed. A few years ago, when the Harper's panel on usage pondered the matter, the condemnation was ferocious. Sydney Harris called it monstrous, Orville Prescott said it was vile, Herman Wouk regarded the usage as pure vulgate, and Willard Espy said it reminded him of a man who would go unshaven to a funeral. As a man of moderation, I have called it no more than a pestilential barbarism.

This is what the uproar is all about. A writer for the Las Vegas Review-Journal reported on the restoration of an antique railroad car: "Some of the interior and exterior didn't seem like it could be saved." When the work was completed, "the Blackhawk appears exactly like it did at the turn of the century." Aaargh! Yikes!

Why this passion? Why do some formulations grate upon our ears? It is because consensus develops in language just as consensus develops in manners. Don't spit on the floor, dear. And don't say that the mutton tastes good like roast mutton should. Say, *as* roast mutton should. The only response to this is, yes, ma'am.

like / such as

On an April day in 1989 I spent an irritated hour reading *Newsweek*. On page 23 my eye caught "neoconservatives *like* Irving

Kristol." On page 40 was a reference to "prominent Swiss *like* Justice Minister Elisabeth Kopp." The same page informed us that money that once went to Switzerland for secrecy "now will detour to less problematic havens *like* Liechtenstein."

On page 42, in an article about baseball, readers learned of franchises "in medium-size markets *like* Minnesota." Page 48 brought "baseball stars *like* Orel Hershiser." On page 62, "Superstar role models *like* Peter Martins and Rudolf Nureyev."

Then this crotchety reader got to page 72, and there—O frabjous day! Callooh! Callay!—I chortled in my joy, for there was an article by Maggie Malone on interior decorators. And there was a sentence about Mark Hampton, "whose clients range from old-money aristocrats to new money moguls *such as* Rupert Murdoch and Estee Lauder." Three cheers for Maggie Malone! She got it right! She got it right!

Newsweek's writers are notorious for bungling this construction. In the home computer industry, "the turmoil has resulted in huge losses for firms *like* Atari, Mattel and Texas Instruments." The Baltimore Orioles have their share of superstars, "most notably .300 hitters *like* shortstop Cal Ripken, Jr., and first baseman Eddie Murray."

Time magazine, I should add, regularly commits these same felonies. *Time* once spoke of a German pornographer who was about to start operations "in sun-and-fun states *like* California and Florida." *Time* has discussed "newspapers *like* the Chicago Sun-Times, Chicago Tribune, New York Post, and New York Daily News." But *Time* occasionally gets it right: "Sunbelt states *such as* Oklahoma and Texas."

The New York Times regularly gets it wrong. Artist Alexis Smith made a name for herself by scrounging bits of flotsam and mixing the pieces "with bits of text borrowed from writers *like* Raymond Chandler and Jack Kerouac." As transitional relationships developed with the collapse of the Soviet Union in 1991, the White House began trying "to influence the relationship between officials *like* President Leonid M. Kravchuk of Ukraine and President Boris N. Yeltsin of Russia." No! I cry again, no! Yet once more, no!

This particular crotchet is dear to my heart. I cherish it fiercely. It was not dear to the hearts of Wilson Follett and Theodore Bernstein. Follett sniffed that only "purists" object to "a writer *like* Shakespeare" or "a leader *like* Lincoln." He found no more than a "shade of difference" and "an extremely slight distinction" between *like* and *such as.*" Bernstein was equally indifferent. "Some nitpickers object to saying, 'German composers *like* Beethoven,' arguing that no composers were like Beethoven and that we should say *such as.* The argument is specious because *like* does not necessarily mean identical."

Peachfuzz! These learned gentlemen are wrong, dead wrong. When *like* is used in direct comparisons, of course there is nothing wrong: "Jimmy Durante had a nose like Cyrano's." More to the point, when *like* is used in larger, indefinite generic application, you will hear no fuss from me: "In considering lives like Lincoln's, we are reminded that humble beginnings . . ." and so forth. The New York Times noted in 1991 that Gov. Mario Cuomo was having a difficult time with "interviewers like Sam Donaldson." Here the reference was not specifically to Donaldson, but to a whole pack of persistent fellows who share Donaldson's aggressive style.

Consider two parallel sentences; (1) *Writers like Follett and Bernstein dismiss the matter out of hand.* (2) *Such writers as Follett and Bernstein dismiss the matter out of hand.* To contend that the two sentences reflect only "an extremely slight distinction" is to exhibit an inability to read plain English. In the first sentence we are *not* told that Follett and Bernstein dismiss the matter out of hand; we are told only that other, unidentified writers, who in some fashion are *like* Follett and Bernstein, dismiss the matter out of hand.

Go back to some of the examples just quoted. *Time* intended to say that the German pornographer was considering outlets in California and Florida, but that was *not* what *Time* said. *Time* said the sleazebag was considering outlets in states *like* California and Florida. Baseball's owners were considering additional franchises in such middle-sized states as Minnesota. The reference to Irving Kristol was specifically to Kristol the individual, not to a generic class of neoconservatives whose views generally parallel those of Kristol.

It takes a measure of temerity to disagree with such eminent authorities as Follett and Bernstein. I am aware that the editors of *Webster's Dictionary of English Usage,* and others like them, regard my crotchet with disdain. Never mind. In this instance all of them are wrong.

literally

Citations of the misuse of *literally* are getting to be rare dodos. This may be a battle we word mavens have won, for a whole generation of journalists has grown up with the understanding, at last, that *literally* means *actually.*

A few citations of Horrid Examples still come along. A writer for Knight-Ridder Newspapers did a turn on the high interest rates charged on credit cards. He quoted a spokeswoman for Bankard Holders of America: "Our feeling is that banks are literally robbing consumers." An Associated Press writer informed us from Los Angeles that "Comedian Richard Belzer literally tore a page from the stage play, *The Man Who Came to Dinner.*" Another AP writer reported that following a welcoming ovation, comedienne Joan Rivers was "literally tongue-tied for the rest of the evening." It would have been a sight to see.

No, indeed. Miss Rivers was not actually tongue-tied. Belzer figuratively tore a page from the play, or metaphorically tore a page, but if he had *literally* torn a page he would have a mangled script to go by. The banks were not actually *robbing* their card holders; they were only charging usurious rates of interest.

Now and then *literally* may be used correctly. The high rollers who bought the weekly news magazine literally had *Time* on their hands. The player who recovers a fumble is literally on the ball. The best advice, as you consider inserting a *literally,* is to leave it out. It adds nothing of value and usually destroys the sentence it is intended to enhance.

livid

Medical examiners may be the last ones on earth to use *livid* as it should be used, meaning ashen, pallid, faintly blue, the color of a corpse. For a good many centuries, that was the only meaning *livid* had. Early in the 1900s, for no reason etymologists can fathom, the word came to mean "furious, enraged, overwhelmed with anger," and a new image developed of some fellow with a face like a Bloody Mary. The adjective has been badly bruised. Use it with care.

lot / lots

In casual speech and in informal writing, *lot* serves a useful purpose: a lot of food at the picnic, lots of fun at the ball. Without this handy collective we would be driven to a "great deal of food" and "plenty of fun," which carry different nuances with them. In more formal expression, *lot* and *lots* are girlish nouns that wisely should be avoided.

luxuriant / luxurious

This is the crotchet of a former schoolteacher in Columbus, Ohio, who feels keenly on the subject. Something that is *luxuriant,* she contends, is something abundant—a luxuriant lawn, a luxuriant beard. Something that is *luxurious* is rich, expensive, first-class—luxurious furnishings, a luxurious cruise. Makes sense to me.

M
Magna Carta / Magna Charta

Either spelling is permissible. I like *Magna Carta* for no particular reason I can think of, except that *Magna Charta* sounds like an Alabama girl playing golf at the club. "Miss Charta, ma'am, you goin' to use a fahv arn?"

Fine point: If you are writing grandly that, "We have inherited many of our guaranteed liberties from Magna Carta," leave out the *the.* If your reference is to something less cosmic, such as "the magna carta of bowling," the *the* is okay.

majority / plurality

There's a large difference. A *majority* is more than 50 percent. A *plurality* is less than 50 percent. In a given election in which 10,812 votes are cast, Edwards gets 4,118, Duke gets 3,224, and Roemer gets 3,270, Edwards wins by a plurality.

Fine point: *majority* takes either a singular or a plural verb, depending on the sense of the sentence. In the runoff, Edwards' majority *was* 390,000. But, a majority of the voters *were* satisfied that Edwards was the better choice.

masterful / masterly

The editors of *Webster's Dictionary of English Usage* firmly assert that the two adjectives are interchangeable. A distinction, they say, is "entirely fictitious," and they scornfully describe the controversy as the invention of Fowler in 1926.

Well, hoity-toity! *Random House* provides a distinction that many writers find useful. *Masterful* carries a connotation of authority, of dominance; a *masterful* conductor is one who imposes his will imperially on an orchestra. Columnist Paul Greenberg had it right when he spoke of George Bush's "masterful command" of foreign affairs in 1991. The AP had it right in describing the masterful cross-examinations of defense attorney Roy Black in a rape trial.

By subtle contrast, a *masterly* performance is a highly skilled performance, the kind of performance we expect from masters.

American Heritage (Third Edition) pooh-poohs the matter. The use of *masterful* in the sense of *masterly*, say the editors, "has long been common in reputable writing and cannot be regarded as incorrect." Fiddlesticks! It's incorrect because I say it's incorrect. Off with their heads!

may / might

In the first instance, we are talking about degrees of doubt. In careful usage, *might* is more doubtful than *may*. The racetrack fan who says he *may* bet on Rosebud in the fifth at Belmont is tilting in that direction. If he says only that he *might* bet on Rosebud, he's cooling.

This nice distinction appeared in coverage of the 1991 hearings on Justice Clarence Thomas. At one point it was reported that Senator Howell Heflin "may be talked into voting to confirm." At that moment, it appeared possible that the Alabama senator could be brought around.

Then things changed. Now it was reported that Thomas's sponsors had given up on Heflin. Sources close to the Judiciary Committee said Thomas "might yet get Heflin's support," but they thought it unlikely.

A different confusion arises in other contexts. "He may have hurt himself" carries one meaning. "He might have hurt himself" carries another. In this construction, *may* connotes uncertainty; we do not yet know what happened. If the fellow "might have hurt himself," the incident has passed; he *might* have suffered harm, but he escaped intact.

Medal of Honor

Don't call the award the *Congressional* Medal of Honor. The most respected of all recognitions of valor is awarded by Congress, but it's the *Medal of Honor,* plain and unadorned.

Mirandize

The Supreme Court's 5–4 opinion in *Miranda* v. *Arizona* led to a piece of jargon that ought to be handcuffed and led away. When police read a suspect his "Miranda rights," they are advising him of the whole panoply of defensive tactics fabricated by Chief Justice Earl Warren in 1966. To say the suspect has thus been *Mirandized* is to commit linguistic mayhem. Bailiff! Lock up the bastard verb and throw the key away.

momentarily

Contrary to idle opinion, *momentarily* does not mean *in* a moment. It means *for* a moment. The word for *in* a moment is *presently.* It's

not a great distinction, but it's a small distinction, and we ought
to treat small distinctions with kindness.

When we write that, "The roar of the crowd momentarily sub-
sided," we have described a familiar phenomenon precisely.
Every sailor knows that a breeze may slacken momentarily. Even
a senator in full oratorical flight may pause for a sip of water. He
thus pauses momentarily. The word is a good word. We should
use it politely.

moot

Treat this tricker with care. In a law school or in a formal debate,
an issue that is *moot* is an issue susceptible to argument. In an
appellate court, an issue that is *moot* is an issue that has been
resolved: It is no longer subject to argument. Something that
once was moot may lose its mootness. By extension, we may hy-
pothesize a lissome lass who cannot decide whether to bestow her
favor on John or George. The question is moot. She marries
John. The question is moot. All clear?

more than one

When we speak of *more than one*, we mean at least two. Right? And
two of anything is plural. Right? Wrong. In ninety-nine out of one
hundred constructions, the idiomatic *more than one* takes a singular verb. "More than one pitcher has won his own game with a
homer." "Chefs agree that more than one sauce is acceptable on
sole." The exceptions arise when the connotation of plurality is
unavoidable: "More than one of the American League's pitchers
have opposed the designated hitter rule." That sentence is a
terrible sentence and ought to be recast.

Moslem / Muslim

They're all the same, but *Muslim* is the preferred spelling.

Ms.

The problem with *Ms.* is a problem of manners, not of prose composition. Regrettably, in my own view, the honorific is here to stay. A significant number of women prefer to be addressed as Ms. Jane Doe. Probably an equally significant number of women detest the appellation, but the pro-*Ms.* faction is louder.

There is no satisfactory solution in the matter of a salutation in correspondence. Some well-mannered women are helpful: The signature will be (Miss) Jane Doe, or (Mrs. Richard D.) Doe, or rarely Ms. Jane Doe. Most women perversely give not a clue. It is part of their mystic charm. My own practice, when all else fails, is to begin, "Dear Jane Doe." This sounds a little familiar, but it would be presumptuous to begin, "Dear Jane," and it would be unthinkable to begin, "Dear Doe." Given the alternatives, "Dear Jane Doe" is the best one can do.

myself

Let me venture this guideline: Never use a reflexive pronoun if you can help it.

Many times, of course, reflexives cannot be avoided: "He hurt himself playing hockey." Reflexives certainly can be used for emphasis: "I myself told him to stay away from wingmen." As the object of a preposition, a reflexive pronoun works just fine: "He offered to give the sideboard to his wife and to keep the blanket chest for himself."

Far more often than not, we should take recourse in plain old homespun nominative and objective pronouns. See how so modest a guideline would resolve these horrid examples:

"The Barnes family and myself arrived at the same time."

"After the hurricane, the three of us—John, Waldo and myself—moved into a small apartment."

"The bartender was about to give a pint to McCoy and myself, but then the temperance ladies barged in."

In each instance the clumsy, self-conscious, pretentious *myself* may be easily avoided: The Barnes family and I . . . John, Waldo, and I . . . to give a pint to McCoy and me.

Some constructions, alas, are quicksand. The writer falls in and can't wiggle out. "I have prepared this memorandum for the board, the auditors, and myself." The sentence is hopelessly awkward, but it cannot be remedied by preparing a memorandum for me.

Nothing can be done with such sentences. They lie on the page like dead mackerel, gazing fixedly into the middle distance. It is as if *myself* were a dissociated third person—Roscoe P. Myself, third door on the left. Sometimes an answer can be found in preparing the memorandum "for my own benefit, and for the information of the board and the auditors," but this makes for a lame sentence. Unless you are very stuffy, you are not going to say the memorandum is for the board, the auditors, and the undersigned.

Probably the best advice is to groan, gaze at the ceiling, and write, "the board, the auditors, and myself." The sentence is clumsy, but other formulations are worse. Use your ear. If the reflexive sounds better—less stilted, less prissy than an ordinary pronoun—go ahead and use it. It's not a mortal sin.

N
naked / nude

The distinction between *naked* and *nude* is barely visible to the eye. With either adjective, we are talking about someone with no clothes on. The choice of *naked* or *nude* offers an opportunity to comment once more on the richness of nuance that contributes so much to the glory of English speech.

In this regard, standard dictionaries fail the writer. *Webster's Ninth New Collegiate* defines *naked* as "not covered by clothing; nude." It defines *nude* as "not covered by clothing or a drape." Other dictionaries are equally unhelpful. Yet we know that a fat man, emerging from his morning shower is not nude; he is naked.

By contrast, the French girls who sunbathe along the beach at Cannes are nude, not naked. (A sailor of my close acquaintance says the self-conscious English girls on the same beach appear to be naked, not nude.) Statues, paintings and photographs of the undraped human figure are nudes. A whore may be naked, but a mistress is nude. We are talking class.

One more note in passing. A body cannot reasonably be "partly nude" or "partially naked." The body is partly clothed.

nauseous

It is more trouble than it's worth to define and to defend this little troublemaker. Careful writers, writing careful paragraphs, will want to reserve *nauseous* in the sense of obnoxious, repulsive, or repellent. To say that someone is *nauseous* is to say something extremely unkind.

To say that someone is *nauseated* is to say that the poor person is about to emulate George Bush in Japan. A lady or a gentleman who is nauseated will soon recover, but one who is nauseous may stay that way forever.

near miss

Think about it: When we read that two airliners had a near miss over Savannah, what are we saying? If they nearly missed, did they collide? The illogical idiom now is firmly embedded in the language. It rests on a curiosity shelf with objects that "fall between the cracks," an interesting thought. We must bear with the idioms of English in the same way that we bear with the idiosyncrasies of our friends. Try *near collision* instead.

needless to say

This is one of the yawing phrases that take a sentence momentarily off course. Curmudgeons will gruffly inquire, "If a thing is needless to say, why say it?" Cut the line out, says the teacher of creative writing. Write tight! Strike every unnecessary word!

Not so fast. Good writers, like good composers, soon discover the need for grace notes and augmented chords. In polite discourse we defer to our readers. We are suggesting, in *needless to say,* that of course it is needless to say something so obvious to them. Others, however, may not be so well informed. For the benefit of these other, less informed, readers, we explain the matter at hand. Needless to say, we don't want to say *needless to say* too often.

Don't be too awed by my strictures, or anyone else's, on this business of unnecessary words. Sometimes we want to go at a paragraph with garden shears. Sometimes manicure scissors are better. Like everything else, it all depends.

neither / nor

Plenty of free advice is available to the effect that *neither* may be treated as either a singular or a plural pronoun. Pay no attention to this bad advice. Except in a very few constructions, *neither* is singular.

Thus: Neither of the senators *was* able to explain his vote . . . Neither of the spices *is* absolutely required . . . If neither brandy nor rum *is* available, use epsom salts. (I put that in just to see if you were paying attention.) . . . Neither of these economic indicators *is* particularly reliable. And so on.

Exceptions occur in this kind of construction: "Neither the priest nor the parishioners *have* much sense of public relations." But note: "Neither the parishioners nor the priest *has* much sense, etc." My thought is simply that it sounds better, and reads better, to say that neither Harper's nor Webster's is necessarily infallible.

none is / none are

Here is the rule that governs the number of *none*. Please keep it firmly in mind: *None* is singular, except when it is plural. That is all there is to it. Some editors and some schoolteachers are obsessed with the notion that *none* is always singular. They should let the notion go.

The choice of *none is* or *none are* depends entirely on the thought a writer means to convey. If the sense of the sentence is *not a single one,* you will want to employ a singular verb: "Four candidates are running for sheriff; none of them is qualified." Suppose the emphasis is on a broader picture. A school bus, let us say, has been involved in a minor traffic accident: *None of the children were hurt.*

These are judgment calls. Nine times out of ten a singular verb will work for me, but if your ear says *plural,* go with the verb that makes you happy.

not only but also

All city editors are nuts about *something.* Charles H. Hamilton, city editor of the Richmond News Leader in the 1940s, was nuts about *not only but also.* He insisted that one half of this pair could not live without the other.

He was absolutely right. A sentence that involves a *not only* will lose its equilibrium; it will topple like a chess piece without the balancing weight of *but also.* Please take care that your placement of the *but also* is precise. Suppose we are talking about a sudden craving for fruit. You will mess up if you write, "She not only wanted apples but also peaches." The proper alignment calls for, "She not only wanted apples but also craved peaches." Or, "She wanted not only apples but also peaches." Order is everything.

not so

This isn't my crotchet. This crotchet belongs to a gentleman in Seattle who once challenged me for writing that finger painting (or whatever) is "not *as* easy as it sounds." In such negative constructions, he contends, we should say, "not *so* easy as it sounds." None of my books on usage discusses this distinction, but I will buy it anyhow. I am as easy to please as a hungry dog, and not so stubborn as an ill-tempered mule. Okay, Mr. Huber?

not true that

Fifty years of covering courts have led me to a regrettable generalization: Lawyers are great talkers but lousy writers. They tend to get all tangled up in the red tape of syntax. The tendency manifests itself in questions of this nature: "Is it not true that you were in Chicago in April?" (The witness was in Houston in April.) The proper answer, clearly if confusedly, is "yes." The confusion can be compounded: "Is it not true that you were not in Chicago in April?" Again, the answer is "yes." Why can't lawyers ask, simply, "Is it true that?" Or directly to the point, "Were you in Chicago in April?"

a number, the number

The rule here is that *a number are* and *the number is.* Thus, "A number of cows are grazing in Rappahannock County," and, "The number of cows in Rappahannock County is steadily declining."

O
of (the superfluous)

English is a wonderfully generous language. Our vocabulary is crammed with so many words that we give them lavishly away. A favorite bauble is *of,* as in, "Susan has all of her books," and "The dish fell off of the table." Some collectors save only those stamps that come "off of nineteenth-century letters." A proper bank robber should instruct the frightened cashier simply to wait "five minutes inside the vault." A careless robber would say, "inside of the vault." No respectable bank should tolerate such an offender.

Most of the time, but not all the time, the *of* is superfluous and ought to be excised. The same advice goes for other little parasitic prepositions that feed on adjacent verbs. Let us saddle a horse and not saddle *up* a horse. In the Senate we should close debate, not close *off* debate. If one senator votes aye and another votes nay, their votes cancel in the tally; they should not cancel *out.*

Another familiar construction should similarly be trimmed. There is no point in painting "too gloomy of a picture" or bearing "too great of a burden." Nothing, however, is wrong with, "Mozart was a giant of a composer," or, "*Phantom* was enough of a hit to finance a dozen lesser productions." Don't be overly crotchety about supposedly redundant words. Sometimes a word that is technically superfluous may be needed for the swing of a sentence.

one (the ubiquitous)

A suggestion: Let us abolish the ubiquitous *one*. Who the devil is *one* anyhow? This is the *one* that poisons such constructions as, "If one leaves one's hat with the check girl, one will have to pay to get it back." Of course, if one does not leave one's hat with the check girl, one will have to put it under one's seat. Yuccch!

An equally offensive construction involves the indiscriminate *you*, as in, "If you leave your hat with the check girl, you will have to pay to get it back." Many a reader is likely to protest that he doesn't wear a hat. Why are you giving him this useless warning? The second-person form works when a writer is instructing, correcting, exhorting, or otherwise directly addressing the reader. Thus I urge you to recast every sentence in which you are tempted to hire the self-conscious, pretentious and prissy *one*.

one of the

One of the many English idioms that puzzle the student is *one of the*. Here I am thinking especially of *one of the only* or *one of the best*. Viewed in the cool light of reason, which is the worst of all lights in which to view an English idiom, it makes no sense to say that the Inn at Little Washington, Va., is "one of the finest restaurants in the nation." It would make more sense to say that the Inn is "among the very fine restaurants." A superlative is a superlative. How could there be more than one restaurant plausibly described as "the finest"?

The same futile objection may be taken to *one of the only*. How could Cecil Fielder be "one of the only sluggers" to hit better than .300 four seasons in a row? Or whatever. The hitter may be "one of the few," but it is baffling to understand how he could be "one of the only."

My feeling is that an adjective in the superlative degree is not to be taken at face value in *one of the richest*, or *one of the ten best-*

dressed women, or *one of the most talented golfers on the tour.* Technically, the "best" is superior to all others in its class, but the technicality disappears if we look upon "the best" as a class in itself. In that view, "one of the ten best" makes sense.

The best advice I can offer is to shake your head and get on with what you are writing. Or else recast the sentence.

only

No syntactical blunder is more annoying than an *only* in the wrong place; and no blunder is more easily resolved.

Let us begin by parsing a simple sentence: *Robert hit Peter in the nose.* Now let us see how the sentence is sharpened and clarified as we move *only* around:

Only Robert hit Peter in the nose. Billy may have hit Peter on the ear, and Roscoe may have hit Peter in the stummick, but *only Robert* hit Peter in the nose.

Robert only hit Peter in the nose. Robert did not bite him in the nose, or stab him in the nose, or otherwise abuse Peter's nose. He *only hit* him in the nose.

Robert hit only Peter in the nose. In this playground melee, Robert may have hit Joe on the arm and Oscar on the chest, but he hit *only Peter* in the nose.

Robert hit Peter only in the nose. He didn't hit him anywhere else.

Now, let us apply Lesson One to the following real-world sentences:

"Ethiopia's problems *only seem* to get worse." The meaning manifestly was that Ethiopia's problems *seem only* to get worse.

"The fourteen family members were *only living* in four rooms." They were *living in only four rooms.*

Some years ago Laurance Rockefeller prudently unloaded 550,000 shares of stock in Eastern Airlines. USA Today reported that "he only had 50,000 shares left." Nope. Rockefeller, poor feller, had *only 50,000 shares* remaining.

The *Journal* of the American Bar Association described certain policies of liability insurance. "These policies *only permit* recovery for claims made while the policy is in force." Better: "These policies permit recovery *only for claims* . . ."

Okay? Am I making sense? Run these through your computer: Goetz Only Indicted on Gun Charges . . . Parkersburg police only reported a few minor accidents . . . An Idaho potato only has 100 calories . . . A broker only makes money when you buy or sell securities . . . The new tax only applies to hotel rates over $100 . . . Digital computers only understand o and 1 . . . [In Oman] homes can only be painted in traditional, pastel colors.

There are times, of course, when the modifying *only* has to go where euphony, cadence, or common sense would put it. *The Lord only knows* is better than *Only the Lord knows*. I could voice a cry of despair: *If writers would put words only where they belong!*, but a better cry would go, *If writers would only put words where they belong!* Amen to that.

opine

Some words, like some people, have a way of arousing instant hostility. They may have done nothing to offend—they may just lie innocently on a page, minding their own business—but they manage to be offensive all the same. A prime example is the puffed up verb, *to opine*. It oozes out of an editorial writer's lexicon along with *to behoove*, as in, "It behooves us to do something at once about the pending crisis." If a writer is minded to *opine,* let the writer opine without saying so.

opt

Why are people sore at *opt*? It means simply to choose, or to elect, to take a certain course of action. I rise to *opt*'s defense because two readers, a continent apart, wrote snarling letters to me after I said Mario Cuomo had "opted out" of the presidential race in 1992. I could have said the governor chose not to run, but *opt* seemed to me brisker. It's an okay verb.

orientate

The Court of Peeves, Crotchets & Irks has had to look at *orientate* several times in recent years on petitions to reconsider, but the court will not be budged. The verb is no more than a blowfish stepson of *to orient*. Why be puffed up? "It will take a week or so for the students to orient themselves to the campus." That says it concisely and offends no one.

over / more than

There ought to be no debate over this minor issue. The principal, primary meaning of *over* is to be above something else. The mistletoe hangs over the door. The hood goes over one's head. The spread goes over the bed. When *over* is used in the sense of *more than*, the reader must experience one of those milliseconds of confusion that interrupt comprehension.

Thus it is better to write that "Ruth and John have been friends for more than forty years" than to say they have been friends "for over forty years." Some tiny fraction of clarity is gained by, "More than four hundred fans turned out to welcome Willie home." True, *over* has been used in the sense of *more than* since the fourteenth century, which lends the practice the respectability that goes with age, but you won't lose anything by opting for *more than*, and you might even get ahead on points.

P

pair

In a column about spring in the Blue Ridge Mountains, I once reported that "two pair of bluebirds have at last moved into residence." Several readers objected. They thought I should have written about two *pairs* of bluebirds.

Here is a rule that works most of the time: Use the singular *pair* if the pair is identified by number: Men's suits once came with "two pair of pants." A teenager might buy four pair of jeans. This guideline gets fuzzy. It offends the ear to write of Imelda Marcos' 942 pair of shoes; *pairs* conveys a better image of shoes all over the place.

The rule on a choice of verbs is clear. Use a singular verb, said Professor Bremner, "in a context of oneness," e.g., "A pair of scissors *is* indispensable to the writer." "A pair of sneakers *is* in the closet." Use the plural verb in a context of separateness: "A pair of skunks *have* invaded our basement." "A pair of sparrows *were* circling the feeder."

Caution: Be careful about "a pair of twins." If we write that Becky gave birth to a pair of twins, we are saying that Becky just had quadruplets.

paradigm

Some words, like some hemlines, come and go with the season. Such a word is *paradigm*. It had great currency in the sixties and again in the eighties, when almost anything could be termed a paradigm. *Webster's* cites one author who used *paradigm* "at least 22 different ways" in a work published in 1962.

The writer who is determined to use this word should use it in its original fifteenth-century meaning. It means an outstanding example or a typical pattern. That is all it means.

parenting

Oh, yuppie, yuppie, yuppie! Jonathan and Jennifer are *parenting* their daughter. They simply love to parent the child. Jennifer says parenting is much more fun than macramé. Don't you think everybody, just everybody, should be parenting too?

partly / partially

In choosing between *partially* and *partly*, be guided mainly by your ear. There is no inflexible rule. The trouble with the adverb *partially* is that it instantly evokes its first cousin, the adjective *partial*. *Partial* in turn evokes a more distant cousin, *partisan*. The principal meaning of *partial* has to do with bias, with favoring one thing or idea over another. With all these bells tinkling in the subconscious, we read that, "Ellen wrote a thank-you note to John with George's gift still partially in mind." What was dear Ellen thinking?

In 1991 Easton Press promoted a series of "the one hundred greatest books ever written." Readers were warned: "If you look closely at ads from other publishers, you will see that some editions are only partially covered with leather." I would have said, "partly covered with leather."

Roughly 8.7 times out of 10, *partly* will work better than *partially*. An alligator snoozes on a log that is partly (not partially) submerged. The victim's body was partly clothed. Her income was derived partly from dividends. At the Palm Beach Post, a music critic's ear should have prevented him from writing that an audience greeted a tribute to Irving Berlin "with a partial standing ovation," an interesting position.

My guess is that *partially* works better 1.3 times out of ten: "The contract terms were only partially agreeable to the buyer, but the sale went forward nonetheless." "Many of the recruits sent to the front had been only partially trained."

penultimate

In 1986 the Marriott hotel people put out a flier for a sumptuous new hotel. A sumptuous adjective, they felt, would add a touch of class, so they wrote: "The incredible Atlanta Marriott Marquis is now the *penultimate* business travel experience in Atlanta."

Well, golly gee, let us hope not. If a stay at the sumptuous Atlanta Marriott Marquis is one's penultimate experience, it is the next to last experience one is likely to have.

That is all *penultimate* means: next to the last. Somehow a notion took shallow root that *penultimate* is a four-dollar substitute for *quintessential*, which costs $5.98. Bury the notion! Forget the word! I was funning around once in my column by submitting half a dozen questions of usage to my readers. The answers, I said, would be found in my penultimate paragraph. When the column went on the wire, the answers were just where I said they were.

Then half a dozen copy editors around the country, seeking to shorten my pearly strands of wisdom, lopped off the last graf of the column. What had been penultimate was now ultimate. So it goes.

people / persons

If an observer can count them exactly, they're *persons*. If not, they're *people*. Thus, a hundred thousand people crowded the mall to hear the rock concert. Forty-seven persons were treated for heat prostration. The sensible reasoning behind this rule may be illustrated by imagining three people waiting for a bus. If two of them take a cab, who's left? One people.

perceive

Lexicographers continue to muddle around with this one. At Random House and American Heritage, editors stand by the old ways. *To perceive* is "to become aware of directly through the senses," that is, to see something as it really is. In the next breath *American Heritage* defines *perception* as the act of perceiving, i.e., to gain "insight, intuition, or knowledge by perceiving." In this fashion kittens chase their tails.

My impression is that *perceive* is now firmly established in the sense of forming an impression. Early in 1992 an industrialist was worrying in The New York Times about Americans who buy Japanese cars because they cling to the notion that Japanese cars are superior. The industrialist encouraged the buyers "to examine whether there is a real difference rather than a perceived difference." He had the current usage exactly right.

Voters have a *perception* of a candidate. They have no idea how the candidate *really is*. All they know is how they *perceive* the woman. There may be a tremendous difference.

personal

Objections are heard to, "the governor is a personal friend of mine," on the grounds of redundancy. What other kind of friend is there but a personal friend? Well, says I, there's such a thing as a business friend. Not all letters are personal letters; many letters are form letters.

The amplifying *personal* is a matter of emphasis. It is entirely in order, having canvassed the expert opinions of Fowler, Follett, Bremner, and Bernstein, for a writer to conclude by saying, "In my personal opinion they are all full of hot air." Most of the time the self-conscious *personal* is better left out. Reminder: The bastard *interpersonal* should be disinherited altogether.

pinch hitter

Inveterate baseball fans will watch the corruption of *pinch-hit* and *pinch hitter* with a sigh. The process has gone too far to be reversed. A pinch hitter has become no more than a mere substitute, with the result that we read without really wincing that Father Hannah pinch-hit for the ailing bishop at Sunday's confirmation.

In baseball parlance, a pinch hitter is a specialist. He is put into the lineup at a particular time to serve a particular purpose. The manager may want a bunter, or a long-ball hitter, or a guy who bats left-handed. We are not speaking of mundane events, such as substituting corned beef for lamb stew on the menu of the Greasy Spoon. This is deep strategy.

As a synonym for *substitute*, poor abused *pinch hitter* has become sadly worn. If all we mean is *substitute*, let us write *substitute* and get on with it.

pistol

A pistol, properly speaking, is what men used to duel with; the chamber is part of the barrel. An automatic also may be termed a pistol for the same reason, though the automatic relies upon the force of recoil to eject a spent cartridge and insert a new one. The duelist, if he survived a first exchange, had to rely upon his second to reload for him. A third handgun is the revolver; its chamber rotates with each shot.

pleaded / pled

The choice here depends mostly upon the rhythm of a sentence. If you need one syllable, go with *pled;* if you need two, go with *pleaded.* They mean the same thing. Because of a life spent covering courts, I prefer *pleaded.* It goes with *pleadings* and a *plea* of not guilty.

There is no such thing, incidentally, as a "plea of innocent." A plea is either guilty, not guilty, or in some instances nolo contendere. Newspaper lawyers are responsible for corrupting the nomenclature. They live in fear that the *not* will inadvertently be dropped from the reporter's story. As a consequence, an acquitted defendant invariably will be described in the press as having been found innocent. Bosh! The fellow has been found *not guilty,* and there's quite a significant difference.

plethora

The word came from the Greeks, and they may have it back. It means "excessive abundance," and is employed only by literary sophomores trying to impress a senior. Howard Cosell, a TV sportscaster of the 1980s, had great affection for the noun. He used it regularly, almost always in a context where it did not belong. It's a swell-headed word. Scrub it.

possession with gerund

This is what the argument is about. Early in 1992 the trustees of South Carolina State College dismissed President Albert E. Smith. Reported the Charleston Post and Courier: "The abrupt dismissal was the result of Smith not living up to a previous agreement to leave quietly." Should it have been, "the result of Smith's not living up"? Most of the time the apostrophe-*s* just looks better and sounds better.

Try this one: "I insist upon your answering the question." Or is it, "I insist upon you answering the question"? I like *your answering.* But look again. Is it better to write, "I tired of the child screaming at me." Or, "I tired of the child's screaming at me." I kind of like *the child screaming.*

For purposes of emphasis, the choice is easy. The fat woman is not likely to say, "I can't see *my* putting on a bikini." She is more likely to say, "I can't see *me* putting on a bikini!"

The editors of *Webster's Dictionary of English Usage* devote nearly three columns to this matter of a gerund's possessive, but they come up empty. Their uncomfortable conclusion: "Many writers use both forms of the construction. Clearly there are times when one or the other sounds more euphonious, is clearer, or otherwise suits the purpose better." Exactly so.

presently

Here is one way to avoid a quarrel with a finicky editor: Do not use *presently* in the sense of *at present,* e.g., "Brown formerly was attorney general but presently is serving in the House." Some editors get red in the face about such a usage. Soothe them. Use n-o-w instead.

pretty

This is one of E.B. White's leech words, the ones that "infest the pond of prose, sucking the blood of words." The others are *rather, very,* and *little.* Rarely, for reasons of style, or euphony, or real absence of conviction, these qualifiers may serve a useful purpose. Ordinarily they can be eliminated to significant advantage.

In his memoir of his service in government, William Bennett recalled a shift in jobs: "Unlike my post as Education Secretary (where I was given pretty wide latitude in performing my job), my effectiveness as drug czar depended to a large degree . . ." The *pretty* didn't add a thing.

preventive / preventative

Forget the mouth-filling *preventative.* It is used only by those writers who mistakenly believe that four syllables must always be 33.3 percent more impressive than three.

pristine

That fine old word, *pristine,* is going through midlife crisis. Emerging from a Latin root and a French branch, it appeared in England around 1530. For well over three centuries it retained its meaning of "early, ancient, original, pertaining to the earliest state." Then the corrupters went to work, and by the early 1900s *pristine* had come to mean "pure, virtuous, untouched, unspoiled." In their lyrical moments writers began to speak of pristine communities and pristine snow. Richard Cohen in The Washington Post extended *pristine* to a "pristine contract."

Jonathan Yardley, one of the nation's top book critics, keeps the old flame alive. He says that true bibliophiles have an obligation to keep rare books "in their pristine condition." Right on! Plenty of words are available to convey the idea of "undefiled." We ought to save *pristine* for paragraphs that deserve it.

prone / supine

Let us have no more nonsense about *prone* and *supine.* In a flabby moment, the editors of *Webster's Dictionary of English Usage* say that *prone* "quite often means merely flat or prostrate, and less frequently flat on one's back." What rubbish! It is *impossible* for a person who is prone to be flat on his back. The contortionist hasn't been born who could pull off the trick. One who is in a prone position is lying face down. One who is supine is lying on his spine.

A reader sent me an unattributed limerick that every writer and editor should commit to memory:

> There was a young miss named Malone,
> Who remarked with a bit of a moan:
> Sex is just fine,
> When you're lying supine.
> It's a pain in the tail when you're prone.

To be sure, *prone* has a more familiar meaning in the sense of "to be in favor of, to incline toward, to have a tendency toward," as in, "Amelia is prone to Twinkies and gumdrops." *Supine* has become a spin word, implying timidity or cowardice.

proximity, close

"Strictly speaking," says *American Heritage,* "the expression *close proximity* says nothing that is not said by *proximity* itself." Well, yes. No question about it. *Proximity* by standard definition means "very close, very near, next to, adjacent, adjoining." It surely would sound oxymoronic if something were in distant proximity.

All the same, at the risk of not speaking strictly, I would be inclined to apply the nape-of-the-neck rule to *proximity.* You know, and I know, where the nape is located; and you know, and I know, that *proximity* implies a relationship so close that the persons or objects may be actually touching. But not everyone is as smart as we are. Some people may not put *proximity* to work every day. Some may never have met the word at all. Give the reader a break! Close proximity.

pupil / student

If a writer needs a bright line to separate the *pupil* from the *student,* perhaps this will suffice: The sixth grade, or the twelfth year, marks the separation point. If children are in elementary school, call them pupils no matter how keenly they may resent it. In junior high school they become students, though you would never know it.

The bright line wavers when we get to musicians and dancers of the concert rank. For some reason embedded in tradition, conductor David Stahl was Bernstein's pupil. He studied under Bernstein but he was never Bernstein's student.

purposely / purposefully

There's a nice distinction here. To do something *purposely* is to do it not by accident, but by design. "The witness purposely lied" suggests that the witness told a falsehood and had a reason for telling it. The act was done *on purpose.* To do something *purposefully* is a little different. "Amelia strode purposefully toward the chairman" suggests that Amelia is about to give the chairman a punch in the eye. She has a specific goal, or purpose, in mind.

Q
quality

"Everybody talks about quality," said the Ford ad. "Ford people make it happen." Ah, me! Someone should have told the Ford copywriters that *quality* is a measure, like speed or growth. It is a manifestation of the sloppiness of our time that we have fallen into a kind of vacuous praise. "That's a quality performance." "The county has quality schools." "The Public Broadcasting channel offers quality programming." O tempora, O nonsense!

Quality comes in infinite gradations, running from *poor quality* to *top quality.* Without a qualifying adjective the word becomes meaningless. The same may be said of *nutrition,* as in, "Animals gain from nutrition." Well, sure.

quantum leap

Whether our quantums are leaping or jumping, or taking the low hurdles, we ought to treat a *quantum* in the same fashion recommended for *parameters.* Give the word back to the mathematicians, and don't even think of using it in a figurative sense. A *quantum jump* (or *leap*) is "an abrupt transition of a system described by quantum mechanics from one discrete state to another, as the fall of an electron to an orbit of lower energy" *(Random House).* It is also "the transition of an atomic or molecular system from one discrete energy level to another with concomitant absorption or emission of radiation having energy equal to the difference between the two levels" *(American Heritage).* Okay? *Now* will you stop talking about Bill Clinton's *quantum jump* on taxes?

quotes / quotations

The choice between *quote* and *quotation* is largely, but not altogether, a matter of taste and context. As a general rule, politicians, sports figures, corporate executives and labor leaders speak in *quotes*. Famous playwrights, great statesmen, and respected clergy speak rather in quotations. One would never excerpt a paragraph from Gibbon and call it a good quote. Thus we have *quotations* from Shakespeare and *quotes* from Joe Gibbs, retired coach of the Washington Redskins.

R

raise / rear

Purists may as well surrender on this one, as they have had to surrender on *lend/loan*. The rule used to be that we raise hogs (or chickens, corn, or cain), and we rear children. That some children are hogs is immaterial. If you go ahead and write about raising children, virtually no one will complain. Except me.

read, a good

One of the more captious complainants in the Court of Peeves, Crotchets & Irks complains of a *good read*, as in, "The works of Mark Twain are always a good read." The judgment: summary dismissal. Respectable writers have been writing about "good reads" since 1825. It's not a phrase one ordinarily would apply to a textbook on the uses of the subjunctive, but for informal purposes it works just fine.

reason because / reason why

Beware of these trickers. "The reason why *reason why* irritates me," said a gentleman in Seattle, "is that *reason why* is redundant. We ought to say, 'the reason this irritates me,' or, 'this is why the phrase annoys me,' but *reason why* merits a resounding *aaargh*!"

In certain constructions, the gentleman is quite right. Many times, perhaps most times, the *why* may be profitably omitted.

But there are times when the *why* has to be there, e.g., "I could give you several reasons why a high-cholesterol diet is unwise." Surely that is smoother than the bobtailed, "I could give you several reasons a high-cholesterol diet is unwise."

It is easier to denounce *the reason is because*, but here too one has to be careful. On the face of it we have a redundancy, and an awkward one at that. The notion of causality is implicit in this employment of *reason*. But as many commentators have noted, when several words separate *the reason* from the following *is because*, the sentence looks not so redundant after all: "The chief reason Denver lost the championship, wholly apart from the injuries that had riddled the team, not to mention the unfamiliar artificial turf, is because Buffalo had a better passing game."

Maybe, even in that contrived sentence, *that* would be smoother than *because*. The choice may be more a matter of euphony than redundancy. Try casting your sentence one way and then another. There's no bright line rule to guide us.

recur / reoccur

Some authorities maintain that *reoccur* is an abomination. Standard desk dictionaries do not even recognize its existence; the *Random House Unabridged* brushes off *reoccur* in a footnote, and *Webster's III* says only that it means to occur again, as any fool can plainly see.

My ear hears a useful distinction here. Single, isolated events may reoccur. A spasm of angina that occurred two years ago reoccurred last week. By contrast, something that is part of a predictable cycle or schedule is more likely to recur. Visits of Halley's comet, I submit, are recurring phenomena, not reoccurring ones.

remains to be seen

It would have been a great invention. My idea was to program the master computer at every newspaper in the land. The computer

would be connected to a system of overhead trolleys with a release mechanism over every writer's head. Whenever the writer
wrote a certain combination of four consecutive words, an alarm
bell would ring, red lights would flash, a stink bomb would go
off, and a bucket of slop would fall upon the writer's head.

The triggering four words, of course, are *remains to be seen.*

Of all the banalities of English composition, none is more
stupid, more portentous, and less profound than *remains to be
seen.* It should be self-evident that everything in this world remains to be seen. Will the sun rise tomorrow? It remains to be
seen. Will the United States lead the world in the twenty-first
century? It remains to be seen. Will the Cubs ever win a world
series? It may seem unlikely, but it remains to be seen.

I grumbled about this at great length in *The Writer's Art,* and
after delivering that tirade in 1984, I continued to collect especially odious specimens of *remains to be seen.* I clipped and filed
another two or three hundred and then gave up. The nation's
editorial writers, political pundits, and lesser oracles are wholly
unregenerate. They will *never* cease writing that things remain to
be seen.

My pessimism deepened in 1986, when Michael Kinsley of *The
New Republic* ran a computer search through *Time, Newsweek,* The
Washington Post, The New York Times, the Christian Science
Monitor, and other such pillars of stylistic elegance. He found
that since 1977, when the data base was established, the publications had declared that more than 2,500 events *remain to be seen.*
Evidently the abominable practice was growing worse, for 1,223
of the citations were from 1985 alone. I continue to believe that a
computer-triggered bucket of slop is an excellent idea.

replica

Every writer has his favorite crotchet, and *replica* is mine. At one
time, careful writers used the noun precisely. A replica was a
reproduction of a work of art (or whatever) produced by the
original creator. Accordingly, the three ships that were built in
Spain to mark the five-hundredth anniversary of Columbus's voy-

age could not possibly have been replicas, for the shipwrights who built the *Niña,* the *Pinta,* and the *Santa Maria* died five centuries ago. The ships of 1992 were reproductions.

Properly employed, *replica* serves a purpose not served by *copy, facsimile, model, likeness, duplicate,* or *reproduction.* Just as I sermonized in *The Writer's Art* about *remains to be seen,* so I poured out my heart for the preservation of poor old *replica.* The effort was in vain. The decline continues.

Since I wrote that eulogy in 1984, the Associated Press has reported on a campaign to raise $18 million to build a replica of Shakespeare's Globe Theatre. United Press International reports a $650,000 replica of a sixteenth-century sailing ship. During the bicentennial observance of the Constitution, one could buy a replica of the ship of the same name. A model maker advertised a replica of the Duesenberg. Yachtsmen could buy a Sterling silver replica of the America's cup. We have been able to buy replicas of a Greek vase dating from 470 B.C., an 1860 photographic studio, Frances Drake's *Golden Hind,* and the fabled trireme of ancient Athens.

Now and then *Smithsonian* magazine gets it right. So does the Charleston, S.C., Post and Courier. Nobody else ever gets it right. Grumble, grumble, grumble.

restaurateur

There's no *n* in it

reticent

A curious and altogether revolting disease has attacked *reticent.* For a good many centuries it meant "restrained or reserved in style." A reticent person was one "given to silence, disinclined to speak." The English, said Emerson, are by nature "slow and reticent."

The old meaning steadily deteriorates. More and more we find it used in the sense of *reluctant* or *hesitant,* or even *unwilling.* Some pop grammarians are not at all reticent about expressing their opinions. From Massachusetts in 1980: "Bluefish are extremely reticent to strike surface poppers." Retailers are reticent to place orders.

No plausible reason can be advanced for corrupting so innocent and so descriptive an adjective as *reticent*. If we want to say someone is reluctant to do something, let us say so. After all, *reluctant* has meant *reluctant* since the 1700s.

reverend

The general rule on *reverend* is that it is an adjective like *honorable* and should be employed in the same way. That is, we should not write about Reverend Jonson, and we should not refer to Jonson as *a reverend*. We should write about the Reverend William Jonson, and identify him as a minister or priest, or whatever. Certainly we would not speak of Honorable Strauss, but rather of the Honorable Robert Strauss. On a second reference we may call him Bob.

The general rule, like most general rules, is subject to exceptions. *Reverend* has been a noun since 1608. It is still a noun today, and several Protestant denominations, notably Baptist and Methodist, routinely speak of their "reverends." From 1859 the *OED Supplement* cities, "I heard a very good sermon from a reverend from Pittsburgh." In 1943, "That car, sir, that's the reverend's." A customary greeting is, "Good morning, reverend." Headline in The Denver Post (1991): "Reverend Advocates Learning as Filter."

It probably is possible to avoid embarrassment or offense by recourse to such clerical titles as *parson* or *minister* or *deacon*. If the Rev. Joan Jonson has her Ph.D., she becomes Dr. Jonson. Creep up carefully on these honorifics. It never hurts to ask ecclesiastical folk if they are *reverends* or *the reverends*, and be guided accordingly.

S
sank / sunk

I have a notion, which I am cultivating carefully, that *sunk* is the proper past tense for ships, and *sank* is the proper past tense for everything else. The Associated Press follows this rule. It reported efforts to salvage a Civil War ship "that sunk when it struck a Confederate mine in 1864." When a ship goes down with all on board, we say that it "sunk without a trace."

A drama critic, interviewing actress Meryl Streep, said that she "sank gracefully into the pillows of a white divan." When the Dow-Jones average drops precipitately, we say the market sank.

So far as I know, *drink* has but one form of the past tense: *drank*. Perversely, *slink* has but one form of the past tense: *slunk*. On the matter of *shrink*, I stand indifferent in the cause; either *shrank* or *shrunk* will do. As for *stink*, I prefer *stunk* to *stank* because *stunk* sounds smellier.

scenario

Will someone kindly make a motion that *scenario* be expelled from general employment? Thank you. Any discussion? The chair hearing none, the motion is adopted and expulsion is decreed. Henceforth *scenario* may be used only in the sense of a script or summary for a dramatic presentation.

Scotch

For inanimate objects, notably whisky, plaid, and pine trees, *Scotch* is correct. For other purposes, *Scottish* is better. Thus, Scottish customs, Scottish universities, Scottish ancestors.

senior citizen

There has to be a better appellation than *senior citizen*. There must be some name or phrase that does not smack so patently of efforts to be kind to the old folks and not hurt our tender feelings. Nothing comes to mind. Here is a void waiting to be filled.

To speak of us as *seniors* fails on a point of gender; women over the age of 70 are not permissibly *seniors*. Are we *elders*? The word evokes images of old geezers ogling the apocryphal Susanna. *Oldsters?* The word has the rumble seat sound of roadsters. To speak of *retirees* is not bad, provided the persons have in fact retired. Nominations are in order for a descriptive phrase that is neither condescending nor cutesy-wutesy.

sensual / sensuous

The magazine *Machine Design* carried a story early in 1992 about new models from General Motors. The headline read, "Sensuous sheet metal makes Buicks voluptuous." The author enlarged upon his theme:

"In case you are wondering why the newly styled General Motors cars activate your hormones, here is an explanation. They are deliberately designed to be sensuous."

Alas, the writer had it wrong. These Buicks weren't *sensuous.* They were *sensual.* This is the distinction. A sensual person is a person of voluptuous tastes, characterized by an exotic or erotic life style. Sensual pleasures are pleasures of the flesh. By contrast, a sensuous person is one with exceptional sensory gifts—someone who could read the Braille signals in an elevator, or detect a touch of basil in the sauce. Sensuous pleasures are pleasures of the senses.

The distinctions are useful to the writer who strives to preserve precise usages in every application. Buick's sheet metal, contoured so as to achieve a "svelte sideview undulation in the belt line with a slight hip over the rear wheel," may have been sensual to the reporter. After all, sensuality is mostly in the eye of the beholder.

sewage / sewerage

Sewage is the stuff. *Sewerage* is the system of pipes the stuff goes through.

On that homely subject, let us note with applause a program presented by the Highland Park (Ill.) Historical Society. This was a slide-lecture on "the gathering places for the effluent of the suburbs." In Omaha, Century Companies of America identified itself as "a nationally recognized leader in financial services for the effluent." Well, the effluent of the affluent is not distinguishable from the effluent of the impecunious. Sewage is sewage. There's a profound moral lesson in that humble thought.

sex

Caught your attention, eh? The issue here involves references to *sex* when we mean *gender*, and references to *gender* when we mean *sex*.

In contemporary usage the distinction gets blurred. The meaning of *gender gap* is perfectly clear. *Random House* defines it as "the difference between women and men in regard to social, political, economic or other attainments or attitudes." In political writing *gender* has a useful place. At the Democratic National Convention of 1988, Ann Richards of Texas made the keynote speech. *Time* magazine said she was "living proof that gender is a Bush, not a Dukakis, hang-up." If the sentence were recast to say that a candidate had a sex hang-up, a very different meaning would be conveyed.

The general rule was summed up succinctly by Robert C. Cumbow in the *University of Puget Sound Law Review* (Spring 1991): "Words have gender; people have sex." That says the whole thing. When one is asked on a questionnaire to check the box headed "sex," the only proper answer is, "often." The term *gender* ought generally to be reserved for its grammatical meaning. In the drafting of wills and statutes, for example, lawyers often insert a provision of gender-neutrality; the masculine pronoun shall be construed to include the feminine, and so forth. If *sex* is used indiscriminately to mean *gender*, we have corrupted *gender* and done nothing to improve the meaning of *sex*.

On the general subject: The Court of Peeves, Crotchets & Irks would be receptive to any printable alternatives to a statement that "the couple *had sex*." A temptation arises to say, "No, they didn't have sex, they had broccoli." To say they *engaged in coitus* is accurate but hoity-toity. Did they *copulate*? The verb has the sound of calisthenics. Did they *fornicate?* That's the word for single folk, but suppose one party is married. Do the lovers *adulterate?*

In their *Thesaurus of Slang,* Albert and Esther Lewin list 130 synonyms for the sexual act. Only a few of these are printable in family newspapers: *go to bed with, go the limit,* and *make like the birds and the bees.* The rest range from light slang to heavy vulgarity. For an interesting note on the etymology of the f-word, see the *American Heritage Dictionary* (Third Edition). The search for an acceptable verb—a verb that will precisely convey the meaning, without euphemism or offense—has been going on since the 1400s. Until something more useful comes along, we probably will have to stick with *they slept together,* which may be both accurate and misleading. After all, even the most romantic couple has to sleep at some time.

shall / will

Don't waste your worrying time on this old crotchet. It used to be the rule that we should use *shall* in the first person future tense, and use *will* to express the future in the second and third person. The old rule has gone the way of button-top shoes.

Exceptions: Use *shall* to express determination, as in "we shall overcome some day," or, "I shall not say another word about your mother's cooking." Use *shall* in legal drafting, viz., "Congress shall make no law respecting an establishment of religion . . ." And use *shall* in an invitational sense for social occasions: "Shall we join the others?"

shambles

At one time *shambles* had a nice, specific meaning. A shambles was a butcher's shop or a slaughterhouse. By extension the word came to embrace any scene of bloody carnage. This was fair enough, but then *shambles* began to fray at the edges. It finally unraveled to the point that it meant any old disarray: "Alina's room is a perfect shambles."

Today dear old *shambles* has reached retirement age. If it must be used, use it only in the plural (a single *shamble* is a kind of shuffling walk), and use it only for occasions of serious meaning. The bedroom of a teenaged granddaughter is not a shambles. It's a mess.

(*sic*)

This snotty little annoyance is a pet device of pedants who want to show how smart they are. Rarely—and I mean *rarely*—it may be used for the specific purpose of emphasizing a variant spelling or some other mistake in a text. The editor who keeps intruding with (*sic*) is an editor not to be admired, but rather to be scorned.

simply

Back in February 1989 a Berkeley law professor, Stephen R. Barnett, was reading thirty-three opinions (including dissents and concurrences) that had just been handed down in the U.S. Supreme Court. He began to itch. Then he began to wheeze and sniffle. Obviously he was suffering an allergic reaction of some kind. As the day wore on he isolated the problem. He was allergic to *simply*.

In a Wisconsin case, Chief Justice Rehnquist held that the state's failure to protect a battered child "simply does not constitute a violation of the Due Process Clause." An earlier case, he said, "simply has no application." In a Texas case involving the taxation of religious periodicals, Justice Brennan asserted that Justice Scalia was "simply mistaken" in his views. Scalia struck back: One argument used by Brennan was "simply not available." Justice Blackmun chimed in: Brennan's approach would resolve a First Amendment issue "simply by subordinating the Free Exercise value." Justice Blackmun, it appeared, was inordinately fond of *simply*. He used it eight times in one opinion.

Justice O'Connor wrote the court's majority opinion in what is known as the Croson case, involving a racial set-aside program in Richmond, Va. "There is simply no way of determining," she said. "It is quite simply impossible to evaluate . . . It is simply impossible to say . . ." Justice Marshall, dissenting, said the majority's position "simply blinks credibility." There was "simply no credible evidence" to support it. Justice Stevens, concurring, found something "simply not true."

Professor Barnett came to one conclusion that merits attention: The more complicated the case, the more the justices used *simply*. His findings ought not to steer us away from *simply* altogether, for the adverb certainly has a use in, "she dressed simply," or "he spoke simply." His piece in the *National Law Journal* made me self-conscious about writing, "the high court is simply wrong . . ." My suggestion is to treat the word in prose as we treat garlic in the kitchen. It simply is something to watch.

since / because

In the fall of 1983 the U.S. Senate briefly considered, and then abandoned, a resolution demanding the resignation of Interior Secretary James Watt. The resolution was abominably drafted, in part because the author failed to acknowledge the nice distinction between *since* and *because*.

The resolution declared that since Secretary Watt had spoken in an insensitive and insulting manner (this was about blacks, as I recollect), and since he had made statements impugning the patriotism of Americans with whom he disagreed, and since such remarks impede his ability to function effectively, and since Mr. Watt's policies have promoted a polarization in the nation, etc., etc., therefore the president should ask the rogue elephant to resign.

To be sure, all dictionaries tell us that *since*, as a conjunction, can mean "in view of the fact that" or "because." *Webster's Ninth Collegiate* offers an example: "Since it was raining she took an umbrella."

At least ninety-nine times out of one hundred, *because* is a better word than *since*. Our purpose as writers should be to make things as easy as possible for our readers. As a general proposition, we ought to eliminate those words or constructions that cause even momentary confusion, and *since* is one of those words.

Its first meaning—the meaning we instantly anticipate—has to do with the passing of time.

Suppose *Webster's* sentence began, "Since it began to rain . . ." What should we anticipate? Is this a *since-temporal* or a *since-causal*? The sentence could go either way: "Since it began to rain, two inches have fallen." Or, "Since it began to rain, we called off the picnic."

Or suppose we launch into a sentence that begins, "Since Father Gilhooley became a priest . . ." Because the first meaning of *since* is temporal, we expect the sentence to end, "he has baptized 1,237 infants." But, no. The sentence actually ends, "he could not marry." If the writer had used *because* instead of *since*, the millisecond hesitation could have been avoided.

The Watt resolution would have been clearer—not only clearer, but stronger, more forceful—if it had set forth that *because* Watt had spoken, and *because* Watt had impugned, and *because* such remarks have impeded, and so on. When we read *because*, we know exactly where we are going.

some (about)

The use of *some* in the sense of "approximately," "roughly," or "about" is a judgment call. Nothing is grossly amiss in writing that, "Some fifty years ago, oleomargarine was a novelty." Or, "By November, some two hundred thousand troops had assembled in Saudi Arabia." On the other hand, nothing much may be said in favor of the usage either. It seems to me that we get sturdier sentences by saying forthrightly, "Fifty years ago," etc., and "By November, two hundred thousand troops . . ." No one is expected to count years or troops. Round figures are always approximations.

When a precise number is known, the *some* becomes absurd. What have we gained by saying that a football game was played "before some 53,218 paying spectators"?

spin words

Now and then a writer will want to lay on an insult—not the usual kind of insult, in which one terms Hunter Thompson a sleazebag, but a different kind of insult. The idea is to say something snide without appearing to say something snide. For this purpose one needs a supply of *spin words.*

The supply constantly is put to work in the world of politics. When President Bush came back from a trip to Japan in 1992, an AP reporter gave him a little spin: The president returned, said the AP, "boasting of 'dramatic progress.'" On another occasion, just after the Los Angeles riot in 1992, The New York Times gave the president a spin job: He toured the riot area "in his armored limousine." There went the eight ball in the side pocket.

The word *politician* itself carries a curl of the lip. Liberals, i.e., *flaming liberals,* may usefully be identified as *left-wingers.* Less formally, a *left-winger* is a *pinko.* Libertarians are generally *far-out* and sometimes *flaky.* Socialists had a tough time for years. In certain quarters, to speak of *socialized medicine* was to rouse a crowd. The rubric had a spin that made it sound worse than *national health insurance.* In some situations it works to identify an antagonist as a *reactionary* or a *mossback.*

Conservatives generally come in two species: *moderate,* and *arch.* At one time, reporters for The Washington Post regularly described Sen. Jesse Helms of North Carolina as an "arch-conservative." I complained to the Post's executive editor, Ben Bradlee, saying that his reporters were editorializing the news. After all, I said, *arch* carries heavy overtones of extreme villainy. He agreed, and told his reporters to knock it off. They suspended for a while, but when Ben retired old *arch* soon reappeared.

During the heyday of Sen. Harry Byrd in Virginia, his friends spoke fondly of the "Byrd Organization." To the senator's enemies it was the "Byrd Machine." The Wall Street Journal, whose editorial writers are the very Minnesota Fats of spin, often comments on politics in California. There the important committees are controlled by "Speaker Willie Brown's henchmen."

Enough. In academia, such nouns as *pedant, pedagogue,* and *educationist* carry a nice spin. A faintly nasty impression may be left by describing a lover of grammar as a *purist.* A woman versifier may be neatly skewered by identifying her as a *poetess.* Do not neglect the litotes, a device that is the spin doctor's friend: "She is not an unpleasant person." The most effective spin words are those that are the least conspicuous. The trick is to be pejorative without saying anything really bad.

state of the art

Throughout the 1980s, a trendy *state of the art* flourished among ad writers of the brie and chardonnay set. It seems to have disappeared, and a good thing, too. The poor old horse was ridden half to death. Put it out to pasture with *dysfunctional, paradigm, epitome,* and *parameters.*

subjunctive

Professor Curme, in his masterwork on syntax, told us more about the subjunctive mood than many of us really want to know. He dwelled at length upon the *optative* subjunctive, which subsumes both the *volitive* subjunctive and the *subjunctive of modest wish.* He instructed us in the *potential* subjunctive in subordinate and adjective clauses. He scared many of his students half out of their wits.

As a consequence of such heavy breathing, many writers grew up in fear and loathing of the subjunctive. They said the hell with it, and who needs it anyhow? Let it go. For at least two hundred years language commentators have been remarking the death of the subjunctive mood. That is a long time to read obituaries for something that won't lie down.

My thought is that we often employ the subjunctive unthinkingly. We say "so be it," or "if need be," or "far be it from me to say one word about her face-lift." We are usually unaware that we have fallen into a subjunctive construction.

Neither do we worry about the moribund subjunctive in many applications involving such verbs as *recommend* or *suggest.* "It was recommended by the House committee that the bank be abolished." "Visitors to Battery Park suggested to the mayor that more trash receptacles be provided." "Ralph Nader demanded that the nomination be withdrawn."

The difficulty arises, so far as I am aware, only in constructions involving situations that are hypothetical or contrary to fact. People get into the most dreadful tizzies over "I wish I *were*" or "I wish I *was*." "I wish I were/was not so fat." "She answered as if she was/were in a dream world." My own preference almost always goes to the subjunctive *were* instead of the indicative *was*. If I were you, I would try it for sound. After all, this was Professor Curme's own feeling. Three thousand words after he began the discussion, he concluded: "In all these examples we may use the indicative rather than the subjunctive. The difference is one of style rather than meaning."

surrounded

Pay no attention to trimmers and temporizers who will beguile you from the paths of rectitude by telling you that a few respectable writers, such as Edna St. Vincent Millay, have written about something "surrounded on three sides." Miss Millay was a fine poet, but she didn't know beans about *surrounded*. It is physically impossible to be "surrounded on two sides," or "surrounded on three sides," or "partly surrounded." It is needless, except for purposes of emphasis, to say that something is "completely surrounded." When something is surrounded, by golly, it is *s-u-r-r-o-u-n-d-e-d*.

T
tandem

Toward the end of the 1980s Congress considered voting itself a pay raise. The raise in salary was to be accompanied by a corresponding end to honoraria. I wrote that the two propositions were in tandem, thinking *tandem* meant side by side, like the horses that pull a two-horse carriage. It does *not* mean side by side. It means one behind the other, like the pedalers on a bicycle built for two.

task force

In the mid-eighties a reverend gentleman in Salem, Ohio, wrote to complain about *task force*. His seniors had appointed a task force on hymnals, for heaven's sake, and another task force in charge of flowers for the altar. *Webster's* defines the term inadequately; *American Heritage* is not much better. *Random House* has it right: A task force is "a group of military units brought together under one command for a specific operation." The term dates from World War II. It ought not to be applied helter-skelter to studies, investigations, or inquiries that have nothing to do with force. Let us rather think of committees, study groups, and blue-ribbon panels, and let them go ad hocking on their way.

temperature / fever

Here is a clear distinction that careful writers will go to pains to preserve. Everybody, alive or dead, has a *temperature.* When we are sick we are likely to run a *fever.* Thus an ailing child may have a temperature of 102.6. She has four degrees of fever.

tenterhooks

"Eight years ago candidates for City Council sat on tender hooks for seven months," reported the Augusta (Ga.) Chronicle. What they sat on were tenterhooks, which are the sharp hooks used for fastening cloth that is to be dried or stretched. The indispensable Barnhart advises that the first usage of *tenterhooks*, in the sense of "painful suspense," occurred in a work by Smollett in 1748.

that / which

You will find everything you need to know about defining and nondefining clauses in almost any book on English usage. Let me skip the usual disquisition and offer only this oversimplified rule of thumb: If a phrase may be set off by commas, use *which.* If not, use *that.* Thus, "The atlas, which is on the bottom shelf, is a new one." But, "The atlas that is on the bottom shelf is a new one."

The distinction between *that* and *which* came home to me in 1984, when I was covering the Republican National Convention in Dallas. The platform committee was struggling with a plank on taxation. A subcommittee proposed to say that the party "opposes any attempt to increase taxes which would harm the recovery and reverse the trend . . ." The *which* in that version should have been a *that,* for the subcommittee was trying to write a defining clause.

Staunch conservatives, led by Rep. Tom Loeffler of Texas, wanted a stronger plank. They succeed in inserting a comma after the word "taxes." This committed the party to opposing "any attempt to increase taxes, which would harm the recovery," and so forth. Their thought was to modify "attempt" by a non-defining clause. Thus they were expressing the thought that *any* attempt to increase taxes would bar the recovery.

till / until

Many editors, for no good reason that comes to mind, have a grudge against *till.* The word has been in respectable use for five centuries, both as preposition and conjunction, and it is still in respectable use today.

The choice between *till* and *until* depends entirely upon the cadence of the sentence. If you need a single syllable, use *till;* if you want two, use *until.* "Jane waited till the blinds were closed" has a better rhythm than, "Jane waited until the blinds were closed." In the former, one hears the subliminal slippers of iambic feet.

times

Lawyers and educators, I have suggested, often are terrible writers. Let me spread the calumny: With few exceptions, writers are terrible mathematicians. The authors of science fiction may have a knack for calculation; business editors may be able to divine in a millisecond the percentage by which a stock has dropped from 15⅜ to 12½. The rest of us cannot even balance a checkbook.

It is thus extremely difficult to educate a writer in the proper use of *times.* People are crotchety about the misuse of *times.* They write reproachful letters. You are not likely to get in much trouble over *times more* or *times as much*. Let us suppose that the Department of Defense spends a billion dollars on canteens this year. Next year it will spend five billion, i.e., five times more or five times as much. Beware of going the other way, by saying that this year's budget for canteens is five times less. The best advice is to give precise figures and to let readers figure out the whole business for themselves.

toward / towards

This is not my crotchet, but it may be your crotchet. In my book there is no discernible difference between *toward* and *towards*. The British prefer *towards*. American usage calls for *toward*. Go fight about something else.

tragedy

It sounds cold-hearted to say so, but not every death is a *tragedy*. The word is too valuable to be frittered away on the tragedy of modern art or the tragedy of American cooking. A tragic event involves either the downfall of a great person or a calamity of massive proportions. Lear's madness was a tragedy. There are tragic overtones in the deaths of young people from cystic fibrosis, and in the birth of "crack babies." If an event arouses both pity and sorrow, it probably qualifies as a tragedy. Handle the word with care.

transpire

In 1984 I expressed uncertainty about the fate of *transpire*. Maybe the verb would survive in its pristine sense. Maybe not. The uncertainty has all but ended. It has to be said, a decade later, that poor old *transpire* didn't make it.

Thus one finds the Associated Press reporting portentously in 1992 that "much has transpired in the world since Bush in 1988 told audiences, 'read my lips—no new taxes.'" In current usage, tennis matches transpire, batting slumps transpire, and celebrity feuds transpire.

This is a sad business, for English offers an abundance of words by which we may say that something happened, or occurred, or took place. In its proper place, *transpire* should mean only that something has become public, or leaked out, or become known. "After the committee met, it transpired that the vote behind closed doors was 14–12." I wish today's linguistic trimmers had left it alone.

try and

People get seriously crotchety about this one. The complaint lies against the use of *try and* when we should use *try to*. I once termed the use of *try and* a barbarism and condemned it out of hand, but passing years have lowered my dudgeon by a couple of feet.

Even so, it still grates to read, "'I just try and live a life of a normal human being,' said ex-Beatle George Harrison." It seems to me that the use of a common, garden-variety infinitive would have sharpened that sentence. The writer who is wedded to *try and* has eminent company—Austen, Dickens, Thackeray, Melville, George Eliot, Henry Adams, E. B. White, F. Scott Fitzgerald all have used the idiomatic form. Even Homer nodded.

tummy

Perhaps there is a place for *tummy* in the writing of books for toddlers, but that's its only place. The mommy who has a tummy ache got it from eating veggies. Or maybe the mommy is preggers. If she is preggers she had better not have more than one drinky-poo before din-din.

tuna fish salad

In Poseidon's name I ask: What in the world is a tuna *fish* salad? Is it in some way different from a mere tuna salad? Would we order a chicken *fowl* salad? Point made.

U-V-W-X-Y-Z
umbrage

It is time to take umbrage at writers who *take umbrage*. In the resentful sense in which it is commonly used, *umbrage* dates from 1604. It was probably a hackneyed phrase by 1610. The word stems from the Latin for "shade," whence come shots from ambush. By extension, the word evolved into the use we know today. The word has an unfunny phoniness about it, a kind of false weight, as if we were dealing with the hollow barbells that function as stage props. The editorial writer who takes umbrage is the same editorial writer who is behooved to take action. Left alone, this portentous fellow will speak of a horse yclept Seattle Slew. He will commit other crimes against literacy. He will propose that we eschew things, which is what ought to be done with *taking umbrage*. Eschew it. And then spit it out.

underway / underweigh

You pays your money and you takes your choice. *American Heritage* says *under way* is two words. *Random House* says *underway* is one word. *Webster's Ninth New Collegiate* obligingly gives us *underway, under way,* and *under weigh*. The contemporary trend is toward the single unhyphenated word: "The Senate session got underway promptly at noon." I admit a fondness for *under weigh* in speaking of ships. The old spelling carries the sound of anchor chains, but not even Tom Clancy uses *under weigh* today.

unique

Has quite enough been said and written about the abuse of *unique?* Probably so, but for the record: *Unique* is one of those absolute adjectives that cannot properly be subject to modifiers of degree. Something may be *almost unique,* or *nearly unique,* or *virtually, practically,* or *absolutely unique,* but it cannot be *very unique,* or *rather unique,* or *most unique.* This is all that needs to be said. For further fulminations, see any book on English usage.

utilize

In most contexts *utilize* is pretentious, a mere six-dollar substitute for the 60-cent *use.* Sometimes, but rarely, *utilize* is acceptable. *Webster's Dictionary of English Usage* suggests that *utilize* is sensibly used in the sense of "a deliberate decision or effort to employ something (or someone) for a practical purpose." We might utilize a certain opportunity rather than use it. A guideline for every day: Put *utilize* on a high shelf with the chipped china.

velocity

Watch this one. Every schoolboy knows that velocity is first of all a measure of speed, as in the velocity of sound. That usage is good enough for every day, but in certain applications, *velocity* is a function not only of speed but also of direction. My suggestion is to creep up slowly on *velocity.* You may hear from gun lovers who will tell you more about velocity than you really wanted to know.

venue

For a good many centuries of criminal law, starting from 1531, *venue* had but one meaning: It had to do with the locality in which a crime occurred, a jury would be chosen, and a trial ordinarily would be held. My Court of Peeves, Crotchets & Irks once ruled summarily that this is all that *venue* means today.

Better informed readers promptly humbled the court. In contemporary usage, *venue* refers to the site of just about anything from a poetry reading to a convention of Elks. The extended meaning still sounds out of place to me, but I concede that in some applications it has become useful. "The Kennedy Center in Washington has four venues for the performing arts" states the matter compactly. It is better than explaining that the Center has one large theater, one small theater, a concert hall, and an opera house.

verbal / oral

The distinction that usually is made is that *verbal* has to do with words, and *oral* has to do with the mouth. This is all very well when it comes to *verbal aptitude, verbal answer,* and *verbal acceptance.* The rule works with *oral hygiene, oral argument,* and *oral sex,* but the rule gets fuzzy when we get to contracts, agreements, or commitments. Either *verbal* or *oral* is acceptable in these word-of-mouth situations. The two words have been used interchangeably for almost four centuries. It's no wonder they cause confusion today.

verdict

Legally speaking, a *verdict* may be rendered only by a jury. Judges (or the anonymous *court*) do the rest. Judges hand down opinions, orders, rulings, decrees, mandates, stays—you name it—but if a judge is hearing a criminal case without a jury, he simply *finds* the defendant guilty or not guilty. In an expansive sense, of course, a *verdict* may be almost any kind of decision reached by almost anyone.

veritable / virtual

Something that is *veritable* is true, or at least figuratively true. George Bush defeated Michael Dukakis in 1988 in a veritable landslide. *Virtual* is different. It carries the meaning of "in effect, though not actually." Thus, "Many families classified as 'low income' live in virtual poverty."

viable

Apart from biology laboratories, *viable* is a nonce word that has just about run out of nonce. It means "capable of living," and as applied to a fetus, *viable* is an indispensable adjective. We overdo it when we write of a viable candidacy, a viable alternative, a viable treaty, a viable agreement, a viable subject, and a viable Little League team. Police in Seattle, tracking down a serial killer, identified a man who had not been charged and denied any involvement: He was a "viable suspect." As an alternative, try *workable, plausible, practical, promising,* or any combination that seems to work.

wake

The principal parts of *wake* are *wake, woke, woken,* and don't let any fossilized professor persuade you otherwise. "Ordinarily I wake at dawn. Yesterday I woke at noon. I rarely have woken so late." It is perfectly permissible to use *awake, awoke, awoken* if you prefer. It is also okay to use *awaken, awakened, awakened.* They all mean the same thing. Your ear will tell you not to speak of someone or some event that awoke up the sleepers.

watershed

At the time I wrote *The Writer's Art,* I had positive views on *watershed* and expressed them positively. I said that properly speaking, a *watershed* is not a single point or a sharp line; it is a whole region or area in which water drains in a particular direction. Metaphorically, the famous school segregation case of 1954 was a watershed in Fourteenth Amendment law.

That was the final entry in the book, and I must have been tired when I wrote it. In a technical sense, beloved of geologists and surveyors, a watershed is of course "a ridge of high land dividing two areas that are drained by different river systems," just as *American Heritage* defines it, and I should have said so. The word appeared in that precise meaning in 1803, but by 1839 it had come to mean what I said it meant. It meant *an entire area* subject to drainage from a particular divide.

The venerable Fowler in 1926 stuck by the old ways. He had been taught "that the senses river-basin & area of collection & drainage-slope were mere ignorant guesses due to confusion with the familiar word *shed.*" This led the editors of *Webster's Dictionary of English Usage* to comment that, "It looks to a Fowlerian as if Kilpatrick has committed a howling blunder, but perhaps his mistake is . . . not all that blameworthy."

Then the editors took it all back: "The physical sense of *watershed* that Kilpatrick knows is, in fact, far more common, at least in American English, than the older sense prescribed by Fowler."

I cannot recollect using *watershed* since I wrote the entry of 1984, and I no longer give a particular damn how the word is used. Metaphorically, the Gutenberg Bible was a watershed. Dancer Gene Kelly described the musical *On the Town* as a watershed. The discovery of DNA was a watershed. But I insist that the consequences, or fall-out, or subsequent developments also constitute a watershed. Henry Fowler knew almost everything, but he flubbed on this one.

well-words

Authorities disagree on how these things should be punctuated. Everyone agrees on, "The court based its opinion on well-founded reasoning." The dispute has to do with, "The court's reasoning was well founded." The Associated Press would hyphenate both fore and aft. The New York Times hyphenates only before the noun, and the Times has the better of the argument.

whence

The *from* in *from whence* is often redundant. It can be jettisoned without much loss, but it is not even a serious misdemeanor to leave it in if a *from* improves the cadence. Thus, I would prefer "the land from whence this whisky came is blessed Scotland," because it has a better swing to it. But, "Get thee hence!" is a crisper command than, "Get thee from hence!" I doubt that anyone uses *hence, thence,* or *whence* any more, except in the sense of "ten years hence, the subjunctive mood will have vanished."

whether or not

One of my crotchety readers confidently contends that *or not* is redundant—that *whether,* standing alone, conveys the idea of a yes-or-no choice. Certainly this is true in most instances. Nothing at all is gained by saying that, "We don't know whether *or not* the curtain will rise on time." Or, "We will have to determine whether *or not* Gramm is interested in running."

But the rule against redundancy is not inviolate. Often the *or not* adds a necessary emphasis. Moreover, a vital element is left out if we say, "Whether you admire Clinton, you have to concede that . . ." It's a fine idea to trim our prose of redundancies, as if we were trimming a pork chop, but this admirable practice can be taken too far.

whiskey / whisky

It's *whiskey* in the United States, *whisky* in Great Britain.

whole nine yards

A gentleman in Savannah wrote me some years ago to inquire about a familiar phrase. He had gone to a hospital for a complete physical examination. He asked the X-ray technician how many pictures she would take. "Honey," she said, "we're going to give you the whole nine yards."

I asked readers for help. All kinds of etymological answers rolled in. A retired army sergeant recalled that a standard barracks used to be twenty-seven feet long. It had to be cleaned every week, wall to wall, "the whole nine yards." A sergeant in the air force had another explanation. An ammunition belt, it seems, is twenty-seven feet long. When the whole works is expended, "we give 'em the whole nine yards."

Several readers said it had to do with textiles. Bolts of cloth once were nine yards long. Carpet, I was advised, comes in nine-yard rolls. A nurse volunteered the thought that human intestines run on for twenty-seven feet. A sailing enthusiast was certain the phrase comes from the days of tall ships. Under full sail, a three-master would fly "the whole nine yards."

In the end, it turned out that the phrase has a homely, humdrum explanation: It derives from the truck that brings ready-mixed concrete to a construction site. Such trucks contain twenty-seven cubic feet of material. When concrete is being poured, the foreman asks for ten feet, or twenty feet, or "the whole nine yards."

who / whom

Confession time. Your mentor, meaning me, is a syntactical coward. Facing a choice between *who* and *whom*, he turns tail and runs. Except when the pronoun is snuggled right next to the preposition, as in "Upon *whom* shall we then rely?", I come down with the fidgets and twitches.

Let me recall a particular dilemma. I was writing a political piece late in 1984. I wrote, "No matter who the Republicans name as majority leader next week, Baker's successor will have a high example to follow." I'm sorry I ever wrote that infernal sentence, for it caused me much grief. I first wrote, "whom the Republicans name." Then I deleted the *whom* and tried *who*. In an agony of indecision I read Fowler anew and reverted to *whom*. Then *who*, I said, and the hell with it.

Fifty readers wrote in, including a precocious brat at a private academy in Glen Head, N.Y., to teach me that it should have been "whom the Republicans name," because the verb *name* demands a proper objective pronoun. Nevertheless I delighted in a supportive letter from a gentleman in Stewart Manor, N.Y. He wrote:

> Keep the word *who*. If you do, you will be striking a blow for natural word order as the guide in matters of English usage.
>
> Ours is a positional language. We expect nominative case pronouns to precede verbs. Hence, we like *who do you trust?* and *who should I give the check to?* In your sentence, we also like *who* in its position . . . All of the inflections that were used in Old English to indicate case are gone. Go with *who*. This is English, not Latin.

I have a notion, and put it forward defensively, that before long the distinction between *who* and *whom*, except in the most obvious constructions, will go the way of the ivory-billed woodpecker. No one has seen an ivory-billed in years. People still worry obsessively about the vanishing *whom*. No question of grammar is presented to me more often, or more futilely, than the choice of the two pronouns.

My pusillanimous tendency is to write around the booby trap; and my heretical thought is to say that in most constructions a *who* is as clear to the reader as a *whom* any day.

wise, word to the

On May 24, 1992, John Smoltz pitched his Atlanta Braves to a 2–1 victory over Montreal. The remarkable news was that he struck out fifteen Expo hitters, thus tying a franchise record set in 1960. Smoltz was elated.

"As far as stuffwise," he said, "I haven't pitched a better game than this."

As an umpire in the lexicographical ball game, I am going to rule *stuffwise* a fair ball—provided its use is confined to pitchers. Otherwise, ho ho, I would use the *-wise* suffix with great care. I would especially abandon *elsewise*. *Webster's III* lists *elsewise* as a variant of *otherwise*, but not in my ballpark.

A letter writer in The New York Times noted that "obscenity," by Supreme Court definition, requires a strong sexual component, but need not contain any form of violence. "Contrariwise, the most vicious, violent and degrading depictions are fully protected by the First Amendment so long as they do not contain strong sexual content." *Webster's* says that *contrariwise* dates from the fourteenth century, but the adverb hasn't improved with age. *Likewise* came along in the fifteenth century. In serious writing, as distinguished from comic writing, we ought to find a phrase that doesn't call so much attention to itself.

Index

265

Index of
Words and Phrases